SPECTRAL EDITION

SPECTRAL EDITION

Ghost Reports
from U.S. Newspapers
1865-1917

Edited by
Tim Prasil

BROM B⬤NES BOOKS

ISBN: 978-1-948084-00-0

The font used for "SPECTRAL" on the front cover and elsewhere is Lycanthrope and is courtesy of Chad Savage's Sinister Visions™. Visit sinistervisions.com.

The "Belated Villagers" illustration on the back cover comes from the *Little Falls Herald* (Minnesota), April 20, 1906.

DEDICATION

This book is dedicated to all the newspaper reporters and illustrators who, if only for one assignment, extended their usual news beats toward the spectral realm.

CONTENTS

INTRODUCTION

Let's Start at the End

In 1916, the *El Paso Herald* editorialized: "Ghosts have gone out of fashion along with haunted houses. One never has a haunted house pointed out to him anymore. It is doubtful if there be one single haunted house in El Paso, and doubtful whether a single soul ever sees a ghost." The brief commentary goes on to speculate that such spectral phenomena might have been lost to electric lights, to "modern indifference," or to a lack of fearing ghosts. There the comment ends— not a springboard to some larger point, only a quick lament of changing times. About a year-and-a-half later, veteran journalist Captain J. Walter Mitchell, writing for the "Looking Back" column of the *Washington Herald,* expressed a similar sentiment: "Not so many years ago there were numerous so-called haunted houses in this city and these places furnished many thrilling stories to the old-time reporter." The remainder of Mitchell's much longer article reviews several of the haunted houses that he recalls had been covered in D.C. area newspapers.[1]

My own hunting for ghosts in old U.S. newspapers confirms the observations expressed in the two articles above. Much as the various ghost-hunter shows on television and the internet in our own era suggest that *once again* there is an audience fascinated by ghosts, American newspaper readers over a century ago were tantalized by a surge of ghost stories. Though fairly easy to find in the latter decades of the 1800s and first decade of the 1900s, these reports plummet in frequency during that second decade of the new century. The wave's rise, on the other hand, seems to have gradually gained momentum in the 1860s and 1870s. Ghost reports were published infrequently before and after those points, and the very earliest I've discovered, dated 1844, opens with this telling statement: "It has been so long since a real case of haunted house has occurred, that many deemed the fashion had

---

[1] *El Paso Herald* (Texas), April 15, 1916; *Washington Herald* (DC), Nov. 17, 1918.

become entirely extinct."[2] The heyday of ghost reporting in U.S. newspapers, then, comes rather neatly—and, I suspect, significantly—between the end of the Civil War and the start of American involvement in World War I: 1865 to 1917.

These ghost reports were often treated with the same journalistic objectivity and seriousness as other news items. For instance, in the news-in-brief section of a Vermont newspaper in 1873, a notice that the son of a Vershire couple had died in a fire is followed by this tantalizing tidbit: "Bennington has a house that is supposed to be haunted by a ghost of a woman anxious to revenge herself on one of the tenants who ill-treated her in life." This is then followed, all in identical font and format, by the announcement of the reappointment of a Lamoille County sheriff whose father held the same office for many years. A decade later, a paper in Ohio reported the death of "one of the oldest and most highly respected citizens of Barnesville" beside this curt statement: "Bridgeport is said to have a haunted house. Tables are said to move about without any visible agency, doors are rapped upon, and noises of all kinds are heard throughout the house at all hours of the day and night." Right below that is a notice about a liveryman whose carriage shed suffered snow damage.[3] Such reports, written matter-of-factly, show that some reporters and editors considered ghostly encounters to be legitimate news.

Some journalists saw such experiences as an opportunity to jokingly undercut their sources' reliability or, at least, to toss off a bit of Shakespeare. Perhaps a glimpse of this less-than-objective tone appears in the "Dakota Jottings" section of a paper serving the Dakota Territory. In the space of a few inches, readers learn that Sully County is moving its records to a fire-proof vault, that "Deadwood has a genuine case of 'haunted house,' where goblins hold nightly revel," and that work on the natural gas well in Gary is proceeding rapidly.[4] Sandwiched between mundanities, the "genuine" haunted house is given conspicuously curt coverage. In contrast, typical ghost reports were significantly longer, at times filling two or three columns, as illustrated by the articles filling the chapters of this book.

Such ghost reports provide evidence that the U.S. experienced a period of particular interest in ghosts as widespread open-minded contemplation of their reality slowly rose and suddenly fell.

---

[2] *Daily Madisonian* (Washington, DC), Jan. 22, 1844.

[3] *Orleans County Monitor* (Barton, Vermont), Feb. 17, 1873; *Belmont Chronicle* (Saint Clairsville, Ohio), Dec. 27, 1883.

[4] *Wahpeton Times* (North Dakota), Feb. 21, 1889.

Newspapers reveal other manifestations of this fascination with ghosts, too. In 1881, the *Daily Dispatch* of Richmond, Virginia, told readers that furniture from a house alleged to be haunted was on the auction block and that this ghostly provenance "attracted a crowd of buyers, and the second-hand buyers met with an unexpected competition. Annie McWaters, the servant girl who had the most startling interviews with the ghost, was there, and still persisted that the house was haunted." In 1885, the *Iron County Register* told readers, "Boston has for months been full of the wildest theories about ghosts and visions. The subject is almost invariably discussed in every social gathering, and wonderful stories are commonly told of personal experiences. As evidence of the kind of minds engrossed in these things, it is noteworthy that four members of Harvard's faculty are members of a society for investigation." The reporter is probably referring to the American branch of the Society for Psychical Research, established the same year, but other groups were forming, too. The Brooklyn Society for the Extermination of Ghosts and Dispelling of Haunted House Illusions, according to a 1904 issue of the *New-York Tribune,* "includes thirty young men between the ages of seventeen and twenty-three," all of them intent upon debunking the borough's haunted houses. More supportive of ghosts, New York's *Evening World* had run a contest in 1889, announcing that one "golden double eagle will be given to the person who sends the best ghost story" based on personal experience. Returning to 1904, newspapers across the nation ran a story about a real estate agent whose client was willing to pay handsomely for "a real haunted house and the ghost must be well authenticated." The client's intention was to convert the building into a lodge and banquet hall.[5]

What explains this rise in U.S. readers' interest in ghosts and U.S. newspapers lending credence to such things? The answer is no doubt complex, but I think that three historical developments contributed. These factors are 1) the trauma felt in the wake of the Civil War and, specifically, its unimaginable death toll; 2) a shift in perceiving distances brought about by technological innovations, especially telegraphy, that affected perceptions of the proximity of the physical and spiritual dimensions; and 3) the uncertain professional guidelines in U.S. journalism in the 1800s.

---

[5] *Daily Dispatch* (Richmond, Virginia), June 30, 1881; *Iron County Register* (Ironton, Missouri), July 30, 1885; *New-York Tribune* (New York), May 21, 1904; *Evening World* (New York, New York), Dec. 24, 1889; *Minneapolis Journal* (Minnesota), May 20, 1904.

Its Ghost May Still Haunt Us for a Time

VICTORY!!!
GLORY HALLELUJAH!!
LEE SURRENDERED
His Entire Army Captured!
GRANT DICTATES TERMS.
The End Draws Nigh!

Thus reads a headline on the front page of the *Cleveland Morning Leader* on April 10, 1865. Beside this column of rejoice ran an article giving a decidedly Yankee perspective on the end of the American Civil War: "Beaten, flying, disorganized, falling into pieces with every mile it moved, . . . the once proud army of Lee had become a mere rabble and rout, and its commander, when he could not save it, surrendered it. In that surrender the rebellion committed suicide. Its ghost may still haunt us for a time, but its life is gone and its deeds are things of the past." Though speaking figuratively about ghosts, the reporter literally predicted one means Americans used to cope with the terrible loss of life incurred by that rebellion and the war to quell it.

A seminal work on how the Civil War challenged and reshaped the ways that Americans lived with death is Drew Gilpin Faust's *This Republic of Suffering*. She writes, "In the middle of the nineteenth century, the United States embarked on a new relationship with death, entering into a civil war that proved bloodier than any other conflict in American history, a war that would presage the slaughter of World War I's Western Front and the global carnage of the twentieth century." After noting that about 620,000 soldiers died during the war waged from 1861 to 1865, Faust points out that this figure neglects the civilians killed by troops spreading disease, waging guerrilla attacks, and leaving communities without food supplies. Along with unprecedented numbers, the average age of the dead was psychologically devastating. While infant mortality was fairly common, mid-nineteenth-century Americans "expected that most individuals who reached young adulthood would survive at least into middle age." The war, of course, took men who were young and healthy.[6] Though the spirits of soldiers rarely if ever appear in the ghost reports following 1865, when a backstory is provided to explain the haunting, it almost always involves someone who died tragically and young: a murder victim, a suicide, a casualty of a railroad accident, etc. The war was over, but troubling

---

[6] Drew Gilpin Faust, *This Republic of Suffering: Death and the American Civil War,* Alfred A. Knopf, 2008, p. xi-xii.

deaths like those of the many, many soldiers persisted, reminding Americans of their war losses—perhaps in more individualized and fathomable scenarios.

In a chapter titled "Believing and Doubting: 'What Means this Carnage?'" Faust provides insights into how the nation struggled with the Civil War slaughter. These indirectly shed light on the ghost reports. Even before the war, science had dealt two powerful blows to the promise of an afterlife so vital to traditional Christianity, complicating how the Bible offered comfort to those in mourning. In the 1830s, Charles Lyell's *Principles of Geology* "challenged the veracity of Genesis by demonstrating that the Earth was millions of years old, not the six or seven thousand postulated in Scripture." More profoundly, at the tail of the 1850s, Darwin's *The Origin of Species* presented a scientific alternative to creation itself, and Faust notes that its claims of natural evolution had been "shared and discussed in preliminary form with American scientists" beforehand. Similarly, the voice of science had spoken loudly against believing in ghosts. For instance, Dr. James Thatcher was a Massachusetts physician and Fellow of the American Academy of Arts and Sciences who authored *An Essay on Demonology, Ghosts and Apparitions, and Popular Superstitions* (1831). Ghostly encounters, according to Thatcher, can be traced to nerves, which under unhealthy conditions "may be subjected to very irregular motions or vibrations. Hence unreal images may be raised in the mind. . . . Superstitions, fancies, or enthusiastic emotions, do greatly disturb the regular action of the nervous system."[7] In other words, avoid superstitions, imagination, and undue emotion (be it gloominess or glee), and you probably won't be fooled into seeing a ghost.

Curiously, most Americans able to dismiss the claims of science and retain assurance of the afterlife promised by scripture might still have had a difficult time interpreting newspaper ghost reports as corroboration that spirits live beyond physical death. Protestant Christians vastly outnumbered other religious groups in the U.S. during

---

[7] Faust, p. 173. James Thatcher, *An Essay on Demonology, Ghosts and Apparitions, and Popular Superstitions,* Carter and Hendee, 1831, p. 6. Thatcher's ideas are similar to those of doctors published earlier in England: John Ferriar's *An Essay towards a Theory of Apparitions* (Cadell and Davies, 1813), John Alderson, *An Essay on Apparitions, in which Their Appearance Is Accounted for by Causes Wholly Independent of Preternatural Agency* (Longman, 1823), and Samuel Hibbert's *Sketches of the Philosophy of Apparitions; or, An Attempt to Trace Such Illusions to Their Physical Causes* (George B. Whittaker, 1825).

the 1800s. Much earlier, during the Reformation begun in the 1500s, Protestants had rejected Roman Catholicism's doctrine of purgatory, a belief that was accommodating to ghostly visitations. In *Ghosts: Appearances of the Dead & Cultural Transformation,* R.C. Finucane explains that, without purgatory, "the likelihood that apparitions were the departed seeking assistance could not be admitted. Other explanations had to be found. Whereas some suggested an angelic origin for these undoubted events, many Protestant writers claimed that such beings were actually emissaries of the Devil." Even if this hurdle could be cleared after the Civil War, Protestant Americans were faced with ghosts who didn't especially seem to be *seeking assistance.* Ghosts of earlier centuries returned for clear reasons, if not to solicit prayers for release from purgatory then perhaps to divulge the location of a hidden will. Those Shakespeare-spouting reporters favored *Hamlet,* which opens with Hamlet's father returning from the dead to expose his murderer. But these ghosts became eclipsed by "apparitions of very limited, or even apparently non-existent, functions," according to Finucane. In brief, most ghosts of the 1800s were reported to be "wispy figures that floated about darkened chambers with no apparent reason for being there at all."[8] Finucane focuses on British accounts of ghosts here, but his description applies well to most of the ghost reports I found in U.S. newspapers of the same period.

Despite such conflicts, there were alternative ways to be assured that the many, many brothers and husbands killed in the Civil War survived in a Great Beyond. One was Spiritualism. After Faust points out that séances tempted science-minded participants with "belief that seemed to rely on empirical evidence rather than revelation and faith," she zeroes in on a series called "Voices of the Dead," which was run in the Spiritualist newspaper *Banner of Light.* These articles featured messages channeled through a psychic medium named Mrs. J.H. Conant. Faust explains that "soldiers of all ranks and origins reported that they had died well, that they had met relatives in heaven, and that, as one voice declared, 'death has taken nothing from me, except my body.'" The communiqués from the next world mirrored "condolence

---

[8] R.C. Finucane, *Ghosts: Appearances of the Dead & Cultural Transformation,* Prometheus, 1996, pp. 114, 194, 204. Writings by American clergymen giving natural explanations, such as dreams and delusions, for ghostly encounters include W.B.O. Peabody's "New-England Superstitions," *New England Magazine,* 4 (Feb., 1833), pp. 139-53, and Enoch Pond's "Spectral Appearances; Their Causes and Laws," *Princeton Review,* 40.2 (Apr., 1868), pp. 293-317.

letters written to inform relatives about the deaths of kin in hospital or battle," and though Faust points out that the soldiers named in the newspaper series do not appear on "the database of 6.3 million records of 3.5 million soldiers that the National Park Service has compiled," Spiritualism provided comfort in suggesting that answers to dire questions about real soldiers would be answered one day. "There would be an ending to uncertainty—perhaps through contact with the spirit world but certainly through reunion in the world beyond," says Faust.[9]

The ghost reports might have given similar consolation. They're vague, fleeting, dubious, and at times, downright silly. However, they were also an alternative to Spiritualism, as seen particularly in those reports that identify the witness of the spectral phenomena as having no Spiritualist leanings. Indeed, ghosts seemed to have a far lengthier and more widespread history than Spiritualism. In an 1862 article titled simply "Ghosts," the Reverend T.M. Griffith points out that there is abundant evidence for spirit visitations in both the Bible and in human history. He goes on to say, "Every land, every neighborhood, almost every family has its startling facts. Witnesses beyond number, of the highest character for veracity and sound judgment, have given their evidence to the world; and the world has rejected their testimony as unreasonable." Griffith spends the rest of his essay arguing that ghosts *are* reasonable.[10] This was published in the *Ladies' Repository,* a journal published by the Methodist Church in Cincinnati, revealing that some Protestant Christians *could* see ghost reports as validation of an afterlife. So long as reporters and the witnesses they wrote about were trustworthy, readers could trust that there was some visual, auditory or otherwise physical proof that death is not final. So long as such proof was appealing to heartsick readers in the long process of letting go of the Civil War dead, the ghost reports retained their popularity.

Distance Does Not Really Exist

In Jules Verne's 1865 science fiction novel *From the Earth to the Moon,* a Baltimore, Maryland, gun club—feeling a kind of post-Civil War boredom—devises a grand plan to construct a cannon massive enough to shoot its payload all the way to the moon. In France, the adventurous Michel Ardan sends the club a telegram requesting they delay their plans. He then charges across the Atlantic on a steamship,

---

[9] Faust, pp. 180-85.
[10] T.M. Griffith, "Ghosts," *Ladies' Repository,* 22.10 (Oct., 1862), pp. 622-623.

intent on convincing the gun club to send *passengers* on that remarkable cannonball. Upon making his pitch, Ardan explains that human history has been one of ever-increasing velocities: from crawling to walking, from horse-drawn carriages to railroads. Technological innovation was essentially making the world—indeed, the solar system—far smaller (and Ardan's previous use of telegraph and steam engines would have driven that point home with his original readers). Ardan proclaims, "Distance is but a relative expression, and must end by being reduced to zero." While the miles to the moon seem daunting, he says, it's merely a 300-day trip by train, a span of time most sailors have exceeded at sea. Compared to a trip to the planet Neptune or the star Arcturus, a trip to the moon becomes very manageable. "Distance is but an empty name," he insists; "distance does not really exist!"[11]

Here, we see a fictional reflection of very real perceptions in 1865. Distances seemed to be collapsing and shrinking. Since the 1830s, the telegraph had been shortening long-range communication from days, even weeks or months, to seconds. At roughly the same time, steam-powered ships were truncating the time needed to travel from one city to another while turning trans-Atlantic travel into a matter of days instead of the weeks that sailing would entail. The emerging railroad travel, in the meantime, was moving faster still, making distances seem to be heading toward zero, as Ardan suggests. Those living through these changes must have experienced a paradigm shift in regard to comprehending distances.

Certainly the Spiritualists were using this new way of thinking to close the distance between the physical and spiritual dimensions. Though spectral knocking has a longer history,[12] rapping served as a primary method of communication between here and the hereafter when Modern Spiritualism burst upon the scene in the U.S. The event typically cited as igniting the movement occurred in 1848, when the Fox Sisters from Hydesville, New York, went public—and later international—with their ability to communicate with the dead. The parallels between their system of eliciting raps from spirits and telegraphy's Morse Code were not lost on those who would promote Spiritualism, perhaps no clearer seen than in the title of *The Spiritual Telegraph,* a founding newspaper devoted to the movement. In a cultural history of the weavings between electronic media and

---

[11] Jules Verne, *From the Earth to the Moon: Direct in Ninety-Seven Hours and Twenty Minutes: and a Trip Round It,* Scribner's, 1890, pp. 93-94.

[12] See Finucane, p.108.

paranormal and spiritual phenomena, Jeffrey Sconce says that "Spiritualism attempted to align itself with the principles of 'electrical science' so as to distinguish mediumship from more 'superstitious' forms of mystical belief in previous centuries. It was the animating powers of electricity that gave the telegraph its distinctive property of simultaneity and its unique sense of disembodied presence, allowing the device to vanquish previous barriers of space, time, and in the Spiritualist imagination, even death."[13] One explanation of why Spiritualism became so popular—attracting millions of followers by the end of the 1800s—involves its borrowing technology's ability to shorten distances and redirecting it toward those grieving the loss of loved ones, thereby fostering the feeling that those who had "passed on" hadn't journeyed so far after all.

That said, stories of spectral encounters have a very long history of locating ghosts in close proximity with the living: a rundown house between this town and the next, the graveyard only a few blocks away, or even downstairs when everyone is asleep. As my categorizing of ghost reports illustrates, ghosts have a habit of attaching themselves to particular houses or other buildings, specific grounds or waters, or limited stretches of road. (Ghosts attached to particular families or individuals seem to have a bit more mobility, but there's still a sense of *closeness* involved.) This tradition of the local, earthbound phantom goes back at least as far as the first century A.D., when Pliny the Younger wrote to Sura regarding a haunted house mystery purported to be true. In Athens, the account goes, a phantom rattled chains and manifested visually in the house. Learning of the haunting, the calm and courageous philosopher Athenodorus investigated. He spotted the specter, followed it to where it disappeared into the ground, and marked that spot. Leading an excavation the next day, the ghost hunter discovered a skeleton in chains. Once the bones had been buried with greater ceremony, the ghost was apparently free to move on from its worldly concerns.[14] In this respect, ghost reports have relied upon a close proximity to the living for millennia.

Still, as I've already implied, opposition to the reality of ghosts was strong in the first half of the 1800s. An 1832 issue of the *American Monthly Review,* for example, opens an evaluation of Dr. Thatcher's

---

[13] Jeffrey Sconce, *Haunted Media: Electronic Presence from Telegraphy to Television,* Duke University Press, 2000, p. 28.

[14] For a translation of Pliny's important "ghost report" and discussion of it, see D. Felton, *Haunted Greece and Rome: Ghost Stories from Classical Antiquity,* University of Texas Press, 1999, pp. 65-73.

essay and a work on the Salem witch trials by saying, "The whole tribe of ghosts, goblins, and witches has been rapidly disappearing during the last century, before the daylight of modern science and philosophy. In our own country the general diffusion of knowledge is driving them out from every corner of the land. . . . It is true that you hear now and then a good old-fashioned story of a haunted house; and meet with some traditional superstitions yet lingering in the minds of the more ignorant. But we have hardly enough left to rhyme or to reason about; and even these few, which remain, are likely in the present course of things to die away ere long and to be forgotten."[15] But the reviewer was mistaken about ghosts: refusing to be forgotten, they became a topic that more and more Americans rhymed and reasoned about by the century's end. This reconsideration of the reality of spectral visitations can be partly explained by this paradigm shift toward perceiving distances as closer than ever—even dimensional distances—bolstered by the odd bedfellows of technological innovation and Spiritualism.

That Press Has Its Evil Eye in Every House

At the start of 1842, Charles Dickens took a six-month journey through the U.S. and Canada. His impressions were published in *American Notes for General Circulation*, and it's there that he comments on the state of the press. While acknowledging that some American publications exhibit "character and credit," these are dwarfed by "infamous journals." Dickens argues that the latter hold greater influence than some might imagine, and "while that Press has its evil eye in every house, and its black hand in every appointment of the state, from a president to a postman; while with ribald slander for its only stock in trade, it is the standard literature of an enormous class, who must find their reading in a newspaper, or they will not read at all; so long must its odium be upon the country's head, and so long must the evil it works be plainly visible in the Republic."[16] Doubtfully the first, Dickens was definitely not the last to express alarm at the potential of the free press in the U.S.—and until radio and television became serious competition for print periodicals in the following century, Dickens was probably right to worry about the powerful influence that newspapers had on shaping opinions of the nation.

---

[15] "Upham's Lectures on Witchcraft," *American Monthly Review*, 1.2 (Feb., 1832), p. 140.

[16] Charles Dickens, *American Notes for General Circulation*, Chapman and Hall, 1842, Volume 2, pp. 294-96.

Introduction

Regarding the publishing of ghost reports, newspaper editors were faced with a dilemma. I've discussed how science and Protestantism leaned toward exposing spectral encounters as deceptions wrought either by overexcited nerves or by the Devil himself. Editors had to decide how the institution of Journalism would handle the subject. One solution was to report a ghostly encounter—and then turn around and discount it—as one paper in Cleveland did in 1866. After a terse description of alleged manifestations at a haunted house in Erie, Pennsylvania, the reporter writes: "One of the Erie papers publishes an editorial account of a visit to the haunted house in that city, giving a detailed account of what was heard in the supernatural line on the premises. The story is on par with some of the highly fanciful creations of old crones who delight to frighten children. Nothing commendatory can be said of those who deal in such inventions." A couple of decades later, a Virginia paper took a similar tactic. After noting a local haunted house's "strange and unaccountable rappings," its disembodied voices (one of which cried, "Come! O, do come!"), and its "securely fastened" doors that open by themselves, the article shifts to smug disapproval: "It seems strange that, in this age of enlightenment, there still are persons who are so superstitious as to believe in the existence of ghosts."[17] Presumably, other papers simply avoided ghost reporting altogether. As my Appendix reveals, rival newspapers in Memphis debated—not just the authenticity of one very questionable haunting—but also the journalistic ethics involved in covering such matters.

One concrete consequence of ghost reports was the damage they could have on renting or selling the property deemed haunted. Some newspapers recognized this and avoided ghost reports as a result. A paper in Idaho sums up the situation well: "Boise has had several haunted houses in the past, but they have seldom been reported by the papers on account of injuring the parties who have these houses to rent. It is seldom that a tenant can be secured for a house that is believed to be haunted." Another paper, this one in North Dakota, illustrated a more direct risk of suggesting a house might be infested by phantoms: "A Hankinson man was sore over the report that there was a haunted house on his land, and endeavored to lick the man he thought had started the rumor." As late as 1915, a Connecticut journal informed readers that two landlords were requesting an abatement of taxes on their rental property because "there has gone abroad a story that a ghost

---

[17] *Cleveland Daily Leader* (Ohio), Feb. 13, 1866. *Staunton Spectator* (Virginia), Dec. 9, 1885.

walks nightly in the Courtland Street mansion."[18] As evidenced by the many reports presented in this book about renters breaking their leases, the problem was a very real one and raised the question of newspapers being complicit with libel.

Despite these detriments, a surprising number of newspapers reported on spectral visitations without commentary on the witnesses' gullibility or the landlords' deficits. This book presents close to 150 articles from newspapers serving urban and rural communities from across the country. They were culled from over 300 ghost reports I found in journals as far-ranging as San Francisco's *Morning Call* to Washington D.C.'s *Evening Times,* from Tennessee's *Southern Standard* to Michigan's *True Northerner,* and from the *Akron Daily Democrat* to the *Arizona Republican.* A few papers showed up more frequently than others in my findings. St. Paul's *Daily Globe* and Pittsburgh's *Dispatch* seem to have been especially amenable to ghost reports, either those written by their own staff or those reprinted from other papers, the latter being a common practice of the period. I confess that I consciously limited reports from New York's *Sun* because of its notoriety for publishing sensationalistic, if not outright fabricated, articles. (When Edgar Allan Poe had invented a tale about balloonists successfully crossing the Atlantic in three days, he confidently marched his manuscript to the *Sun.* The newspaper agreed to publish the piece as authentic news, and the excitement it stirred put Poe into the literary spotlight.) If other papers were following the *Sun's* practice of printing whatever would sell papers when running ghost reports—or if their editors and publishers were genuinely open-minded about ghosts being real—is an issue now left largely to speculation. It would be a mistake, though, to presume that all papers printing such reports were putting sales over ethical journalism. There is simply too great a diversity of newspapers that did so to make that a valid generalization.

These varying editorial policies show one way that U.S. newspapers lacked a strong tradition or consensus guiding what should and shouldn't be reported, something that Dickens's British newspapers had. This helps to explain why the ghost reports appeared when they did. No professional guidelines or self-imposed censorship had developed to stop them, even though some editors clearly recognized that such articles might negatively influence those "who must find their reading in a newspaper, or they will not read at all." In

---

[18] *Caldwell Tribune* (Idaho), Nov. 26, 1892. *Pioneer Express* (Penbina, North Dakota), April 1, 1904. *Bridgeport Evening Farmer* (Connecticut), Jan. 14, 1915.

Introduction

this regard, the ghost reports give some indication of the American press exercising its freedom to partake in the debates of the day. In this case, the debate wasn't about politics, technology, literature, or national character. Instead, it was about the boundaries of reality and, indeed, about the survival of humanity beyond death.

Some Closing Comments before We Begin

I've arranged each chapter's ghost reports in chronological order. In other words, we start in the 1860s and proceed from there—until the next chapter, when we jump back and start the trip forward over again.

In addition, I've made slight alterations to some of the original texts. Perhaps due to deadline pressures, these articles originally appeared with a fair number of grammar and spelling errors, including some doozies. One headline, for example, reads "STRANGE GOINGS NO," presumably intended to be "STRANGE GOINGS *ON.*" Along with such errors, nineteenth- and early twentieth-century newspapers adhered to a now-curious convention in which "street," "county," "river," etc. would not be capitalized when part of a proper noun, resulting in "Throop street," "Logan county," or "East river." Another outdated rule was to hyphenate words such as "to-night" and "to-morrow." I have unobtrusively corrected and modernized such matters.

My purpose in making these alterations is to help readers from over a century later be less perplexed by the articles' language and, in turn, be more baffled by what's being described within them. Why did so many people react to ghosts by shooting at them, for instance? Did the hordes of people who flocked to a haunted house expect the ghost to make a speech from the porch? There's also the question of what we're to make of those articles that claim the spectral phenomenon had been witnessed by *several* "substantial and reliable" people.

And then there's the ultimate question. Lurking somewhere in these very odd ghost reports—published between two horrific wars—is there proof that ghosts actually do circulate among us? Regarding this compelling mystery, the humble editor of this book adamantly avoids either belief or disbelief, but very much hopes to encourage his readers' sense of *wonder*.

Tim Prasil

13

HAUNTED HOUSES
with Backstories

The overwhelming majority of ghost reports that I unearthed involved haunted houses, so many that I split them to fill this and the next chapter. The articles here include backstories. By this, I mean the ghost's earlier existence in the physical world is discussed, even if that discussion is brief or guesswork. This, then, suggests the range of who was depicted as likely to become a ghost: from murder victims to suicides and from misers to those with unfinished business. A few of the backstories feature spirits who, after dying quietly, simply seemed unready to leave home.

This chapter also introduces the array of houses that can be reported as haunted. Be it urban or rural, old or new, decaying or in fine condition, a mansion or a cabin—it seems Longfellow was correct in writing: "All houses wherein men have lived and died / Are haunted houses." Or, at least, they can be, if we trust these ghost reports.

Here, then, we launch a house-hunting expedition. But instead of solid construction, good air circulation, and ample storage, we're seeking nocturnal groans, glimpses of a melancholy figure, chairs that move by themselves, and if we can stand it, the touch of a hand that is both clammy and unseen. All of these await you in this chapter.

A Haunted House in Joliet.

Our readers have heard of the haunted house in St. Louis, of the haunted house in Chicago, of the haunted house in Philadelphia, of Mrs. Surratt's haunted house in Washington, but we doubt whether they ever heard of a haunted house in Joliet. Yet such is a veritable fact. There *is* a haunted house here. It is near the Michigan General Railroad depot, in the Eastern part of the city. The last family that resided in the doomed tenement has numerous and unmistakable proofs of the fact, the premises were infested with "ghosts, or spirits, or goblins damned."[1]

It is represented by the late inmates, who are acknowledged to possess more than an ordinary degree of courage and are of undoubted respectability, that no sooner than the lights are extinguished then noises, earthly and unearthly, are heard in all parts of the house, including sounds of footsteps, moans, the moving the chairs, and the whirling of pans upon the floors. And we are informed that the wife of the man who last lived there, between sundown and dusk one evening, actually saw the figure of a tall woman, dressed in black, which disappeared without noise or opening the door on her moving towards it. These manifestations became so annoying that finally the family was compelled to take their residence up elsewhere, and the house is now untenanted.

There are various dark stories in circulation in the neighborhood in regard to the cause of these unearthly visits. It is alleged that, once upon a time, the house was owned and inhabited by a lawyer, who had an amiable, loving and beautiful wife, but between whom there existed anything but connubial bliss. In time the body of the poor woman was taken from the water, a cold, stiff, snowy-white corpse. It was thought by many at the time that she had come to her death by unfair means; and the mildest view of the case was that she had been driven to commit suicide by the unconnubial conduct of him who had vowed to love, cherish and protect her.

Such at present is the story of the Joliet haunted house; and in due time we shall make further investigations and report the facts to our readers. But we advise all to hold their breath and not be skeered.

Ottawa Free Trader (Illinois), Dec. 29, 1866
Reprinted from *Joliet Signal* (Illinois)

An Indiana Haunted House.

Greenberg, Indiana, has a sensation, it being nothing short of a haunted house. *The Herald* of that town says the house is situated near the railroad track and had been occupied for some time by an Irish family. The ghost makes appearance every night just as the clock strikes twelve and, for half an hour, makes itself at home by throwing chairs,

---

[1] A paraphrase of Shakespeare's *Hamlet*. Stunned by the appearance of what appears to be the ghost of his father, Hamlet responds, "Be thou a spirit of health or goblin damn'd / . . . Thou com'st in such questionable shape / That I will speak to thee" (1.4.40-44).

tables, cooking utensils, etc. about the room in a promiscuous manner. The family stood it as long as possible and then moved out. Another family moved in, but got enough in one night. The owner offered twenty-five dollars to anyone who would 'lay' the ghost, and a young man, possessed of more courage than money, offered to do the job. He armed himself and repaired to the house. Just as the clock struck the hour of midnight, a slight noise was heard, followed by a groan. About this time doors in the upper part of the house commenced shutting in a mysterious manner. This continued for some time, when the door of the room in which the young man was sitting suddenly opened, and a lady, dressed in black and deadly pale, stood before him. He started toward her, when she vanished through the door, and on going to the door, she was nowhere to be seen. The house several years ago was the scene of a most brutal murder, in which a man killed his wife by cutting her heart out. He left the country and did not return until the war broke out, when he enlisted in a New York regiment and was killed during the storming of Vicksburg.

Union Flag (Jonesborough, Tennessee), Nov. 27, 1868

A GHOST!
A Disembodied Woman
Prowling About in Topeka

It is very seldom that this city is treated to a ghost sensation, and then the people are slow to believe in it. But now we have a ghost story that is vouched for. The appearance of this strange being is confined to the east side of the classic Shunganunga,[1] in and around a stately residence. The house has not enjoyed a very good reputation for some years. The former occupant was charged with a heinous crime, but acquitted upon technical points of law. The present occupants are adventurous women, who had rather court sensation than live quiet, unobtrusive lives. But this has little bearing upon the case. Something over a year ago, a lady who had, in her younger days, been a wild, reckless girl, lay upon her deathbed. She had, in former times, been an associate of one who now lives in the stone mansion, who we will call Rachel, and she, in her anguish, yearned to see her friend once more, and sent for her to come to her. She wanted to plead with Rachel to forsake her worldly ways, and make her entrance into the better world sure. But death came too soon, and the last request was never made.

---

[1] A creek.

On the same night, after all in the stone mansion had retired, a form of a woman with long flowing black hair was seen to slide into a room where two girls were sleeping. The apparition moved towards the head of the bed and sat down on a chair and awakened the sleepers. They, thinking it to be Rachel, asked her what she wanted, when the spectre turning a mournful look, which could be seen in the darkness, upon the speaker, arose and moved towards the door. Footfalls on the floor could be plainly heard as the spectre vanished through the door. A stilted moan as of deep despair proceeded from the darkness, and a small voice seemed to be chiding someone and pleading in agony. Soon were heard sounds of returning footsteps, and then all was silent. Those to whom the spectre appeared lay half-conscious and soon dropped off to sleep.

The next morning they were surprised to learn that Rachel had not left her room, but that she had heard the soft footfalls and the voice. No mention was made of this occurrence to anyone until one of the neighbors came during the day and inquired if anything unusual had taken place during the night before, and he was informed of the circumstance. He then said he had noticed the woman go up the front steps, sit down and bury her face in her hands, and seemed as if in distress. This man lives on Tenth Street and is a spirit medium, and felt the influence of the spirit before he saw it. These people agreed to watch for further demonstrations without letting anyone else know. The spectre has never made itself visible since that time, although it has been around the premises, as the opening and closing of doors, walking across the floor, and sounds of voices have indicated. Quite frequently, when all is still, that little voice, which is very sweet and sad, will break the silence with an exclamation of pity or of grief that seemed to come up from a heart that is broken. When spoken to, it ceases its woeful sounds, and the only response that is drawn out is "Oh, for pity!" which has been distinctly understood. When the night is darkest or the elements raging, then the troubled spirit is certain to be in the house, pleading with somebody or for someone, and the voice is saddest and startling.

Recently three prominent gentlemen of this city called at the house to investigate the phenomena. Towards midnight, as they all sat together conversing in low tones, the backdoor was distinctly heard to open and close, and footsteps were heard upon the carpet, advancing toward the party. When the sounds ceased, the party went in the direction of the sound, but felt nothing except a sensation peculiar to a light draft of air passing over them. When pursued, it flees and will not converse with anyone. It is harmless and is disinclined to fill anyone with terror. Those who have witnessed the demonstrations say that they have not the least particle of fear. They are satisfied that what is related here has actually occurred, although some are not believers in spiritualism. The stories of different ones correspond exactly. Further investigation is to be made, when facts may be developed that will throw more light upon the matter.

Leavenworth Weekly Times (Kansas), May 4, 1876
Reprinted from *Topeka Blade* (Kansas)

PERSISTENT MRS. COOK.
The Ghost that has Haunted
an Evansville House for Eighteen Years.

An intelligent and trustworthy citizen has furnished us with the facts about certain apparitions (twice) seen in a dwelling in the suburbs of this city.

About eighteen years ago there lived in this city a Miss Harris, who was young, amiable, and engaged to be married. She had a very intimate friend, Mrs. Cook. The two had often discussed the doctrine of Spiritualism.

One day it was proposed, half in earnest and half in jest, that the one of the two who should die first should appear to the survivor in order to set at rest all doubt. They agreed that the one dying first should, if possible, make the demonstration.

In less than a year Mrs. Cook was dead, and in a short time Miss Harris broke her engagement when her wedding day was near. On the evening which had been set apart for the wedding, she retired early. About midnight, finding she could not go to sleep, she raised the mosquito bar and arose to walk to the window.

As she did so she confronted a veiled figure standing at the side of the bed. One quick, earnest look, and the girl recognized the features of her dear friend, Mrs. Cook. She was terribly frightened, and uttering loud shrieks, ran past and downstairs into the room of her uncle and aunt, and there, trembling with fright, cowered behind their bed. She was so unnerved that she was unable to speak, and they were trying in vain to ascertain the cause of her fright, when another scream was heard, and a servant girl, who had a room opposite Miss Harris, bounded into the room. The girl said that she had heard Miss Harris scream and thought it was her aunt. She arose to go to the old lady's room. As she entered the hall she saw a white figure kneeling at Miss

Harris's door with her hand shading her eyes. She looked again, recognized the dead woman and ran downstairs.

A close search of the house failed to reveal any intruder or any signs of one. The doors were all locked, and the ground windows closed.

Miss Harris afterward married a most worthy minister of the Gospel and is now residing in the Far West.

About two months ago two young ladies arrived in this city from New Albany, Ind., to visit the aunt of the former Miss Harris. Two weeks before they left, they were both sleeping in the room formerly occupied by Miss Harris. Just about midnight, both awoke suddenly. There, standing by the side of the bed, was a white-robed figure, but evidently that of a woman. Each girl, in great fright, softly attempted to awake the other. As they looked, the figure, dim and shadowy, glided slowly backward and disappeared into the hall, though the closed door. They both arose instantly, fearing it was some thief. The gas was lit, the host and hostess alarmed, and a thorough search of the house made. It was in vain. Every door was closed and locked. Every window and shutter was fastened.

And thus it stands. The last visitors had never heard the story of Miss Harris and the spectre. If anybody can explain this away by natural causes, we should like to have it done.

Somerset Press (Ohio), Jan. 26, 1877
Reprinted from *Evansville Journal* (Indiana)

MIDNIGHT MEADERINGS
of a New England Spook—
Sensation over an Alleged Ghost
in Cambridge, Mass.—
Its Story and How It Was Investigated.

Boston, April 8.—Cambridge is prolific in news of late. Today she furnishes a sensation which forms the chief topic of comment here. The story has for its basis a haunted house, in which the spirit of a girl is supposed to have appeared almost nightly of late. The house is situated in the shades of the classic Harvard, was built fifty years ago, and has sheltered many of the most respectable families of Cambridge. Twenty years ago it was said to be haunted, and for some time the owner could not get an occupant. Two years ago it was occupied as a clubhouse for Harvard students, and afforded them many an all-night's sport. The present occupants are Henry Marsh and family, who, during the past six months, according to their statement, have been almost driven wild by midnight gambols of the spirits. The ghost has been heard to walk and run all over the house; to place its clammy hands on the heads of the occupants, both while they have been about the house and abed. The windows have been opened and slammed in rooms where the occupants of the house are positive there was no earthly being, and beds have been moved and the house generally shaken up.

A few nights since, Marsh's wife says she met the spirit suddenly in the kitchen, and, almost scared to death, listened to what the ghost had to say. The spirit said her name was Bertha Stoughton, and that she had been murdered many years ago, and was buried in the cellar, and that her object in staying in the house was to recover a diamond ring worn by her when murdered. The Marsh family are professed Roman Catholics, and, as they have heretofore been skeptical, their story received more consideration than if it came through believers in Spiritualism. The latter here have not allowed an opportunity to pass of attempting to prove the doctrine of their faith, and that there was no illusion. Late Saturday night, with Mrs. Wilde, who is said to be the most powerful medium in the country, a number of Spiritualists, with reporters, held a séance at the house. The spirit of the Stoughton girl manifested its presence and, through the medium, described the details of the murder. She lived in the house with a man now living in Cambridge, a tutor in a well-known educational institution, giving at the same time his name, that she was seduced by him, and he, finding her *enceinte*,[2] attempted to poison her, but gave her an overdose; that he then choked her in her chamber on the second floor, dragged her downstairs to the kitchen, and then through a trap to the cellar under the L portion of the house; that, although here begging her life to be spared, he killed her by striking her four times on the head with a club, and then buried her four feet deep in the cellar. The medium went so far as to point out the spot where she said the body was buried.

Shortly after midnight this morning an *Enquirer* correspondent dug up the cellar to a depth of five feet, but found no semblance of a human body. This fact, in a measure, goes to support the theory of the skeptics that the phenomena is a humbug. The Spiritualists, on the other hand, believe the story and express confidence of yet bringing the murderer to justice as well as finding the body. Marsh's house is now the attraction for thousands of visitors, and the sensation has not been equaled here for many years.

Memphis Daily Appeal (Tennessee), April 11, 1878
Reprinted from *Cincinnati Enquirer* (Ohio)

---

[2] From the French, meaning pregnant.

A HAUNTED HOUSE.
A Dead Miser's Uneasy Spirit
Revisiting His Earthly Dwelling.

In the village of Glenville, on a lonely road in the suburbs of Cleveland, is a frame house of one-and-a-half stories, about which there is at present considerable excitement among the neighboring residents on account of some singular manifestations that occur therein. The family living there have become disgusted with its peculiar attributes and are about to leave. Frequently, and at all hours during the daytime as well as after dark, the most singular sounds can be heard in different rooms in the house, knocks being given so loudly as to frighten people living in a brick mansion many rods away. Watches have been frequently kept to discover if someone was not practicing a fraud, but the investigators have invariably decided that the house is supernaturally haunted.

An old miser who formerly lived there and who bore a bad reputation in other ways besides the hoarding of money, is said to be continually walking and pounding about the premises in order to bring to light a large sum of gold which disappeared mysteriously about the time of his death.

Lancaster Daily Intelligencer (Pennsylvania),
Nov. 19, 1880

The people of Downs, Kansas, are considerably excited over a haunted house or, rather, dugout.[3] About half a mile from town is an island nicknamed by some of the old soldiers of the town and vicinity "Island No. 10," containing some eighty acres and surrounded by the waters of the Solomon. There are no improvements except a dugout, and this is constructed upon a more modern plan than the large majority of them, having a board and shingle roof. Several families have tried to live there, but only succeeded for a short time, having been driven away, as they said, by strange noises, appearance of unknown faces, ghosts, etc.

---

[3] A flood of white settlers from the eastern states and Europe established homesteads in the Great Plains in the decades following the Civil War. On arrival, many relied on dug-outs for temporary shelter. The scarcity of trees for logs inspired these settlers to dig down into the soil or at an angle into a hill and then to secure a roof over the hole. In contrast, a sod house used "bricks" of sod to build walls upward, though the two forms of construction were sometimes combined.

Until quite recently the place was abandoned, but lately a family consisting of husband, wife and two children have been living there. Complaint was also made by this family of the house being haunted, and several of the citizens of Downs went over to the dugout, determined on investigating the matter, and this they did to their entire satisfaction. The party consisted of honest and conscientious citizens and good businessmen. Arrived at the dugout they stationed themselves in and around the house, and there awaited events. Everything was still for a time, but in a little while strange noises began to be heard and soon a voice, "I'll kill you; I'll kill you; I'll kill you," was heard, three times in succession. At this the party set up such a scream that they could be heard in town and, yelling with all their might, did not "let up" until reaching Downs.

There is no doubt of the dugout being haunted. In sight, and but a short distance away, was committed, some two years ago, one of the most cold-blooded murders that has ever been heard of. Further particulars are awaited with anxiety.

Red Cloud Chief (Nebraska), April 27, 1883
Reprinted from *Kansas Paper*[4]

A MURDERED GIRL'S
Spirit Appears Every Night, Accompanied by That of Her Assassin in an Old New England Farm House, and Together They Rehearse All the Ghastly Details of an Awful Crime.

The old Hammond homestead, situated near the boundary line of Wareham and Middleboro, Mass., has recently been the scene of remarkable spiritualistic manifestations. The old house, for years without a tenant, stands in a wild and lonely spot, a half mile or more from any habitation. It is an old New England farmhouse, erected over 100 years ago, two stories and a half in height, and is of that rambling style of architecture which characterizes such structures. The old farmhouse has been the scene of frightful crimes. Many years ago a murder was committed in this house, and five years later a young and beautiful girl was murdered, and her headless body was found in the cellar. No clue to her murderer was ever discovered, and as time went

---

[4] Though several newspapers from this period were called simply *The Paper,* I have been unable to locate one anywhere in Kansas.

on the horrible deed was forgotten, only to be recalled by the recent remarkable phenomena which are said to be witnessed here. It has been but some three weeks since the manifestation commenced, and those who have investigated the phenomena are entitled to much confidence.

The first was witnessed by a party of school children, from eight to thirteen years of age, who day after day were obliged to pass and repass the house. They report seeing a young and beautiful lady dressed in black rush out of the house, closely followed by a man who held in his hand a heavy piece of wood. When but a few steps from the door, the young lady suddenly turned round and faced her pursuer; then knelt down and, with uplifted hands, implored him not to injure her. The man, not appearing to heed the supplications, whirled the stick two or three times over his head and with fearful force brought it down upon the poor victim's head, prostrating her to the ground. The man then quickly took the body up in his arms, reentered the house and was seen to go down into the cellar. As soon as the two were lost to view, the most horrible and distressing cries were heard, as though coming from a multitude of female voices. The children said they were frightened at first, but that afterward they seemed to be magnetized and could not move; but after the man had, as they said, murdered his victim and when he had entered the cellar, they all seemed to realize what had transpired, and when the mysterious cries were heard, frightened almost to death, they ran for their homes, which they reached in an exhausted condition.

All available means were at once taken to ferret out the so-called phenomena and ascertain, if possible, the truth of the children's story. A party of citizens the following evening visited the old homestead, taking up a position in the woods nearby, where they could have a commanding view of everything that transpired within and without the house. The party consisted of eight young men of the village. Suddenly the house within was brilliantly illuminated, and forms, both male and female, were seen to pass and repass the open windows. The excitement in the place seemed to be intense, and the most unearthly shrieks were distinctly heard. Suddenly all was darkness in the place, and a death-like quietude reigned half an hour, when all the apartments[5] from the cellar to the garret were again all ablaze. The young men then started for the house on the run, but when they came near, the manifestations ceased and all was dark again. One of the young men, becoming much excited over what he had seen, started to notify the village people, when he fell fainting to the ground. Further investigation failed to reveal

---

[5] In the 1800s, "apartment" was often used to mean a room.

anything more, and the young men returned to the village and related what they had seen.

Two nights afterward, a gentleman from New Bedford, accompanied by his wife and daughter, on the way from Bridgewater to the above city, were passing by the old house just after dark, when they heard screams from people within. The disturbance frightened the horses so that they were not got under control until they had run a quarter of a mile. The gentleman then drove back to the scene of the disturbance. To his horror he observed while approaching that the house was on fire. Before he could arrive at the place, he had to pass through a densely thick piece of woods that entirely shut out from view for a time the supposed conflagration. Upon getting through the woods he could not see any house, all appeared like a dream. After waiting in the locality for over an hour he proceeded to the city, where he related his adventure.

Several well-known professional Spiritualists have of late visited the locality. They have not seen the phenomena, but they have heard female voices within the old structure, and singing interspersed with frantic shouts and beating upon some instrument resembling a bass drum.

William R. Luce, who resides near the Middleboro line, informs your correspondent that, a few evenings since, he was passing by this old house when he noticed a bright light within. Thinking tramps had taken possession of the place he stopped his horse and, in a moment, observed several females pass and repass the door. Soon they were all seen to proceed up the old rickety stairs into the apartment above. After a while he heard a scream, and the body of a female was hurled down the stairs amid fearful shouts from the inmates. Mr. Luce sprang from his vehicle and quickly proceeded to the house, when suddenly the light was extinguished, and all was still as death in the old mansion. Mr. Luce was not a little excited over what he really supposed was a tragedy and was more surprised when he had investigated affairs at not finding the house occupied or showing any signs of having been inhabited for the past fifty years or more. Mr. Luce is a gentleman of some sixty years of age, well known in this vicinity. He is sure he witnessed the above phenomena, although he does not believe in Spiritualism, never attended a Spiritualist gathering and would not have a Spiritualist in his house.

The manifestations have created considerable excitement in the vicinity. It was not generally known outside of the immediate neighborhood until within two weeks, when it has become the theme of conversation in households within five miles of the place. The people who have been in the habit of passing by the place evenings now go two miles out of the way rather than brave the ghostly figures that haunt the old house. The residence of the owner of the place, Mr. Gibbs, is daily besieged by the neighbors, imploring him to tear down or destroy the old house in some way. It is thought by many that someone will yet set the old structure on fire, as it may be the means of affecting the minds of several who believe in the late manifestations that have occurred there. It was first thought to have been a capricious prank of some village joker, but the investigation clearly demonstrated the theory that no human beings could carry on such an exhibition as was presented a few nights ago to the eight young men.

Your correspondent interviewed several who were present when the manifestations took place, and this account of the affair was related in a straightforward manner, and they seemed to be laboring under great mental excitement over the matter. By invitation of one of the party who witnessed the phenomena, your correspondent was driven to the scene, where the spirits hold high carnival. He was shown the rooms they passed and where the spirits were seen, and the exact spot where the young lady was struck down, and the secluded spot taken by the young men who witnessed the spiritualistic phenomena. Before he had taken his departure some twenty men, women and children had congregated around and within the old structure, and with but two exceptions they believed what had been related about the place.

Memphis Daily Appeal (Tennessee), Nov. 25, 1883

A HAUNTED HOUSE.
The Strange Story Told by Connecticut Villagers.

New Haven, Conn., Feb. 25.—The residents of Killingworth, a quiet town on the sound, are very much exercised over a haunted house. On a lonely road, near the center of the town, stands an old house of peculiar construction. It was in this mansion a decade ago, Mrs. Horace Higgins cut the throats of her three children while they were asleep. They were buried in the village churchyard, and, although the other graves there are covered in summer with abundant growth of grass, not a blade ever grows on the graves of the children. Their mother was adjudged insane and confined in a room overlooking the graves, and every night until she died she would stand at the window gazing on the clock in the church tower nearby, moaning and craving pardon for her crimes.

For many years the house had the reputation of being haunted, and it almost continuously remained tenantless until last summer, when the Ray family of Boston took it as a summer residence. The first night they slept there, the two tenants were nearly scared to death by the apparition of a woman in white standing at their bedroom window. Loud and unearthly noises echoed through the house. The next night Mr. and Mrs. Ray say they saw the apparition, and they promptly gave up the house. Recently only these facts were learned by the villagers, and since then several weird sights have, it is said, been seen in the old mansion.

St. Paul Daily Globe (Minnesota), Feb. 26, 1886

Wheeling (W. Va.) is excited over the discovery that, in spite of the re-shingling of a house alleged to be haunted, there still appears upon the roof a coffin-shaped mark, which has been noticed upon it ever since a man murdered his wife and concealed her remains in a coffin in the loft. For twenty years the house remained tenantless, and when sold recently a new roof was put on, but as stated, the coffin mark has again appeared.

St. Landry Democrat (Opelousas, Louisiana), May 1, 1886

A SPIRIT MYSTERY.
Citizens of Bucksville, Logan Co., Much Excited Over the Manifestation of a Supernatural Agency.

Russellville, March 20.—A very sensational ghost story has been going the rounds in the northern part of this county which at first was thought to be only the work of some imaginative newspaper correspondent, but upon investigation the story turns out to be substantially true, and the deeper the investigation the more startling are the facts.

Bucksville is the name of a post office, store and blacksmith shop situated on the extreme northeastern border of Logan County, and near the Warren line. Among the farmers in that neighborhood none is more substantial than one S.H. Glidewell. His house, an ordinary two-story log and frame structure with an "L," is located in one of the most picturesque spots in the county. The country in this neighborhood is very hilly—almost mountainous—and his farm lies between two of the highest and most rugged of these hills, nestling just under the foot of one in a thick grove of forest trees. There is nothing uncanny or forbidding in the surroundings, but it seems that a veritable ghost has taken up his (or her) abode there and persists in remaining in spite of the determined efforts made to discover and dislodge him. The people of the neighborhood are terror-stricken as the mystery increases and defies all attempts at solution.

The ghost at first confined itself to the upstairs rooms. Here it would remove chairs from one room to another, pull the covering off the beds, tear up the carpets, and on one occasion a roaring fire was found burning in a room which had not been occupied for years, and the door to which was securely locked. Again, the family below stairs were startled from the sleep by the sound of a violin and dancing in the same room. No one was bold enough to venture into the room, but when someone suggested that one of them should call in one of the neighbors, the sound immediately ceased; and when finally the room was entered, no evidence of its recent occupancy could be found except that a candle, which had been left fresh in a brass candlestick on the mantelpiece, was burned nearly to the socket.

On the following night three neighbor boys volunteered to sit up and watch for his ghostship. Nothing unusual was heard until an old clock in the family room struck the hour of midnight, when the almost-sleeping watchers were frightened almost out of their wits by loud peals of laughter, which seemed to come from a closet under the staircase. At first no one dared move or speak, but at last one a little braver than the rest ventured to open the closet door and, with a tallow candle nervously held aloft, peered cautiously inside. Hardly had he passed the threshold when suddenly his light was extinguished, and before he could retreat he was nearly drowned with a deluge of ice-cold water from above, accompanied by another burst of merriment. The watchers fled in graceless confusion, leaving the family shivering with terror. Nothing more was heard that night, but upon entering the dining room the next morning, a skull and crossbones were found upon the head of the table, and at each plate was a small sprig of cedar.

The family could stand it no longer and at noon moved to the house of a neighbor. While they were preparing to remove the household goods from the rooms downstairs (the upstairs rooms not being touched) the table and chairs suddenly began to move as if going through the figures of a dance, and when Mr. Glidewell's son attempted to take hold of one, he received a shock as if from an electric battery, and another peal of laughter sounded in his ears.

However chimerical this may sound, the half has not been told. The above facts were gathered from conversations with some of the very best men in the county, who live in the neighborhood of Bucksville and know that the facts above related are true. All that countryside is shaken to its very center and during the daytime, so I was told by a reliable gentleman, people flock there by scores to look at the haunted house. Mr. Wm. Gulon, the Marshal at Auburn, with a posse of armed men, undertook to probe the matter to the bottom, but although they heard numerous mysterious noises and at prolonged intervals the wild laughter, they were unable to solve the mystery and returned home worn out and thoroughly convinced that there must be something supernatural about it.

Numerous theories have been advanced about the matter, but all seem equally incorrect. The most prevalent belief is that the ghost is the spirit of a man who was drowned in the creek that runs near the house many years ago and was buried on the spot on which Mr. Gildewell's house now stands. Another theory is that it is the ghost of a young girl who committed suicide in that same house in the fall of 1869, only a short time before Mr. Gildewell moved into it; but the mystery remains unsolved and seems to deepen as it grows older.

Semi-Weekly South Kentuckian (Hopkinsville), March 29, 1887

CHICAGO'S HAUNTED HOUSE.
Weird Tales of Ghosts Have Frightened Tenants for Many Years.

Chicago, July 10.—A curious example of how the popular superstition that a house is haunted ruins the name of the property is shown by the destruction of the handsome two-story brick house at No. 126 Langley Avenue. This residence is in perfect repair, and were it not for the fact that it is known as a haunted house, the workmen would have no reason for disturbing it. But the weird tales of what the spooks do there in the midnight hours have frightened all tenants away, and the house has been an unprofitable property ever since the ghosts moved in.

It is in a fashionable quarter of the city, and ten years ago its occupants were three maiden sisters named Trowbridge—Elizabeth, aged forty-three; Anna, aged forty; and Nora, a half-witted woman of twenty-five. They lived modestly, dressed well and had some property. On the evening of July 21, 1879, a policeman was summoned to the house. He turned the slide in his lantern and led the way to the second floor, where, hanging in the archway of the folding-doors, they saw the bodies of the oldest sisters, each suspended from a hook that had been screwed into the woodwork.

Within a week a sign "For Rent" was put up on the house, but renters passed by on the opposite side of the street and pointed out where the tragedy took place. Soon strange stories began to circulate about the neighborhood. Servant girls going to early mass asserted that they saw the ghosts of the "old maids" moving through the deserted rooms, while some insisted that they heard shrieks and moans. People of intelligence laughed at the idea of spooks, yet, in spite of the fact that the house had been put in thorough repair, it remained without a tenant for several years. Finally a family from the East who had heard none of these stories moved in. Within a week they were occupying another house, and the sign "For Rent" was again put up. Their domestic said that every morning the furniture would be arranged differently from the way it was the night before, while after midnight the sound of feet was plainly heard pattering around the hallway and on the stairs. Since then several tenants have lived there, but only for a short time. They all laughed in a half-hearted way at the idea of the house being haunted, but nevertheless they could not be induced to stay.

The double suicide of years ago and the stories of the revels of the spooks has cost the owner many thousand dollars. He is now tearing the house down and will have it rebuilt from the very foundation.

Evening World (New York, New York), July 10, 1888

A MUSICAL PHANTOM.
Violin Solos by a Ghost that Haunts a Mine.
The Strange Story Told
of a Deserted Cabin Down in Alabama—
Sweet Strains from an Invisible Musician.

Down in the abandoned Arbacoochee gold fields, twenty miles south of Edwardsville, Ala., says the *Pittsburgh Dispatch,* stand the ruins of a log cabin where years ago a mysterious and bloody crime was committed. The place is haunted, but not by visible ghosts. No white-robed phantom forms walk with noiseless tread across the broken, vine-covered floor of the old cabin. No specter lights gleam through the one window or across the rotten threshold of the shutterless door. The ghost is heard, not seen, and no one who has once heard the sounds that come from the old cabin at midnight will ever again doubt the existence of spooks.

The ghostly sounds are the music of a violin. The playing is not that of a master, but it is good, and it is soft and low as though the soul of the player was in sympathy with his music. Night after night for many years this ghostly violin played by ghostly hands has awakened the echoes of the deserted cabin. First, there is heard thrumming on the strings, a tuning of the instrument, and then the bow is drawn across the strings when they are all in perfect harmony. A sweet Scottish love ballad of olden days is first played, then comes the familiar music of the Scot's Highland fling.

Then there is a brief pause, another thrumming of the strings, and then on the night air softly floats the music of that old Scottish song: "Within a Mile o' Edinboro Town." One stanza is finished, another is begun; the music is softer, sweeter than before, when suddenly it stops in the middle of a bar, and is heard no more until the following night, when the same programme is repeated.

Of course, there is a story attached to the old cabin, a story to explain the ghostly music, and a weird story it is. In 1868, when the Arbacoochee gold fields were filled with prospectors, two old California miners turned up there one day. Their names were Martin Burke and Daniel McLeod. They were past middle life and had been mining in California and Nevada for twenty years with indifferent success. McLeod was a Scotchman, and to the newly discovered gold field he brought an old violin, which he never tired of playing when asked to perform.

The two miners rented the cabin and went to work prospecting among the hills. They had been there only a few weeks when other miners and prospectors noticed they went out early in the morning, always going in the same direction, and did not return till night. Many suspected they had struck it rich somewhere in the hills, but as no one else had been able to find gold in paying quantities it was finally agreed that Burke and McLeod were merely following some blind lead.

One day the two men were missed. Next day they were still missing, and the cabin was visited. The dead body of McLeod was lying on the floor of the cabin. He had been shot through the head while sitting in front of the fire, playing his violin. When he fell, his fingers stiffened on his violin, and when in removing it from the dead man's hands, the bow was drawn across the strings by accident. The old fiddle emitted a wail for the dead musician which, it was stated, made those who heard it shudder.

Burke was gone, and naturally he was suspected of the murder of his partner. There seemed to be but one reasonable theory of the crime—that the two men had made a rich find and that Burke had murdered his companion and, taking all the gold, had fled. The theory was generally accepted, but as there was no positive evidence against Burke, no effort was made to find him.

None dared to charge him with the murder of McLeod because they had no evidence. Burke spent his days and nights in the one saloon of the little town. About that time the ghostly violin playing in the old cabin was first heard, and one night a frightened countryman was giving an account of it in the saloon at Arbacoochee. Burke heard the story, and it was noticed that he turned deadly pale and, staggering to the bar, called for a glass of liquor. From that night Burke drank more and more, and in a week he was on the verge of the jimjams.[6]

Late one night he reeled up to the bar and called for liquor. A crowd of countrymen were drinking in a backroom, and one of them was playing a violin. Burke paid no attention to the music at first, but just as he raised the glass to his lips the country fiddler began to play: "Within a Mile o' Edinboro Town." The glass of liquor fell from Burke's trembling fingers, and with a gasp, he fell to the floor. The look of terror on the man's face was one never to be forgotten. He fell all in a heap, and in five minutes he was dead. The doctors said he died of heart failure, caused by drink and sudden excitement.

St. Johns Herald (Arizona), May 7, 1891

Mr. Quinn's Ghost.

John Quinn, an old man, died at his residence on Bowman Avenue, Danville, Ills., about two weeks ago. After his death the family vacated the house, which was soon occupied by another family.

Yesterday afternoon, after locking all the doors, the family left for a few hours' visit with some friends in another part of the city. On their return home about dusk they were started to see Mr. Quinn, dressed in his ordinary wearing apparel, walking up and down the floor of his former sleeping room.

Several neighbors were called to witness the strange spectacle, among who were Wilber Walker, Mary Wilmer and Mrs. Henry Kirby. Mr. Quinn's ghost came twice to the window, bowed to the people gathered in the street and then sat down in the window.

Suddenly every trace of him disappeared. Mr. Spreht and Miss Wilmer mustered up courage enough to enter the house and found that not a lamp in the house would burn. Lights were obtained from the

---

[6] The jitters or "heeby-jeebies," but when this article appeared, implying the delirium tremens.

neighbors and search was made throughout the house. Everything was found securely locked, and there was no trace of anyone having entered. The neighborhood is greatly excited over the occurrence.

The Dalles Daily Chronicle (Oregon), Oct. 3, 1891
Reprinted from *Indianapolis Journal* (Indiana)

Broken Up by a Ghost

Fort Dodge, Io., Dec. 11.—A husking bee at the Rasmus Thompson farm, near this city, was broken up by the appearance of a ghost at the festivities. The frightened farmers are ready to take their affidavit that it was a ghoul, though none of them waited to made sure. The ghost is said to be that of Mrs. T.F. Mahar, who died in the house a couple of years ago. Several people claim to have seen the apparition.

St. Paul Daily Globe (Minnesota), Dec. 12, 1891

A KENTUCKY SPECTRE.
THE GHOST OF A MURDERED TRAVELER
Still Visits the House in Which He was Killed—
Uncanny Stories Told of the Old Ross Place.
DEEDS OF DESPERADOES

Five miles west of Mt. Vernon, in Rockcastle County, Kentucky, on the crest of a high hill stands an old log house in the midst of a fifteen-acre clearing. Dilapidated and desolate, the house presents a weird and uncanny appearance. The fields are barren wastes overrun by herds of cattle that roam the mountain for pasture during the spring, summer and autumn seasons.

The building is reputed to be the oldest in Rockcastle County, having been erected early in the present country by one Ross, and was occupied by him and his descendants for many years. The property at the present time is owned by Mr. Tom Frith, one of the most substantial men of his section. Though the stories told of it are in the main gruesome and uncanny, they are related and believed by the best people of the county.

One of the most weird stories related of the old place is that of the murdered traveler, whose uneasy spirit haunts the premises and makes it decidedly disagreeable to the tenants. This story, vouched for by some of the most reliable and solid citizens of the county, is about as follows:

Some years previous to the outbreak of the Civil War, the "Ross place," as it is called, was occupied by a family named Holder. These people bore a bad reputation, and it was conceded by all that there was no crime too mean for them to commit. In addition to being known as

THEIVES AND ROBBERS,

It was hinted that they were counterfeiters and murderers as well.

The Holders were desperate people and did not hesitate to commit any crime. Those that were not in the gang with them feared them, and so they carried on their wickedness for years without being molested.

One day in the summer of 1859, a stranger, mounted on a splendid horse, stopped at the little station now known as Brodhead and made inquiries as to the route to Cumberland Gap. According to a bystander, the traveler gave his name as James Travers, from Ohio, and stated that he was on his way to the mountains, where he alleged that he and his brother were the joint owners of a mining interest. He was evidently a man of wealth and seemed to have plenty of money in his possession. What directions the countryman gave the stranger as to the route is not known, but some months afterward Travers' brother appeared in Rockcastle and set on foot to make inquiries concerning James Travers, whom he had traced that far. Careful investigation disclosed the fact that the mining man had taken the wrong route to the mountains and had stopped for dinner at the house of the Holders. Here all trace of him was lost.

Mr. Travers was convinced that his brother had met with foul play and that the Holders knew more about the missing man than they would tell, so he left immediately for Cincinnati to enlist the services of experienced detectives to assist him in fastening the crime upon the Holders. However, when he returned with assistance, the Holders had disappeared as completely as if the earth had swallowed them. No information could be elicited regarding them. They had gone, and that was all that could be learned. The house and premises were searched, but no trace of the missing Travers could be found.

THE OLD HOUSE

Remained unoccupied for a long period, and then Tom Ross, a grandson of the original owner of the place, moved with his family into the house. Previous to this, however, strange tales had been circulated regarding the lonely farm. It was haunted, the people of the neighborhood said. Strange sights had been seen and strange sounds had been heard in and around the old house, and he was considered a brave man, indeed, who would pass there alone after dark.

Despite all this, Ross, who was a coarse-natured man of the ruffian type, took up his abode there and defied the "h'ants," as he termed them. But after a time his manner changed, and he openly acknowledged that the place was haunted. In addition to hearing unearthly noises through the night, Ross solemnly avowed that, since he had been an occupant of the house, promptly at noon of each day a strange voice, seeming to come from the direction of the gate opening on the road, would shout "Hallo!" three times quite distinctly. On going to investigate, nobody could be found. Ross at first thought it was some of his neighbors trying to play a trick on him, and he would revile the "thing," as he called it, in the most terrible manner. This had no effect in bringing forth the possessor of the mysterious voice, and all would be quiet until the next day at noon, when there would be a repetition of the cries of "Hallo!" from

NO APPARENT SOURCE.

One of Ross's more skeptical neighbors, hearing of this, went over to satisfy himself that the stories were or were not fabrications. He related afterward that he was satisfied that the tales told of the ghost were based on a solid foundation. He distinctly heard the voice at noontime shout "Hallo!" and in addition to this said that, when Tom Ross poured forth a volley of oaths at the mysterious visitor and challenged it to come forward and show itself, a large and ferocious watchdog that belonged to Ross, and which was standing midway between the house and gate, suddenly dropped his tail and retreated to the house, snapping, snarling and barking as if pursued by some terrible object intent upon doing it bodily harm. On reaching the dwelling the dog took refuge under the bed, from whence no persuasion could induce it to come for some hours. The skeptic stated that his own feelings at this time were not of the calmest and added that, while he was by no means converted to spiritualism, he had no desire to repeat the experience.

Ross shortly after this moved to another section, and tenants for the old house followed in rapid succession. But each occupied the premises for a short time, all getting away as soon as practicable and with singular unanimity telling the same story of the mysterious noonday visitor and his blood-curdling cry.

The ghost, according to one tenant, a German, John Dietzman by name, did not restrict itself to shouting "Hallo" at the gate, but extended its operations into the house. John told that the ghost would come lumbering down the stairs from the little room above, making a noise similar to that of an empty flour barrel rolling down the steps.

THE UNCANNY VISITOR,

At all times invisible, would proceed to the fireplace, stir up the embers and cause a roaring fire to blaze up the chimney. This performance was repeated nightly, and all the time John and his good wife would lie in bed shivering with terror and not daring to move. The German could not stand this, and he soon moved away.

The house then remained vacant for a long period. One night during this time, a party of young men, returning from a dance in a spirit of bravado, determined to spend the remainder of the night in the haunted house. On ascending a hill about half a mile distant from the old house, they discovered that the building was on fire. Angry flames were pouring from it in all directions, and it was evident that it would soon be burned down. The young men hastened their steps, being eager to witness the end of the fated structure. To reach the building they had to pass through a strip of woods which momentarily obscured the burning house from view. Their astonishment can be imagined when they emerged from the woods and, quite near the old structure, found it standing dark and gloomy and intact. The young men did not stop to make any investigations, but hurried from the haunted spot as rapidly as possible.

Of course it was generally supposed that the spirit which was playing such pranks at the old Ross place was that of James Travers, and this supposition was confirmed not long since in a very remarkable manner.

A party of the best citizens of Rockcastle County determined to thoroughly search the entire premises for some

KEY TO THE MYSTERY,

And to that end the floors of the house were taken away and every foot of ground turned up to a considerable depth. But nothing was discovered. An old outhouse that stood in one corner of the neglected yard and which had years before served as a corncrib, was next visited, and the rough puncheon floor of that taken up. Here the searchers met with better success, for after digging awhile, a man's skeleton was unearthed. The back of the skull was badly crushed, showing in what manner death was inflicted. A printed handbill, containing a description of James Travers, had been circulated at the time of his disappearance, and one of these had been preserved in the Circuit Clerk's office at Mt. Vernon. Thereupon was described certain defects in the teeth of the missing man. The teeth of the skull unearthed in the old outhouse tallied exactly with the printed description, and the identity of the skeleton as that of James Travers was established beyond peradventure.

The bones were given a decent burial, and it was hoped that by this means the premises would be rid of the tormenting ghost, and the place was immediately rented to a family of negroes. But it seems that the burial of the bones had no effect toward quieting the ghost, and the colored people soon moved away after being nearly frightened to death by the unseen noontime visitor and his unearthly cry. Since then the old home has remained unoccupied and is fast going to decay.

Hartford Herald (Kentucky), June 12, 1895
Reprinted from *Cincinnati Inquirer* (Ohio)

GHOST SEEN ON SPORT HILL
SPECTRE HAD MADE
SEVERAL APPEARANCES
According to the Testimony of Two Very Reliable Witnesses, the Ghost of
Thomas McAndrew Appears Every Few Nights at the Second Story Window of a House on Throop Street Occupied by Charles Brewer—
The Stories Told by Those
Who Have Seen the Visitor.

The residents of that portion of Dunmore which bears the name of Sport Hill have been very much excited during the past few weeks over the appearance of an alleged ghost, which a number of absolutely sane and singularly unexcitable people maintain they have seen on several occasions. The story of the spectre's visitations runneth thus:

Last summer, Thomas McAndrew, an old man, who lived in a pretty little house on Throop Street, across the street from the Bliss silk mill, died, and almost immediately all sorts of queer stories about the appearance of his ghost began to be rife in the neighborhood.

The old man's children are said to have seen the spectre on several occasions in the cellar, and it is said that it prowled about the house at night, uttering all sorts of weird and uncanny noises and cutting up all kinds of high jinks, even going so far, as one man told *The Tribune* reporter last night with bated breath, as to play Irish jigs on the piano.

After the ghost had been doing its turn for several months, the family moved to New York City, and the house was vacant until the end of June, when Charles Brewer, the night foreman of the silk mill, and his young bride moved in. Mr. Brewer, who is a bright, intelligent, clean-cut and matter-of-fact young man with no spiritualistic leanings, is the man who has seen the ghost more times than anyone else and is therefore more able to give a succinct description of the alleged unearthly visitor than anybody else.

DESCRIPTION OF GHOST.

A *Tribune* man had a long conversation with him last night, and he described in detail the appearance of the deceased McAndrew's ghost. The ghost, he said, makes its appearance in the two second-story windows of his house overlooking the stoop. The house faces the silk mill, which is kept running all night. The peculiar part of Mr. Brewer's narrative is that he has never seen the ghost while at home and in the house, but always sees it from the windows of the mill.

When he rented the house he was told that it was haunted and was warned against living in it, but, as he said last night, he pooh-poohed these stories and decided that the best ghost in the world couldn't force him to give up a house he liked. Now he thinks otherwise.

He first saw the ghost in the front room windows on the night of June 25, he says. He was looking over at the house from the silk mill and says he distinctly saw the figure of an old man with a white beard pass back and forth before the windows. A sort of light seemed to diffuse itself from the spirit's body and lighted up the windows and the porch.

He inquired of his wife the next day as to whether she had heard anything, and she replied that she had not, but that she had been asleep all the time. Mr. Brewer was inclined to doubt his own senses, he says, and he accordingly spent all his spare time watching for the reappearance of His Ghostship.

He says he saw the spectre again a few night afterwards, and this time the window curtains were pulled down. After that he saw it several other times, and he has now arrived at the conclusion that what he saw was really a ghost.

"I didn't believe it at first," said he last night, "but I must say that I am forced to now."

THEY HEAR NOISES.

He said that he and his wife decided to move their bed downstairs finally, and that since this has been done they continually hear all sorts of strange noises. The other night, he says, they distinctly heard someone get into bed upstairs, but found no one in sight when they rushed up. So convinced has Mr. Brewer become that the house is haunted that he has decided to move out.

Another person who has seen the spectre is Lafayette Decker, the engineer at the mill. Mr. Decker is a tall, fine-looking old man, with cheery blue eyes and an open, honest face. He told *The Tribune* reporter that he used to laugh himself sick when he heard the folks talking about spooks, but said that since he himself had seen the ghost, he does not laugh anymore.

38

He says he was called to the window by Mr. Brewer a few weeks ago and saw the spectre distinctly. It didn't appear to him as much like a man as it did like a bundle of old clothes, he said, but a light shone from it, and it moved past the windows and finally disappeared. "It called to me, too," said he, "but I didn't go."

The Tribune reporter suggested to the two men that they might have mistaken the light from the silk mill or a chance ray from one of the electric lights nearby for the ghost, but they guessed they knew light when they saw it. The suggestion of a practical joke on the part of Mrs. Brewer or some of the mill hands was almost indignantly frowned down.

The Tribune reporter spent some time at the window of the mill, waiting for the ghost to appear, but he was apparently off duty, for not a sign of him showed up, despite Mr. Decker's announcement that he generally appeared on Monday night, between the hours of 10 and 12.

SPORT HILL STIRRED UP.

At any rate, the ghost story has stirred the residents of Sport Hill up to a high pitch of excitement, and the street in front of the haunted house is nightly thronged until 12 o'clock with an anxious throng desirous of getting a peep at something from the other world.

As might be expected, the rather plain and unvarnished tale of Messrs. Brewer and Decker has been touched up by others in the vicinity. For instance, one youth assured *The Tribune* man that old McAndrew, before he died, announced to his family that no fruit would ever grow on the trees in the yard after his death, and added that not a single bit of fruit has since appeared.

Scranton Tribune (Pennsylvania), July 30, 1901

GHOST RULES HOUSE.
Queer Doings in Alleged Haunted Residence Caused Excitement at Dunkirk, N.Y.

Residents in the Fourth Ward of Dunkirk, N.Y., are greatly excited over an alleged haunted house in Lincoln Avenue. The house in which the ghosts are said to hold sway is a small, gloomy, vine-covered cottage, resting back from the street, almost hidden from view by deep shrubbery. It was the house of an aged woman who was found lying on the floor one morning dead. For years she had led the life of a recluse, and her every action had been shrouded in mystery. After her death considerable money was found secreted about the place.

39

Within the past two years over a dozen families have lived in the house. None remained longer than two weeks. A family who had moved into the house Monday last moved out on Thursday. They stated that continually about midnight the sound of footsteps, groans, blood-curdling chuckles of laughter and the clanking of chains could be heard throughout the house.

The lighted lamp on a number of occasions was blown out without any apparent cause, and several times the bedclothes were forcibly pulled from the occupants of the bed. The old woman during her life never allowed a person to enter the house. The opinion is that she has come back to the world to keep people out of the house, which she guarded so jealously before her death.

Washington Bee (DC), Dec. 13, 1902

HAUNTED
House in Chicago Draws a Mob
Which Is Dispersed by Firemen
Ghost Puts Eleven Policemen to Rout
When Furniture Dances

Chicago, Aug. 1.—Thousands of people—police estimate is 5,000—jammed the streets for a solid block around the "haunted" house, 181 Twenty-Third Street, for three hours last night with the hope of seeing the "ghost" which had driven two families from the premises and put eleven of the "bravest" to rout.

So demonstrative was the mob that the police were forced to send in riot calls for fifty reserves to clear the streets. Time and again the police charged the crowds without avail.

They were driven to the expedient of calling out the fire department and throwing streams of water, pumped by two engines into the struggling mass of humanity before the ghost was left in peace.

At 9 o'clock last night, after the last drenched straggler was sent on his dripping way, the police from the Hinman Street station, led by Sergeant Lyman, closed and locked the little house of mystery and stationed a strong guard around the premises to watch all night—from the outside.

The Bacheldor family, which occupies the house in the daytime, when the ghost has retired, went to the home of Mrs. Bacheldor's mother, Mrs. Will Ludington, 1046 Twenty-Second Street, to spend the night.

All of their possessions are in the "haunted house," and it works a hardship upon them to remain away. None of the members of the family are willing to undergo the blood-chilling, nerve-freezing horror of the table rappings, the stopping of clocks, the moans, moving of pictures and jumping of furniture that has cursed the place.

Mrs. Bacheldor says that today she will probably call upon her church to hold sacred services in the house with the object of propitiating or laying the evil spell that is woven about it. She says she has called upon scientists and the cold, everyday reasoning of the police to explain the phenomena without success. Now she will try the power of prayer.

As early as 6 o'clock in the evening the crowds flocked to the vicinity of the house last night. By 6:30 o'clock there was a howling mob that swirled through Twenty-Third Street from Hoyne Avenue to Leavitt Street, jammed the abutting thoroughfares, and made the night hideous with moans, cries, catcalls and hootings.

"Let me at the ghost," screamed a young girl in shrill treble. "If I catch him I'll kiss him."

"Show it to me," said a big laborer. "I eat ghosts for breakfast. Let us at him."

Police stationed at the doors of the little house had all they could do to keep the fighting, tugging mob from breaking through. When the press became too hot for the little army of officers, a call for reserves was sent in.

The response swelled the little army of officers to fifty, but they were swept about in the turbulent mob like straws in a Niagara.

"The fire department," shouted Sergeant Lyman in inspiration. A call brought engine companies 23 and 36. The engines were coupled up. Three firemen manned each nozzle. Aiming the streams in the air, as a direct blast from the water would have been sufficient to all but kill, the firemen sprinkled the mob until it disbursed, blubbering and gagging.

The ghost, through stage fright or some other reason popular with ghosts, failed to make itself manifest last night.

But Mrs. Bacheldor regaled such of those as could hear her with many hair-raising stories of the ghost's appearance before.

"Three persons died in the house just before we took it," she said. "For all I know, there may be three ghosts. There is enough noise for three.

"We took the house from the Citrke family, which owned it, the Saturday before the Fourth of July. I thought that they acted queerly when I asked them why they wanted to give it up so cheaply, but I was not told that Mr. and Mrs. Citrke and a daughter, Kate, had all died in the house.

"The spook started spooking Sunday. First, a picture, one, I believe, of the dead Mr. Citrke, over whose body his two sons were said to have fought about the will until a candle ignited his clothing, jumped around and then fell to the floor.

"Then the chairs began to moan. They didn't squeak or creak; they moaned—long, low, like the sounds emitted by a pigeon. Then the clocks took the notion of stopping at 7 o'clock in the evening.

"This is the hour that old Mr. Citrke is said to have died.

"These manifestations continued about four times every week until I felt that I was about to suffer with nervous prostration. My husband laughed at me until a week ago tonight. He had always called it some kind of a practical joke.

"But a week ago last night, Harry Ludington, my brother, was seated in the dining room. Mr. and Mrs. Charles Hesher and others of my family were in the front parlor.

"Suddenly Harry, white as paste, came running into the room. 'I hear it,' he cried. But there was no need for him to warn us. A long, low moan that ran up my spine like a mouse clinging to the spinal cord, came from the room just vacated. The great dining table lifted itself in the air and moved about the room. We fled.

"The police were called. Sergeant Lyman and other policemen entered the house with drawn revolvers, saying that it was only a human imitation of a ghost and that they would shoot the joker. The pictures started bobbing, the moan came again, and they didn't know where they were going, but they were certainly soon on their way."

Bismarck Daily Tribune (North Dakota), Aug. 2, 1908

HOUSE HAUNTED, THEY SWEAR.
Eight Policemen Bear Witness
to Ghostly Sounds by Night.

Eight policemen of Gary are convinced, after having made a personal investigation, that a certain small cottage a mile from Tolleston is the abiding place of a genuine ghost. The squad of officers came to this decision after having spent a night of terror in the haunted house. Moans, raps and other sounds continued in a mysterious manner through the night they say. Until two months ago the house was vacant. Steve Gradochic and family then moved in. Wails and sounds of a struggle have nightly disturbed the new tenants, and they called the police to investigate. Several years ago a farmhand committed suicide in the cottage.

Plymouth Tribune (Indiana), Feb. 4, 1909

Haunted House, All Right.

Los Angeles, Cal., Aug. 19.—Haunted houses may be all right in novels, but when they pop up in real life they are apt to be a bit of a bore. One of the prettiest bungalows in the Pasadena Avenue neighborhood got the name of being haunted. Tenants said the spirit of Dr. Mills, spiritualist who perished in the Titanic disaster,[7] kept them awake nights by pounding on the walls. After scoffing, the landlord slept in the house two nights. Then he ordered it torn down and rebuilt.

Topeka State Journal (Kansas), Aug. 19, 1915

N.Y. Society Is Taking Tea with Ghosts
By J.H. Duckworth

Ridgewood, N.J., June 15.—The ghost of a murdered Hessian soldier whose phantom body can be heard falling on the worm-eaten oak rafters of a bat-haunted attic is the latest novelty offered to attract motorists to a wayside tea house.

This spectre-haunted place is the picturesque Rosencrantz homestead at Ho-ho-kus, N.J. on the old Albany Turnpike, the scene of Aaron Burr's romantic wooing of Madame Provost in 1777. It has been opened as a tea house by the Misses Rosencrantz, last of the family of Gen. Rosencrantz of Civil War fame.[8] Taking tea with the ghost here is now a popular pastime with wealthy automobilists from New York.

---

[7] I can find no one named Mills known to have died in the sinking of the Titanic. However, one identified victim was W.T. Stead (1849-1912), a prominent advocate of Spiritualism and an editor of two collections of "real" ghost stories. After he died, Estelle Stead, his daughter, and Pardoe Woodman, a medium, "recorded" *The Blue Veil: Experiences of a New Arrival beyond the Veil* (1922). This book is framed as an account of the shipwreck and the afterlife "communicated" by Stead's spirit.

[8] While the ghostly Hessian soldier rings of the headless horseman in Washington Irving's "The Legend of Sleepy Hollow," this historic house still stands and can be visited by the public. Called the Hermitage, it is indeed where Theodosia Prevost married Aaron Burr and where the Rosencrantz family lived from 1807 to 1970.

"The story is," said Miss M.E. Rosencrantz, "that at the time the Hessian troops were encamped at Paramus, a mile from here, a Hessian soldier was murdered upstairs for his bag of gold. A well-stuffed money belt, at any rate, was found hidden in the wall of the attic during the lifetime of the late Col. W.D. Rosencrantz, cousin of the Civil War general.

"The Hessian's ghost has haunted the house ever since, according to tradition. We often hear at night a queer sound in the attic as though a dead body had fallen on the floor.

"We rushed upstairs to discover what made the noise, but never had our curiosity satisfied. Not even have we found the dust disturbed.

"It is all very uncanny, but we are used to it. We cannot, however, get friends to pass the night with us."

Students of historic buildings are as much interested in the place as are the delvers into psychic phenomena. Here Aaron Burr met, wooed and won the fair Mme. Provost. The young soldier was in camp at White Plains, 25 miles away. He used to ride over to Tarrytown on horseback, take the ferry across the Hudson to Nyack, and ride on to Ho-ho-kus, getting back to his regiment just before daybreak.

It was during these momentous times that the Hessian soldier met his untimely end and bequeathed his restless spirit to send cold chills up and down the back of hot and dusty automobilists.

Bismarck Tribune (North Dakota), June 15, 1917

THEN THE FAMILY MOVED OUT.

From "GHOST RULES HOUSE," page 39.

HAUNTED HOUSES
with Ghosts Unknown

The final report in the previous chapter hints that, over the 1910s, haunted houses had grown quaint enough to attract tourists for tea. This chapter charts the transition from hardnosed disbelief to a more fair-minded consideration of haunted houses. One article I found— published just a few months after the Civil War—opens by reporting on "a dwelling really believed to be haunted," but it quickly shifts to editorializing about such beliefs: "We talk of the nineteenth century; how enlightened it is, and how bravely we have got over the superstitions of other ages. While the fact is there is just as much belief here in witches, hobgoblins, spirits and haunted dwellings as there ever was." The writer then describes a man who, despite having lost thousands of dollars in an investment, never lost faith in the Spiritualist medium who had given him financial advice.[1] Similar skepticism surfaces in the first few articles here, but it's gradually eclipsed by the practice of attributing claims about ghosts to "credible and trustworthy" sources. Were journalists and their readers becoming less confident that ghosts didn't exist?

Whatever the answer, this chapter is focused more on ghost reports that provide no backstory to explain why their respective houses are haunted. The mystery surrounding these hauntings is greater, and this might explain why we begin to see more attention paid to the investigation of the supernatural phenomena. Indeed, ghost hunters step forward here with candlesticks at the ready.

Our house-hunting continues, but the night has grown darker.

A Haunted House in Pittsburg.

The *Pittsburg Chronicle*, the other day, published a long and sensational story to the following effect:

---

[1] *State Rights Democrat* (Albany, Oregon), Oct. 14, 1865.

A gentleman newly arrived in Pittsburg from New York rented a house on Pennsylvania Avenue. He soon discovered that his house was haunted. He saw male and female spirits flitting across the room and heard the usual unearthly sounds. He became much alarmed and invited a number of his friend to his house for the purpose of solving the mystery. Among those present was a reporter of the *Chronicle,* who writes as follows:

Books were lifted from the tables and slammed down upon another; bells were rung all through the room; the piano (although tightly locked up) was played; a guitar suspended above the chandelier, where no human hand could reach it, was made to discourse most excellent music; doors tightly locked were opened and slammed shut; sparks of fire were carried about the room; one fellow, a disbeliever in spiritualism, was choked by an unseen hand and almost frightened out of his wits; and many other marvelous things were witnessed. The phantoms which appeared were a beautiful woman, and a most horrid demon, who seemed to attend upon her. The skeptic above alluded to made a frantic attempt to seize the female figure, which instantly vanished and left him insensible upon the floor, when the landlord tried to put a bullet through the demon by firing a pistol at him. The place, after these violent demonstrations, became "too hot" for either occupants or visitors, and the house was vacated and is not "to let."

The other papers of that city pronounce the report nonsensical, but state that it is producing mischievous results. The *Dispatch* of Friday says:

During all day yesterday, the crowd visiting the home in which the "Startling Revelations" were supposed to have occurred were very large. Last night, about eight o'clock, a credulous assembly, numbering not less than five hundred persons, congregated around the "haunted mansion" to see what could be seen. Their "enthusiasm" arose to such a pitch that for a time a demolition of the structure was seriously threatened, and as it was, many of the windows were broken and other parts of the house abused by missiles hurled by the crowd. Alderman Butler, Mayor Lowry, Chief of the Police, and the officers of the emergency force were present and dispersed the curiously inclined after some difficulty. No arrests were made. All we have to say is that the property is depreciated at least two-thirds in value by the publication of such manifest absurdities.

Dayton Daily Empire (Ohio), May 4, 1865

A Good Old-Fashioned Ghost in Pennsylvania.

The town of Bristol, Pa., according to the *Philadelphia Press* correspondent, has a haunted house, where a ghost of the most approved style holds midnight revel to the great alarm of the townsfolks. Here are some particulars:

WHAT THE GHOST DOES.

This fine mansion is deserted. On dark nights or at the midnight hour it is avoided, and the luckless wight who has to pass it walks on tiptoe like the opposing pickets used to do on the Peninsula when a soldier in the copse was unwittingly exposing himself to death.[2] Moans have been heard to come through gaping, broken windows—shrieks, imprecations, soliloquies—as if there was something or somebody in agony—something or somebody that wanted to die yet was commanded to live—and lights often glare out in the darkness or pass by the windows with such rapidity as to leave a long line of light behind. But the appearances are not by night alone, but by day also. The orgies of the ghost do not disappear, like mountain mists, before the sun. In sunlight as well as by the "glimpse of the moon," the spirit walks to the affright even of those who are bold enough to enter within the haunted precincts. Its manifestations differ in the daytime, however. A few days ago two skeptical young ladies, learning that the ghost could be seen at precisely six in the morning, determined to brave ghostly displeasure by entering his domain and plucking a wild flower or two. They went as promised to the affright of servants, who were surprised at unwonted early rising—and now let them tell their own tale:

"The sun had got up when we got to the gate. When we opened it, it creaked on its rusty old hinges and went back again with a slam after we had passed through. That frightened us a little; but still we kept on right through the tangled bare grass in the path and the twisted stems of boxwood, wet with dew. We went around the side of the house right to the back, where there is a large flowerbed that has been growing to weeds, and growing and growing longer than I am growing old. We went right up to the flowerbed, and Annie was just pulling a sprig of geranium, when there came a rapping—such a rapping—at a window just over our heads (a little shudder) and a shower of tiny pebbles—and where they came from we didn't know. We were frightened, I tell you.

---

[2] In 1862, General George McClellen led Union forces up the Virginia Peninsula in an attempt to overtake the Confederate capitol of Richmond. However, General Robert E. Lee defeated the plan, which went down in Civil War history as the Peninsula Campaign and the Seven Days' Battle.

But we weren't going to give up. So we tried to get a flower again, and then there was a rapping again, only quicker and louder than before—a shuffling of feet, and a groan. We looked up at the window, but saw nothing, and then we ran away as fast as we could, and I fell down in the tangled path to the gate."

ANOTHER ACCOUNT.

The manifestations at night have more of horror for susceptible and superstitious minds and weak nerves, for darkness invests with terror what daylight shows even to be quite usual and commonplace. I will not enter into any detailed description of them, but give you the statement of an old farmhand who, after speaking of the "haunted mansion," gave his own experiences.

"You see, sir," he said while he stopped his horse (he was plowing at the time) and gathered up the rein-ends in a lump in his brawny fist— "you see, sir, I was just the way I am now (he wore a shirt, muddy kersey pants tucked into his boots, and a battered straw hat). I was going down to the store for the old man, and I had a bit of a kettle in my hand and a big basket slung over my shoulder. I walked along first rate till I got down to *that* place" (nodding his head toward the mansion with a motion half muscular, half nervous). I felt queerish-like and hitched myself up to go by right and square. It was only about nine o'clock or thereabouts—maybe it was close to tea—but what should I see when I got to the far end of the fence but a tall person in white with a brown kind of a handkerchief on its head—and it had a candle in one of them old-fashioned candlesticks. It walked along on the tops of the flowers and box-bush like, and didn't bend them."

"'Ah!' was my involuntary exclamation while I assumed an air of great interest and entire belief.

"Yes, sir," said the ploughman decisively, "and it walked right towards me, and then I got up and left, and that's all I know."

"And do you really believe in the existences of the ghost?"

"Well, I guess I do!" answered he decisively. "Has not everybody believed in it these twenty years gone?"

We did not demur, but left him and wondered how anybody in Bucks County could believe in ghosts at this day. It was an evidence of want of knowledge as well as of superstition. But Bristol was an old borough; it was a Democratic County; that explained the matter—partially.

WHO THE GHOST IS.

That I cannot begin to tell you. There are many intimations of black deeds in that old house years ago, and fifteen other conjectures as are usually indulged in in such cases. Those who have seen the ghost all

50

differ in their descriptions of him or her, so that the "oldest inhabitant" cannot fix anybody, once in the flesh but now departed, who looked like it. The property is said to be owned by a lady in your city, who does not occupy it because she is afraid. She knows not who the ghost is, only that he or she is.

Ottawa Free Trader (Illinois), Sept. 9, 1865

A Haunted House.

A curious story is going the rounds of the press concerning a haunted house in Penn Yan, New York. A visitor thus describes what he saw and heard: "Our village clock was striking the hour of twelve when we entered the haunted room. The stillness was disturbed first by what seemed a guitar, played but a few feet from us, and as sweet a voice as ear ever heard singing to it in a low tone. In an instant the sound of voices and footsteps were heard all about us, but although the room was lighted as a lamp could make it, we saw nothing. The singing continued until the same sweet voice, in the most piercing and sharpest utterance, cried, 'Help!' As the unearthly yell broke forth we felt our hearts beat quickly, our breath come heavily, and every nerve tingle. Three times did this mysterious voice cry, 'Help!' After this followed what seemed to be a dance of madmen, together with the most demonic screams ever heard."

Weekly Panola Star (Mississippi), April 10, 1869

HAUNTED HOUSE.
A Cloud-Like Ghost—Clanking Chains—
Family Terrified—A Hasty Move.

Some time ago we noticed the fact there was a house in Chartiers Township which, according to the assertion of the people of that neighborhood, was a haunted house. A family recently moved to the place not knowing that spirits walked through the rooms and over the roof at "the witching hour of night." Their account of what they heard and saw has led some persons to believe that there is something wonderful going on within the old moss grown walls, and they have determined upon an investigation.

The house is an ancient one and is in a dilapidated, tumbledown sort of a condition. On the outside, the walls are blackened and broken whilst within the mold grows green and the rats leap about in a startling way. It is just such a house as ghosts are said to dwell in—dark, gloomy

51

and cheerless, and to be within the old walls alone, even if no ghost should appear, is said to be enough to give one the horrors and send the cold chills a-capering down the back.

The Chartiers ghost is said to appear in the form of a black, shadowy cloud, and at times to assume the shape of a female with long, trailing clothes as it glides around the room. The gentleman who rented the house is a laborer in this city, and his wife and family are generally left alone. The first night they occupied the house, however, the husband and father was with them. No noises were heard on this occasion, and it is presumed that if the spirits did appear, the family, after the fatigue of moving, slept soundly and did not hear them. After spending one night at home, the husband and father returned to the city, and the wife and children were left alone.

Then the spirits appeared—they glided from one room to another, upstairs and downstairs, through the hall, over the roof, out of the windows, across the yard, anywhere and everywhere that they could create the most surprise and consternation. The lady of the house was a courageous woman, and she stood the "scare" remarkably well. The next night, determined to give battle to his ghostship, she brought into the house a ferocious dog—one so ferocious and fearless that they were obliged to keep him chained lest he should attack persons who made friendly calls on the family. The dog being in the house, the wife and children felt safe, but when the shadowy ghost appeared lo! even the bold and bloodthirsty dog slunk and skedaddled away like a whipped spaniel. His tail fell suddenly, and there was not any more fight and growl in him.

The lady of the house had no belief in ghosts, and she *womanly* resolved that she would stand by the old house yet a few days longer, expecting that the mystery would be cleared up. She accordingly sent a message to her husband in the city, acquainting him with the facts, and asked him to come out and see the shadowy cloud and hear the wonderful noises.

The husband pooh-poohed—he didn't believe in ghosts—not he—it was only rats and imagination that was alarming the family. Nevertheless he went, but continued to pooh-pooh at the idea of ghosts and haunted houses in Allegheny County and in this enlightened age. The husband invited two or three other gentlemen to come and spend the evening with him that they might receive the ghosts in proper style. They accepted the invitation, and one of them had a bottle of spirits with him and asserted that, if the ghost should prove to be His Satanic Majesty, he would invite him to take a drink. Another one of the party, like Hamlet the Dane, declared that if a ghost should appear he'd "speak to it, though hell itself should gape and bid him hold his peace."[3]

It appears that the men were having a pleasant evening together, chattering, laughing, etc., when a clanking of chains was heard. Thinking there must be something wrong with the horses, one of the party went out to investigate, but everything about the stable was found in its proper condition. About this time the dark, ghost-like cloud appeared, and the man who was under the impression that the ghost, if there *was* a ghost, was His Satanic Majesty, forgot altogether to ask him to take a drink—it slipped his memory altogether. The other gentleman also forgot to "play Hamlet" and "speak to it."

The husband and father was convinced—he declared that "seeing was believing," and he accordingly moved his family to another house without delay.

Three or four "brave boys" of this city have heard of the matter and are determined to investigate for themselves. If they should see the dark cloud or hear the clanking of the chains and should escape to unfold the tale, they will take pleasure in unfolding it. Or course there is nothing supernatural about the mysterious presence of the cloud. A volley of buckshot or a shower of pebbles might soon develop the substantial and terrestrial character of the supposed-to-be supernatural visitor.

Democratic Press (Ravenna, Ohio), June 22, 1871
Reprinted from *Pittsburgh Gazette* (Pennsylvania)

STRANGE GOINGS ON.

A week or more ago we alluded to some mysterious occurrences in a house in Dunn County, Wisconsin, but the story lacks the completeness which subsequent investigation has given it, the more wonderful phenomena not having been mentioned. According to a reporter of the *St. Paul Pioneer,* the family occupying the house is named Lynch and consists of husband and wife and three children. The trouble commenced eighteen months ago, when household utensils began to disappear and various articles of raiment were cut and torn up.

The eldest son was accused of being the mischief-maker, but he maintained his innocence, and a short absence from home convinced his parents that he was not the moving cause of their distress. Matters became so serious that an appeal was made to the neighbors for their

---

[3] *Hamlet* 1.2.244-45.

intervention, but they regarded it as some cunningly devised scheme to play on their credulity with a view to obtaining money from them, and held aloof. At last, however, two persons were induced to visit the house and investigate. They took with them some pieces of cloth, which they placed in a bureau drawer, in an upper room. Locking the drawer and the room, they waited an hour downstairs and then found the cloth had been cut and torn to shreds.

A five-year-old child, left alone for a few minutes without thought of the consequences, had her hair cut close to her head and was unable to say how it was done, as she had seen no one. A venerable elder, who thought the Good Book all-powerful to exorcise the demon influence, entered the room where the liveliest manifestations were experienced with his bible under his arm. He was surprised to see a broadax traveling toward him, apparently of its own volition, and he dropped his book and precipitately retired. When he regained his courage and reconnoitered, his surprise was increased at finding that the broadax had chopped the bible to pieces. Other incidents, equally strange and startling, are awaited.

Tri-Weekly Astorian (Oregon), Nov. 4, 1873

STRANGE SOUNDS
HEARD IN A MILWAUKEE MANSION.
THEY ARE LAID TO SPOOKS—
AND ARE ACCOMANIED BY FLASHES OF LIGHT—
ADVENTUROUS SPIRITS
SEARCH THE HOUSE IN VAIN—
A PROFOUND MYSTERY.

Just at present Milwaukee rejoices in a sensation of the ghostly nature, and the attention of scientists is invited to the following facts narrated in the columns of the *Sentinel* of that city: For some time rumors have been in circulation to the effect that an old house in the Sixth Ward was haunted. Strange stories were told by people who had lived in the building, and the neighbors noticed that few tenants stayed for any considerable time on the premises. This latter fact need not be wondered at, as the building is one of the oldest in the city, so old, indeed, that it is credibly reported by old citizens that on the eventful morning during the Bridge War, when East Siders loaded their old cannon to the muzzle with the full intent of blowing the wicked West Siders into the hereafter, they pointed their grisly gun at this identical building.⁴ It stands on the bluff overhanging the river, southeast of the reservoir, and commands a fine view of the city. Just below it on the west is the deep ravine in which many a desperate deed was done in the early days of the settlement.

Reports of the wonders done nightly in the building induced a skeptical *Sentinel* reporter to visit it yesterday with a view of examining into the truth of the rumors. It is a square-built, two-story house, roughly weather-boarded on the outside and dark, dismal and dingy within. It has never known either paint or window blinds. With some difficulty the reporter procured the key from a neighbor who has the letting of the house. It is uninhabited by the living at least at present, and the worthy Teuton's eye twinkled as he saw what he imagined to be a prospective tenant. The building contains a cellar, four rooms on the first floor, two large ones and two closets on the second, and a garret. The walls were bare and battered; large patches of plaster had fallen off, and in the room which had been used as a kitchen, the floor was worn through in two or three places. The stairs were quite rickety, and the old-fashioned stepladder which led to the garret was thickly
COVERED WITH COBWEBS.
The whole scene was sad and dreary enough; the wind howled fitfully through crevices and broken windowpanes, and the heavy drip of the rain through the leaky roof gave an air of unutterable desolation to the place.

When questioned regarding the disturbances said to take place, the crafty German, Herman Hegner, at first denied their occurrence. Questioned more closely, he admitted that such stories were current in the neighborhood and even admitted that he himself had been a witness to some things there, which he solemnly averred were of preternatural origin. He had moved into the neighborhood two years ago and, having heard some wonderful stories of strange lights and sounds in the house, determined to investigate the phenomena. A Polish family had been living in the building and had moved away through fear. He watched

---

⁴ In the early 1840s, tensions rose between those living east and west of the Milwaukee River—two autonomous and competing villages—over having to pay for a series of bridges connecting the two villages. The bridges had been ordered by the Wisconsin Territorial Legislation, and in 1845, resentment had intensified enough that the west siders sabotaged their half of the Chestnut Street Bridge. Offended east siders readied for battle, even pointing a loaded cannon across the river, though they never fired it. The destruction of the bridges escalated until, in 1846, the City of Milwaukee was formed, bringing the rival settlements under one jurisdiction.

55

the house the first night that it was vacant and noticed that, shortly after midnight, the room in the southwest corner of the first floor suddenly filled with light. Thinking that the house was on fire he hastened to the window to see what was the matter, but just before he reached it, the light disappeared. He stood for a moment and then started for the front door, of which he had the key. Before he had moved two steps, the light flashed forth again with blinding brilliancy, shone for about a minute, and again disappeared. He entered, groped his way through the rooms and found no living thing. This appearance of light, produced by no human agency, he had often seen repeated. At times nothing would be seen of it for months, and again it would appear nightly for weeks.

He had never heard of any spectral appearances nor of any movement of any kind in connection with this phenomenon until about a month ago. Then a Bohemian family, lately arrived in the country, took possession of the house. The first morning after their entry they came to complain of having been disturbed repeatedly the previous night by the sound of footsteps, falling bodies, and occasional suppressed screams upstairs. All the members of the family, five in number, slept on the first floor. The next night, it seems,

THESE NOISES WERE REPEATED

with even greater violence than before, for about 1 o'clock, the whole family came rushing to Hegner's house and, terror stricken, refused to go back. Next morning they packed up their traps and moved away.

The story got abroad and was multiplied by the neighbors. Last Sunday evening, two Englishmen applied to Mr. Hegner for permission to spend the night in the house for the purpose of exposing the delusion and capturing the ghost. He gave the key, furnished them a blanket apiece, and they went in. Early next morning Hegner went to the house, found the front door open, his blankets lying in one of the lower rooms, and the visitors gone.

The reporter inquired their names. Hegner knew one of them, George E. Heath, a blacksmith working in the shops of the old roundhouse near the reservoir. The reporter sought him out and, having ascertained his identity, questioned him regarding his experience at the haunted house on Sunday night. After some hesitation he consented to tell what occurred, saying beforehand that he still disbelieved in ghosts, although he could not explain what he had seen and heard. His story briefly told is as follows:

I knew the reputation of the house, but only laughed at the stories I heard about its being haunted, so last Sunday I bantered a friend of mine named Henry Jordan to go with me and stop in the old house that

56

night. He agreed, and we got the key and some blankets at a house at the foot of the hill and went up to the house. The sun had just set, but there was light enough to see well, so we went from cellar to garret to make sure there was no one inside. There wasn't a living thing, not even a rat, to be seen, so we pocketed the key and walked down to the roundhouse, where we stayed till after 10 o'clock. We went back and, after smoking awhile, made up our minds that we were a pair of fools for coming to an old house as still as the grave to look for ghosts that were not to be found. Soon we got sleepy and lay down. I was awakened by Jordan, who told me he had heard some noise upstairs. We sat up for a moment, and then I heard

SOMEONE WALK STEALTHILY

across the floor above; then there was a pause followed by noise as of someone leaping on the floor. A scuffle followed. I heard a smothered cry and a heavy fall, and then all was still. I proposed to go upstairs and was just about to strike a match with which to light our candle when the room we were in was filled with a blinding light. For a moment my eyes were dazzled so that I could distinguish nothing; then I saw Jordan point toward the stairway, visible through the open door. I looked but saw nothing. The light seemed to last for about a minute and then went out. It might have been longer or shorter, I cannot certainly say.

I lit the candle and looked at my watch. It was 25 minutes past 12. I was not frightened in the least and insisted upon going upstairs. At first Jordan hesitated, but when I moved he followed me. We searched both rooms and closets, but found no trace of anything living or dead. I even climbed the ladder and looked into the garret, but there was nothing there. We descended, blew out the light and determined to stay awake and watch. In about fifteen minutes we heard again that stealthy step; the same pause, leap, cry, struggle and fall followed, succeeded by the same strange light. I wanted to search again, but Jordan refused to stay another moment in the house, and so I was compelled to leave.

On being asked what explanation he could give of these strange phenomena, he could give none; but he didn't believe that ghosts had anything to do in the matter. He expressed himself perfectly willing to stay there again any night if anybody would stay with him. He bantered the porter to stay there last night, but the latter hadn't time. Jordan is a worker in the Milwaukee & St. Paul car shops and is said to be an honest, trustworthy man. The same is true of Heath. The affair has created the wildest excitement and no end of talk in the neighborhood, and the brown old building is a perfect terror to all the children and not a few of the grown persons living around it.

Indiana State Sentinel (Indianapolis), Aug. 19, 1875

New Berlin, that staid and steady old town on the banks of Penns Creek, is just now thoroughly shaken up by a ghost story. The ghost seems to have a partiality for Mrs. Gephart's house opposite the Evangelical church. He behaves very badly at times, and it is a wonder that people are willing to put up with such cuttings up, even by a ghost. The other Tuesday night, between the hours of 10 and 12, he upset a bureau, threw books on the floor, rolled up the carpet, made blinds rattle and hurled a stone through the air outside the house, and all this without showing himself to anyone. The same thing was repeated on Thursday night. All this is vouched for by sundry persons who were present, and yet we cannot but confess to some doubts in the matter after all.

Millheim Journal (Pennsylvania), April 24, 1879

A special from Seymour, Ohio, says that there is intense excitement in Seymour over a ghost. Wednesday night it entered the "haunted house," walked upstairs and disappeared. It was white and appeared to be the ghost of a man. Thursday night the spook appeared headless and horrifying. It passed upstairs into a bedroom. The lady of the house locked it in a room. It tried to open the door, but could not get out. Yesterday morning it had vanished.

Stark County Democrat (Canton, Ohio), July 8, 1880

A MICHIGAN SPOOK.
The Furniture of a Dwelling House Waltzes Around.

Reed City, Mich., boasts of a real old-fashioned haunted house sensation. An old house in the east part of the village was lately leased and occupied by a gentleman of this village. Soon after he occupied it, the family began to be disturbed at night by sounds as if some person was walking about the rooms. This annoyed them greatly, but there were no violent demonstrations until one night last week, when they were awakened by a great commotion in the house.

The gentleman got up and attempted several times to light a lamp, but could not do it. He finally gave up the attempt and concluded to make an examination in the dark. While groping around he would be seized apparently by a person who attempted to throw or push him over. He finally got hold of a poker and attempted to strike it, but every time failed to hit anything material. He repeatedly attempted to light

58

the lamp; and still the unseen force would seize and attempt to push him over, and it would take all his strength to resist.

Finally there came a great clatter and noise, and every piece of furniture in the house seemed to rattle and dance around. By this time his wife could not stand it any longer, so they dressed as best they could in the dark and started for one of the neighbors. As they went out of the door they heard distinctly the report as if three pistol shots had been fired in the cellar. Calling up the neighbor, the gentleman left his wife in the house, and the two men returned with a lantern. They searched the house and cellar thoroughly, but could find nothing that could explain the cause of the disturbance. The effect upon the man's wife was such that she would not live in the house, and they have moved into another dwelling.

The night after the disturbance, a party of men sat up until morning. They had lights burning all over the house, and played an accordion all night, and reported the next morning that they did not hear anything. A great many ridiculous stories are afloat in regard to the sensation, but the above were the only disturbances heard. We have this from the gentleman himself. He does not believe in "ghosts."

Daily Globe (St. Paul, Minnesota), Oct. 9, 1882

EVICTED BY BAD SPOOKS.
Queer Doings on Broad Street—
Why a Lease Was Broken and
Why a House Agent Will Not Sue
for Its Enforcement.

One of the finest residences on north Broad Street is for rent. The last tenant moved out a few days ago and defies the irate house agent, who threatens to hold him liable for several months of unexpired lease. The lessee, who is a prominent lawyer, claims that he has been evicted by ghosts. He declares, moreover, that the landlord knew that the house was haunted, and he swears that he will contest the payment of further rent in the courts if necessary. Indeed, he is preparing his defense in case the issue comes to trial. The family physician and every member of his household have more or less direct testimony to give regarding the supernatural inmates of the house. The story has been known to several friends of the lawyer who live on Spruce Street near Broad and on Arch Street near Eighteenth. One of these gentlemen passed the night with the lawyer in his library in order that he might be able to corroborate the tales that were told him. The house is near Columbia Avenue on Broad Street.

TAKING POSESSION.

The lawyer became tenant two-and-a-half years ago. The site of the house is one of the most desirable on the great boulevard, and the occupant furnished it sumptuously. The drawing room was large, and sliding doors separated it from the library behind, which was filled with professional and miscellaneous books. The dining room was in an extension. Several months passed after the lawyer had taken possession before anything unusual occurred. Then the incident was so trivial that it excited curiosity rather than fear. It was this:

The gentleman returned from the theatre one night. Finding that everybody in the house had gone to bed and that the building was perfectly quiet, he stepped into the library to smoke a cigar. The lamp on the table had a heavy shade upon it, which kept the room in shadow. Seated almost sideways to the grate, the gentleman could look out through the open doors leading to the drawing room and could distinctly discern a light in a house on the opposite of the street. As he sat smoking, thoroughly wide awake, the gentleman imagined that he saw one of the sliding doors move slightly. In a few moments the light outside was shut from his view. He thought little of it at the instant—hardly enough even to ascribe it to an optical illusion. When he looked again both doors were moving, and as he sprang to his feet, they came together with a crash that reverberated through the silent halls. The lawyer, to whom the idea of supernatural agency had not yet occurred, stepped promptly to the doors, opened them, and passed through the front room into the hall. All was silent. Hall and drawing room were empty. Still thinking that a servant had been closing up the house he called aloud. Then he lit the chandelier, shook out all the draperies at the sides of the windows, and peered behind the sofas. Nobody. Not a word about this was said to any member of his family.

THE MYSTERIOUS FOOTSTEPS.

Several weeks passed. The lawyer's wife spoke to him one morning about hearing persons going up and down stairs several times during the night. There was a step near the foot of the second flight that creaked. Their bedroom door was quite near, and when awake, the creaking stair could be readily distinguished. All members of the family were asked in the morning, but all denied having been up or down stairs during the night. The servants were equally positive. The lady of the house doubted the credibility of the witnesses.

A night or two after, the doorbell rang, but though the lawyer sprang at once to a window, which was open, nobody was on the stoop.

It was a bright moonlight night, and there was no place for anyone to hide. The lawyer then took matches and went down through the halls. The front door was bolted. Not a sound was to be heard. His last match was burned at the door, and he started up the stairway in the dark. Close behind him came the footfall of another person. When he reached the landing he lost no time in gaining the door to his room. There was a bright light within. He pushed the door open, hoping that he had at last caught the servant who had been annoying him. The sound of the footfall pursued him and, as he had stood there in the full glare of the gaslight from his own room, passed up the second flight of stairs to the floor above. The squeaking stair again registered the weight of a human body. The wife within heard the step. "Who is it," she asked without a suspicion of anything more than a belated servant. The lawyer could only slide into the room, bar the door and stammer, "— if I know."

A GHOSTLY CARNIVAL.

For more than a month after this incident the house was full of spooks every night. Still the lawyer was resolute and plucky. The gas would suddenly go out in the library. He only cursed the gas trustees. Cold gusts of wind would blow through the house, though the weather was mild. He only abused the Signal Service Bureau.[5] The folding doors closed and opened so often that the crash did not even disturb him when he was engaged in reading up references for a law case. Noises like the howling of a dog could be heard in the cellar, though he did not keep an animal about the premises. Sounds as of two persons whispering together could be distinctly heard in the wide hallway, though several prompt investigations showed that the place was deserted. The lawyer did not give serious attention to these matters, though the other members of the family were in open mutiny. The cook refused to go to the cellar for coal. The waitress gave notice to leave because the lady of the house forbade her to spill grease over the stair carpets from the candle with which she insisted on lighting herself up to bed. Neither servant would answer the doorbell after dark or light the gas in the drawing room if by mischance it was forgotten before nightfall.

---

[5] The Signal Service Bureau was formed by the U.S. military after the Civil War ended. The Bureau recorded and collated meteorological data from widespread stations with the goal of warning citizens about storms developing over the Great Lakes and the Atlantic and Gulf Coasts. The Bureau has since evolved into the U.S. National Weather Service.

THE FINISHING SCENE.

Just about this time a lady, related to the family, came on a visit. She occupied a room at the back of the house on the second floor. About midnight she threw herself against the door of the room occupied by the lawyer and his wife, frantically demanding shelter and protection. She was admitted, pale, almost fainting. She explained that someone was secreted in her room. She had heard groans and deep sighs. Not the slightest intimation had been given her of the stories current in the house. The wife accompanied the visitor to her room. The gas was lighted. Nothing; nobody! On the following day the visitor left.

A new chambermaid was hired soon after, but at the end of three days she positively refused to remain in the house because she declared that at intervals during the night the halls rang with hysterical laughter and screams.

These are only a few of the incidents that have been related to the writer. Others, not set down here, are more glaringly improbable than any in the above record. These statements, whether hallucinations or susceptible of proof, were received from persons otherwise thoroughly credible. One thing certain is that the lawyer has vacated the house and declares he will stand a suit rather than fulfil the terms of his lease.

Daily Dispatch (Richmond, Virginia), May 20, 1883
Reprinted from *Philadelphia Times* (Pennsylvania)

"THE HOUSE IS HAUNTED."
An Extraordinary Ghost Sensation
Near a Hoosier Hamlet.

Indianapolis, Ind., March 24.—The people living in the neighborhood of Castleton, a small village thirteen miles from Indianapolis, are greatly excited over a most extraordinary ghost sensation. Several hundred persons from the surrounding country have been crowded about the haunted spot since last Friday. There is an old log house on the farm of a man named Mart Garrison, which was built half a century ago and has been

UNINHABITED FOR SEVERAL YEARS.

Last week Mr. Garrison began tearing the old structure down and hauling away the timber. Between sundown and dark on the evening of the first day's work, while loading his wagon, he says he became conscious of a peculiar feeling which made his hair stand erect with horror, and as he turned, he claims he saw three figures, two of them quite large, flitting around the ruins. He did not stop to investigate, but abandoned his work and fled for home, when he related his experience to his wife and was advised to the let the old structure alone. He talked about the strange apparition, and then it leaked out that an old citizen living near had often seen unearthly figures and so had his family, and he had heard

CRIES AND GROANS

like those of a woman in distress, but he feared to speak of it for fear the people would call him childish and superstitious. Another neighbor testified in much the same strain, and several persons investigated, but were unable to explain the character of the phenomena. They saw shadowy figures indistinctly resembling two adults and a child, and so did perhaps a half score of others able to muster courage enough to visit the ruins.

Yesterday the farm was literally overrun with people and reports reach the city that they found a grave in the cellar, which they proceeded to open, but were stopped in their work by a lady interested in the property. Hundreds of people have visited the haunted house, and there is great excitement over it in the neighborhood.

St. Paul Daily Globe (Minnesota), March 25, 1885

THEY COULDN'T STAND IT.
A MANSION IN TROY, N.Y.,
IN WHICH NO ONE CAN LIVE.
The Imposing Residence Said To Be
Haunted by Supernatural Beings—
Mysterious Tramping of Feet,
and Opening of Doors—
The Face at the Window.

Troy, N.Y., Jan. 20.—In one of the most fashionable neighborhoods in the city and in the midst of some of Troy's finest residences stands an imposing three-story stone mansion. Until three years ago it was never without a tenant, and in those days was the scene of many joyous social assemblies wherein figured wealth and beauty. The mansion was suddenly vacated, but its splendid appointments and desirable location soon brought it other occupants. Their stay was brief, and again newcomers took up their abode within its walls. Moving out and moving in then became a common occurrence until finally it was noised about that the building was haunted, and for nearly two years the "To Let" card which is nailed to the door has brought no response. The experiences of persons who have sought to make the stately structure a pleasant home, but who were driven to other shelter by what they earnestly aver to have seen and heard, furnishes a ghost story that occasions unusual thought from the fact that the recitals are those of residents of eminent reliability and not prone to sensational narratives.

In the dead of night, it is alleged, occupants of the mansion have been awakened by sounds like the tramp of many feet. Doors have been opened in the most mysterious manner and shut with a slam that startled. Tables have moved across the floor, and chairs have fallen as though pushed by unseen hands. One man who had resolved to brave the peril of an investigation followed the sound of the tramping feet from the first story to the topmost, and his only reward was a thrilling shriek from, as he presumed, a supernatural being. Another member of the family who occupied the house declared that one night, just before the usual racket began, a white-clad figure was seen to move across the parlor, look at the clock on the mantel and, with a sigh or groan, vanish as though turned into air. The declarations of others who have passed sleepless nights among the strange visitors vary in their descriptions of the agonizing sights, but all point toward the presumption that no mortal can live peacefully in the grand house.

Policemen who patrol the beat on which the mansion is located tell of a pale face pressed against the window panes after midnight and of strange lights flickering within. The shop girls in coming from their work at night either avoid the block that contains the haunted house or else hurry past on the opposite side of the street.

Last winter the owner, William Crowley, determined to occupy the structure, but after a brief occupancy with his family, he removed to other apartments. Recently a party of young men volunteered to pass one night in the building. When the appointed time came, only two of the company appeared to receive the keys, and then their courage weakened and they concluded not to interrupt the revels of the ghostly band. Mr. Crowley, convinced that the mansion must fall into decay, has just sold the property for $9,500, about $30,000 less than its real value were there nothing to detract from its worth. What the new owner will do with his purchase is not yet decided upon. It is reported that he will dislodge the "spooks" by demolishing the house and erecting another residence.

Argus (Rock Island, Illinois), Jan. 20, 1886

Disagreeable Texas Ghosts.
THEY COME AROUND AND PUT THEIR HANDS ON THE FACES OF SLEEPING PEOPLE.

Dallas, Tex., March 11.—The second ward of Dallas is in a ferment of feverish excitement over a haunted house. The inmates of the house have moved out, unable longer to withstand the terrorizing feeling of cold hands nightly placed on their faces. The experience is of a most blood-curdling nature. The neighbors were called on to watch the manifestations of ghosts and were stampeded and cannot now be prevailed on to reenter the house. The sensational feature of the unearthly manifestations will be developed when a party of men explore the house at night and make their report.

Evening Star (Washington, DC), March 11, 1887

An Unpleasant Visitor.

An old resident of this city, who lives on H Street and in whose family there was a very tragic occurrence many years ago, has for the past year been annoyed by a ghostly visitant, who haunts the house night and day, generally making his or her presence known about midnight, though the gentleman has at noon had such reminders that he was not alone as having a paper that he was reading snatched from his hands, though he could see no one near him. At night there are loud and mysterious noises, as of heavy weights being thrown down, slamming of doors, murmuring of voices, etc., and at times the lights are blown out. The haunted individual declares that there is no "foolishness" about the matter and has at various times invited friends to visit the house and judge of the manifestations for themselves. He has got used to them now and gives them little attention; but occasionally, when he does not want to be annoyed, he has obtained quiet by doing some energetic swearing.

Sacramento Daily Record-Union (California), July 20, 1887

Haunted.

Near the corner of St. Charles and Jackson Streets is a haunted house, sure enough haunted. It is a fine residence sitting back in the yard which is richly and tastefully laid out with flowers.

A letter came to this office last week asking us to make enquires about the place, that they thought it was haunted or occupied by a gang

65

of burglars who were making the people in that neighborhood believe that the place was haunted. We went up there last Sunday night to investigate it and found the writer, Mr. Loenburg, pretty correct in what he stated in his letter to us. Arriving there at 10 p.m., we posted ourselves in different places and commenced our watch on the building.

It was fully four hours before we saw anything. A light appeared in the backyard and commenced to advance toward the front. We could see the light but could not see anyone carrying it. It suddenly went out. A half hour after that, a white object appeared on the gallery. Coming down the steps it went among the flowers; at the same time the light we had seen came shooting from the backyard and stopped directly in front of the figure in white, who held out his hand and took it.

This was more than we could stand. Picking up a good many bricks we commenced pelting the figure in white. We are positive we sent several bricks through it. But it still stood there. Finding no more bricks or rocks handy, we stopped throwing. We watched the figure and the light for fully ten minutes before it disappeared and then went up the side of the house to the roof. It walked on the guttering of that roof for some time and suddenly vanished. We heard chains rattle, bells ring, and several shrieks. It was nearly five o'clock Monday morning before the noises ceased. We left deeply impressed that the house was surely haunted. Those who do not believe that it is haunted go up there and see.

Weekly Messenger (St. Martinville, Louisiana), July 21, 1888
Reprinted from *New Orleans Observer* (Louisiana)

A SMALL WHITE HAND.
Captain Burris Has Quite an Interesting Experience in an Empty House.

Another ghost has arrived in the city and made her debut yesterday morning at 9 o'clock. Very little is known of her except that she has a delicate white hand. She had a male partner, and he arrived in the humble guise of a paperhanger. As a general thing ghost stories are not reliable, but this one is as well authenticated as the Constitution of the United States or the Declaration of Independence. It is not necessary to locate the haunted house, for of course the pair of ghosts were seen in a house at that hour of the day. It is not necessary, but it is not right as the house is a good one and commands a handsome rent when occupied.

It will be noticed that no one believes in ghosts, but it will also be noticed that when a house is known to be afflicted with one it generally remains empty, no matter how admirably it is located or how handsome its apartments.

If you want to ascertain how many people believe in ghosts, consult a rental agent who has a haunted house on his hands, and he will tell you.

Another singular thing about ghosts is that those who "believe in them" are not afraid of a legion of them while those who do not believe in them are the very people who are afraid as death of them. Well, to the story.

Captain Burris is a quiet, respectable, credible gentleman that resides at the Goodyear House.

Wednesday night he would break his sides laughing over the absurdity of a ghost story; last night it is doubtful whether he slept a wink from the time he went to bed till the rooster's clarion voice was heard in the distance, commanding the spirits to hie themselves off to their own habitation. Yesterday morning at 9 o'clock Captain Burris was taking a quiet walk, and being a man of business and interested in a property, he looked at the houses along the streets which he traversed. He came to one excellent house, which he found empty, and being of an inquisitive disposition, he went in to ascertain something about its appointments. He walked slowly from one room to another until, in one of the rooms, his attention was attracted to a little closet. He leisurely walked up, caught hold of the knob, and partially opened the door, when to his surprise it was drawn shut again with a slam. He tried to open it again, and to his astonishment the same thing was repeated. He concluded that there was a powerful spring somewhere, and his curiosity was aroused. He braced himself against the wall with his left hand while with the right he made a terrible effort to open the door. One jerk opened it, but to his horror and fright, a small white hand caught hold of the knob and pulled the door back despite his efforts to hold it. It was a lady's hand, but there was no lady visible, and Mr. Burris' hair raised on this head as straight as the quills of the most angry porcupine that ever lived. Cold chills went chasing each other along the spinal column, and still he didn't believe in ghosts.

He was determined to solve the mystery, and he stood by that closet and watched the street with the eye of a hawk, determined to call the first man that passed to his assistance. In about twenty minutes a man appeared on the sidewalk, and Mr. Burris called him in. He told him the story and asked him to try whether he could open the closet door. To his surprise the man called his attention to the fact that the closet door was open. Mr. Burris was more astonished than ever when he found the closet was too small to contain any living being larger than a mere child. He was still more surprised to find that there was no possible exit from it except through the door over which he kept watch all the time.

The two men stood on the threshold of the room door, talking about the strange affair when a little boy with a bundle of schoolbooks came along. When the boy arrived in front of the house he came to a sudden standstill, as if something in the house attracted his attention. He entered the yard and went straight up to the door when he started around the house to another entrance. The men asked him where he was going, and he said he was going into the house to see "what that man wanted."

"What man?" asked Mr. Burris.

"Why, the man in the house," said the boy.

The house was again searched, but no man was found.

The boy said that, when he was passing, he saw a man kneeling on the floor in the house as if he was papering it and that he beckoned to him to come in. When he arrived near the house, the man beckoned him to come around to another door, and it was there he was going when Captain Burris and the other man accosted him. Every door in the house was locked except the doorway in which the men were standing, and it was impossible for any man to be in the building; and yet the boy was positive that there was a man in the room and that he beckoned to him to come in.

Captain Burris was more astonished than ever, and he came right downtown and took John Goodyear into his confidence. Both of them went to the house again, but no more ghosts were seen. It was learned in the neighborhood, however, that a tragedy was once enacted in which a lady lost her life, and while Captain Burris does not believe in ghosts, nevertheless, he halfway believes that the hand he saw was that of a dead woman.

A spiritualistic test will be made in the house in a few nights, and if there are any troubled souls there, they will be brought to the front and made to make explanations.

Wichita Daily Eagle (Kansas), Oct. 20, 1893

A Night with a Ghost
Hair Raising Experience of a
Man in Haunted House

Weird tales are being told of a haunted house in the little village of Carroll, Ind., and the stories of ghostly happenings are apparently backed up by the very best evidence—that of persons who have seen the spirit and beheld its work. The house is owned by a resident of the village, Frank Yater. It is an ordinary dwelling with nothing about it to suggest the supernatural. Mr. Yater has had dozens of tenants, but none would stay. Six months ago he announced that anyone who would move into the house could have it rent free for a year. In three months eight tenants had moved in and as quickly moved out again.

In some respects the stories of all the tenants tally. Footsteps are heard at all hours of the day and night, doors open and close without any visible agency, the crashing sound of dishes comes from the dining room when there is no one in it, groans of the most agonizing character are heard, while many have actually seen the spectral visitant, a being so terrifying in appearance that the spectators do not even like to tell of it.

Mr. Lape, who has to his credit the longest tenancy of the haunted house, tells some marvelous stories of his experiences. The house had been untenanted for some time when Mr. Lape took it, and the night before his family was to arrive he took possession and decided to spend the night there. He had a bed, table, chair and lamp moved into one of the rooms on the lower floor and built himself a fire in the grate. Having an utter disbelief in the supernatural, he felt no fears as to any probable visitors and was, in fact, rather in hopes that some would appear so that he might expose the mischievous pranks of some of the neighbors.

Mr. Lape had a fox terrier, an animal with the most intense curiosity and a disposition to nose around in corners and out-of-the-way places, and this he took along with him. On arriving at the house Mr. Lape's attention was directed to the peculiar actions of the dog. As a general thing the animal was disposed to roam ahead of his master, and when the door of the house was opened he darted in. He immediately darted out again and betrayed a manifest disposition to run away. He came back at Mr. Lape's command, however, but kept close to the latter's heels, all the while showing the greatest uneasiness.

Having completed his preparations, Mr. Lape sat down near the table containing the lamp and began to read the paper. The dog had taken a position on the floor in front of the grate fire, but his head still kept moving about as if following the actions of some person, and his eyes were set.

It was nearly 12 o'clock when Mr. Lape distinctly heard the sound of footsteps in the adjoining room. He arose softly and moved toward the door of communication, which he had locked and the key of which he held in his hand. His intention was to suddenly throw open the door and catch the mortal visitant that he was sure was there. As he reached the door, however, he was amazed to see it noiselessly open in spite of the fact that it had been locked. Mr. Lape was not daunted by this fact and boldly walked into the room, the dog all the time at his heels. The sound of footfalls still continued, yet by the light of the lamp which Mr. Lape carried in his hand, he could see that the room was vacant.

At one of the farther corners of this room was a door that opened into the hall, and toward this Mr. Lape moved. As he did so the footsteps seemed to move directly in front of him, and on looking down on the floor, which was thickly carpeted with dust, Mr. Lape was amazed to see the imprint of a naked human foot made before him as the footsteps moved. Arriving at the farther door, it swung open as noiselessly as the other had done, although it had been locked by Mr. Lape. The footsteps moved steadily and audibly along the hall, leaving their trail of impressions in the dust, and went up the stairs. Mr. Lape followed in time to see the door of one of the bedrooms open noiselessly and then close again. The trail of footprints led to this door, yet when Mr. Lape reached it, it was locked securely. He opened it with a key which he had with him, but the room was empty. There was no other door by which it could be entered, and the only other egress from it was by the window, which was securely fastened.

When Mr. Lape turned to go out of the room, he found the door closed. He heard no sound of closing and had left the key in the lock on the other side when he opened it. He set his lamp down and tried to force the door open, but couldn't budge it. When thoroughly exhausted with efforts to get out of the trap in which he had been captured, Mr. Lape paused with the intention of getting out of the window. As he picked up the lamp from the floor, he was surprised to see the door slowly and quietly open, and then he walked downstairs. There he found all the doors closed and locked, although he had left them open when he went upstairs.

Most men would have had enough by this time, but Mr. Lape had his "dander up," as he expressed it, and was resolved to see the show out. He again placed the lamp on the table and sat down by it to read one of the papers he had brought along. His reading was soon interrupted by a sensation of intense cold, and at the same time, the light from the lamp began to grow dimmer and dimmer. Not only the lamp, but the fire in the grate began to grow dim, while in the air before him what appeared like a cloud with the outlines of a human face was visible.

Mr. Lape's attention was now attracted to the dog, which had forsaken his position in front of the fire and had sneaked to the farthest corner of the room. There he stood with his back to the wall, every muscle strained as if about to leap on something, his hair erect and his teeth bared, while the froth dropped from his lips. Mr. Lape called to him, but the animal paid no attention. Then Mr. Lape's attention was called from the dog to the cloud-like shape that was before him and to which he attributed the intensely cold feeling that affected him. From this cloudy shape could be plainly seen two eyes—eyes that were the essence of malignity and devilish hate. The light had grown so dim that the room was, by this time, almost in darkness. Once or twice Mr. Lape said that he felt an icy clutch at his throat, but this he brushed away.

"If I had betrayed the least fear," he said, "I am certain I would now have been a dead man."

This horrible appearance was in the room, as near as Mr. Lape can reckon, about fifteen minutes. Then the cloudy shape disappeared, and the figure of a young and beautiful woman was seen sitting at the table where Mr. Lape had sat. She appeared to be in the deepest distress and groaned and wrung her hands in agony. The woman sat thus for several minutes and then, rising, moved toward the door leading into the hall and vanished.

Immediately the lamp, which had been burning so dimly, blazed up to its natural flame, and the fire in the grate became bright again. Mr. Lape then looked toward the corner where the dog had stood and saw the animal lying down as if sleeping. The dog did not answer to his call, and when he walked over to it and stooped down to pat it, he found that the poor animal was dead. This was all that Mr. Lape could stand, and he left his house. [6]

---

[6] Prints made by ghostly bare feet; a door that traps then releases an investigator; an intense cold; a dying flame; a formless shape with eyes; an effort to suppress fear; a phantom of an agonized woman, even an ill-fated dog also appear—in that order—in Edward Bulwer-Lytton's haunted house tale "The Haunted and the Haunters; or, the House and the Brain." This novella was first published in *Blackwood's Magazine* in August, 1859, and had been republished several times before this newspaper ghost report appeared. One might assume that Mr. Lape, the reporter, or perhaps the ghost had read this famous work of supernatural fiction.

Dallas Crume, another of the tenants, is a nervy and original young man who recently married and started housekeeping in the haunted house. One bright afternoon he heard a noise in the parlor, and on turning he was positive he saw the dim head and shoulders of a woman dodge behind an open door. He kept his eye on the door until he secured his camera. Then he seated himself in a rocking chair in the room with the supposed ghost, ready to take a snapshot should the apparition again appear. Mr. Crume said it did appear—came from behind the door and quickly glided behind the dresser just as he pressed the button. His surprise was intense when the photographer developed the plate and showed him a photo of himself seated in the parlor holding a camera, just as he did on that day.

Rock Island Argus (Illinois), April 5, 1902

Ghost Lacks Head and Arms.

The Helmer neighborhood, eight miles northeast of Kendallville, is wrought up by the appearance of a tall, headless and armless ghost, robed in flowing white garments, in an old house known as the Jacob Bickle homestead, long since abandoned. For three nights in succession the ghost has been seen, the first time on Saturday evening when a party of boys were playing about the premises, the next time on Sunday, and again Monday night.

The first evening the eight-year-old son of Henry Beckbarger was so badly frightened that he fainted three times before his comrades succeeded in carrying him home. One of the other boys is a son of Joseph Weirick, and the others were three sons of Rena Presskey, all well-known citizens. The second night Ward Miller and Earl Deetz, two well-known young men of the neighborhood, who had heard the story of the boys, went to the place, and they in turn saw the apparition, and were so badly frightened that Deetz did not stop until he had reached his home, a mile distant.

On the third night a posse of citizens of the Helmer neighborhood, probably fifty strong, headed by William Klinesmith, went to the haunted house to solve the mystery of the strange apparition, and although they were armed, the appearance of the ghost struck terror to their hearts, and they fled. Klinesmith was the only one of the party who entered the house, but he, too, failed to remain long enough to complete his investigation after the ghost appeared.

The incident has aroused widespread interest, and ghost parties are being formed by a number of the local people who propose to visit the house one night this week and brave the ordeal of meeting the ghost. So far no reason can be assigned for the appearance of the mysterious apparition as no unusual history is connected with the place, other than that the house has been abandoned for many years and has frequently been a shelter for tramps and vagabonds.

Topeka State Journal (Kansas), Oct. 26, 1908
Reprinted from *Kendallville Dispatch* (Indiana)
via *Indianapolis News* (Indiana)

SEES GHOST EIGHT TIMES
MYSTERY SURROUNDS PURPORTED APPEARANCE OF GHOST AT FARM HOME NEAR JESUP.
BULLETS AND BUCKSHOT MAKE NO IMPRESSION ON IT.
William Kreuger Has Given Up Trying to Frighten "Phantom," Which Has Frequently Visited His Farm— Story Verified by Kreuger's Brother, Who Has Also Seen the Ghost.

Waterloo, March 26.—The chain of mystery surrounding the purported appearance of a ghost at the home of William Kreuger, a farmer residing near Jesup, has never been unraveled and bids fair to remain one of Spring Creek Valley's unsolved problems.

It will be recalled that the reported appearance of the ghost at the Kreuger home early in February had the entire western section of Buchanan County in a state of excitement. Mr. Krueger, while husking corn from the fodder one evening shortly after dark, was suddenly confronted by a phantom-like figure that stood motionless and stolid. It was white as unsunned snow and immediately struck terror to his heart, so he says.

When a reporter called at the Krueger home and inquired as to the present whereabouts of the "ghost," the Jesup farmer in a tremulous tone of voice declared that it has been almost two months since the strange phantom made its eighth appearance and that it has gone as mysteriously as it came.

"I feel certain it wasn't a 'spook,'" declared Mr. Krueger, "for I never did believe in 'spooks.' The strangest thing about its appearance was the fact that neither bullets nor bucksthot could make any impression on it.

"The first evening I saw the figure, which certainly wore a graveyard appearance, I rushed to the house, procured my rifle and shot at it. When I leveled the barrel of the gun and fired, the demon, ghost or whatever you want to call it was standing still and stolid. Crack went the rifle, and I rushed up to claim my prey. Lo! It had suddenly disappeared.

"The next time 'ghosty' came, I used my shotgun with like results. Confident, then, that the strange phantom was both bullet proof and shot proof, I left it to help itself and visit us whenever it felt like doing so."

Mr. Kreuger declared that, if his story of the appearance of the ghost or a strange figure resembling a phantom is doubted, all that is necessary is to interview his brother, Albert, who likewise caught a glimpse of the supposed cemetery messenger.

Evening Times-Republican
(Marshalltown, Iowa), March 26, 1913

Paterson Ghost
Routs Trio of Society Men

PATERSON, N.J., Dec. 9.—Paterson has a ghost it wants laid. It is a real, old-fashioned ghost that clinks chains, groans at twilight and makes a nuisance of itself generally. Its habitat is a crazy old brick house not far from Lambert Castle on Garret Mountain.

A laborer employed by Michael Lynch, working in the vicinity, first saw it. He quit his job. Then Mr. Lynch, who is a contractor, questioned persons who lived near the house. All confessed seeing the ghost. Three young society men from Passaic went to the haunted house to spend the night. They stayed a quarter of an hour, then fled in dismay.

Washington Times (DC), Dec. 9, 1915

LAPE CONFRONTED BY THE SPECTER.

From "A Night with a Ghost," page 69.

HAUNTED BUILDINGS
Other than Houses

Houses aren't the only structures in which ghosts lurk. Prisons are conspicuous in this chapter's reports, which is interesting in that many ghosts seem to be imprisoned in a particular location. Perhaps one of the lessons that ghosts teach is to not become too confined to any one spot—or you're likely to be stuck there, even after death. That said, this chapter's reports on ghostly libraries have a curious appeal to me, since I've already spent a good deal of my life haunting them.

Along with prisons and libraries, this chapter takes us to churches, schools, law offices, a saloon, a mill, and other kinds of buildings that aren't typical houses. It seems like every theater with even a short history has some kind of ghost story attached to it, but my research uncovered only a few ghost reports set in such places. The article about the eerie morgue in Marin County prompted me to wonder why I also didn't find more specters lurking in this kind of building.

Nonetheless, the variety of buildings represented here illustrate how almost any structure can become home to a spectral mystery.

Remarkable Affair in a Church!

Considerable excitement has arisen in Jersey City in consequence of groans, yells and unearthly sounds said to emanate from a church in the upper part of Jersey City for some nights past. The first known of these mysterious sounds was some ten days since, when the pastor had occasion to return to the church after evening services to procure some manuscript which he had forgotten and had occasion to make use of. The edifice had been closed for the night and was in total darkness.

The New York Times says:

"On entering, he lit a match to guide him along the aisle, and when approaching the altar at the rear, his attention was attracted by a low moaning sound, which gradually increased and, at the same time, drew nearer to him. To this he at first paid no heed, presuming it to be the antics of mischievous boys, but presently the sound changed to seemingly unearthly yells, shrieks and groans from innumerable invisible beings clustered around in close proximity to his person, until finally his feelings were so wrought upon that he felt impelled to leave the building with all possible haste. The above are substantially the facts of the case as stated by the pastor of the church to Chief of Police McManus after reports were beginning to be circulated in the neighborhood that the church was haunted. The pastor requested that the matter be kept as quiet as possible, believing that in a few days at furthest he would be able to unravel the mystery and satisfactorily explain the cause of the sounds.

"Since that time the church edifice has been thoroughly examined, inside and out, but without unravelling the mystery, and meantime these dismal and unearthly yells and cries are heard almost every night. A couple of nights since, Chief of Police McManus, accompanied by Aid Doyle and Detective E.L. McWilliams, determined to pay a visit to the reported haunted church. They accordingly procured the keys and entered the edifice shortly after midnight. Taking their position in the center of the church in total darkness, they had remained there but a short time when they heard a low moaning sound, apparently proceeding from the vicinity of the pulpit, which gradually grew louder and came nearer until it finally culminated around their heads into howls, yells, groans, etc., and then gradually died away as it came. After a few moments of perfect silence, Chief McManus drew from his pocket a revolver loaded with blank cartridges and fired one charge, when almost instantly the edifice seemed to be filled with thousands of infuriated demons, making the most hideous noises and apparently bent on tearing them to pieces. The officers describe having experienced a very peculiar sensation in the head, and finally the noise became so hideous and unearthly that they made a hasty retreat, apparently pursued by the infuriated demons to the door, which they closed and locked.

"The officers then crossed the street to the opposite walk and remained there until daylight, but heard no further sounds and made no discoveries which would tend to explain the mystery. The people residing in the immediate neighborhood claim to have been disturbed at all hours of the night by these demonic sounds, and a number of them have determined to leave the neighborhood."

Keowee Courier (Pickens, South Carolina), Oct. 28, 1865

The Ghost in the Chicago jail seems to be an uncommonly lively one. Whether he is gas, odor, or a legitimate "sperrit" seems to be a matter of doubt with the journalists there. His first appearance was at the early hour of eleven o'clock, one night when the gas burned dimly, and the sounds he made were unearthly and awful—loud, prolonged wailing and gnashing of teeth. Prisoners heard it, the deputy sheriff heard it, and they declare the voice distinctly enunciated "oh! dear, oh! dear!" For a week it kept silent and then suddenly and fearfully wailed again, making a moaning noise that chilled the blood of all who heard it. The officers, prisoners and certain curious outsiders all concur in their descriptions of the visitant.

Some think that it is a murderer's ghost, others that it is a banshee, others that it is a peripatetic spirit indulging in an unearthly merriment; but all are convinced of its genuineness as a ghost—a revenant. The prisoners are in a fearful state of mind at the repeated manifestations; solitary confinement has now such terrors for them that good behavior is the rule and not the exception.

Staunton Speculator (Virginia), Dec. 24, 1867

A Ghost in a Calaboose.[1]

Hackensack, in Bergen County, has a sensation in the shape of a genuine ghost which haunts the county jail and creates the utmost consternation and alarm among the prisoners and other inmates. The spirit has been recognized as that of John W. Avery, the young man who was hanged in the jail on June 28, 1872, for murder. The mysterious phenomena which accompany the appearance of the spirit were at first attributed to some plan of escape concocted by the prisoners, but recent developments prove that such is not the case. A prisoner named Wallace, who was confined in the jail in October last and who was familiar with Avery, solemnly affirms that his spirit appeared one night and was distinctly seen to walk around one of the tiers and pull the bed clothing off a German prisoner, who was confined in the cell formerly occupied by Avery. The German, who is still a prisoner, confirms the story, and many persons who visited Avery now remember that he made a solemn promise before his death to revisit the jail after his execution.

The story of his latest appearance seems to be well authenticated, several of the prisoners thoroughly agreeing in their statement of all the

---

[1] A jail or prison.

facts. The phenomena occurred about midnight on Sunday, and there is no doubt that the utmost consternation and alarm prevailed among the prisoners. As is customary in all well-regulated ghost stories, the clock had just ceased striking 12 when a soft, unnatural light filled the whole interior of the jail and awakened all the prisoners. Some of them were terror-stricken and buried their heads beneath the bed clothing, while others seemed to be paralyzed so that they could not move and were thus compelled to be unwilling witnesses of the supernatural scenes and sounds that followed. They solemnly aver that they heard one of the windows raised and felt the cold air rush in. Then the shadowy form of a man, all plainly visible except the legs, seemed to glide between the bars and up the stairs to the top tier of cells. The figure stopped in front of the cell which had been occupied by Avery and, opening the door, entered. The opening and closing of the door were distinctly heard. After a lapse of a few minutes the figure reappeared, and its footfalls on the steps as it descended again were distinctly heard. The figure passed around all the tiers of cells, and then floated down on the washroom, and was heard to turn on the water. Finally the ghost returned to the window and disappeared as it had entered, and the bluish light gradually faded away. This is substantially the story as told by several of the prisoners, who claim to have been eyewitnesses and express their firm belief that they saw Avery's ghost.

Morristown Gazette (Tennessee), March 31, 1875
Reprinted from *New York Times* (New York)

An Editorial Ghost.

Syracuse is agitated over what appears to be a well-authenticated ghost story. For a number of years Daniel J. Halstead was publisher of the Syracuse *Courier*. He died in August last, but his spirit seems to have taken a fancy for visiting the old haunts, as the foreman and a reporter of the *Courier* are ready to swear that they had seen Mr. Halstead in the office on more than one occasion. He was seen as recently as last week by the pressman of the paper, who entered the counting room soon after midnight, that witching hour when churchyards and night editors yawn, and saw him standing within a few feet of him.

There is trouble at the residence of the deceased Halstead also, where his widow resides. A noise, as of a man walking about with a cane, is heard at night, and Mr. Halstead, as is known, was in the habit when in the flesh of carrying a cane. This doesn't appear to have disturbed the widow Halstead much, but a gentleman and wife who rented rooms of her vacated the premises on account of it.

It is all very strange, but the strangest part of it to us is why an editor should want to come back to earth again after once getting clear of it. Many people who have been to Niagara Falls in years past will remember the little steamer "Maid of the Mist" that used to carry passengers up under Horse Shoe Falls. The late Mr. Halstead was captain of that craft. Perhaps the remembrance of those turbulent voyages has made his spirit uneasy.

Country Paper (Oregon, Missouri), April 28, 1882
Reprinted from *Cincinnati Saturday Night* (Ohio)

Weird Lights and Ghostly Figures.

SPOKANE FALLS, W.T.,[2] March 27.—Great excitement prevails here over the discovery of an alleged haunted house. Last summer a young man named Robison was murdered in a saloon by a desperado named Mike Conover, who was arrested for the crime and is now in prison. Soon after the tragedy occurred, the saloon was closed up and the building has not been occupied since. It is stated on authority of a number of respectable persons that the building is really haunted. For a number of nights unearthly noises have been heard, accompanied by weird, flickering lights, and ghostly figures have moved through the deserted house. At first the citizens of the place believed that certain persons were perpetrating a practical joke to frighten the town and scare the owner and thus purchase the property cheap, but careful investigation confirms the opinion that there is something supernatural in these nocturnal sights and sounds. The strange affair creates a widespread sensation and excites fear among all superstitiously inclined persons.

St. Paul Daily Globe (Minnesota), March 28, 1885

---

[2] Washington Territory, which became a state about four years after this article appeared.

DR. CHAPMAN'S GHOST.
The Murdered President of
Old Andalusia College.
A LAWYER'S TERRIBLE NIGHT—
THE HAIR-RAISING EXPERIENCE
OF MR. ESHBACK AND MR. TYGH.

There are two men in this city who are willing to take oath that the building at Andalusia known as "old Andalusia College" is haunted. One of them is H.W. Eshback, a member of the Philadelphia bar, having an office at 508 Walnut Street, and the other is Frank Tygh, a cigar manufacturer at Locust and 6th Streets. A short time ago these two gentlemen passed the night with a friend, John F. Endicott, in the old college, and since that time they have been startling their acquaintances with frightful stories of a ghost seen there. As proof of his statement Mr. Eschback exhibits a bad-looking upper lip, which he says was swollen up by coming in contact with a bona fide ghost. Their stories have gained considerable credence at Andalusia, where the affair is said to have taken place, and the citizens look upon the old college building with more than ordinary suspicion.

Old Andalusia College is a three-story wooden building with a mansard roof and is nearly fifty years old. It is situated at the junction of two roads about ten minutes' walk from the Pennsylvania railroad station. The structure presents a ghostly appearance and, being entirely surrounded by large, tall cedar trees, is not a place where any citizen would wish to pass a dark night alone. It has been said for many years that the house was haunted.

DR. CHAPMAN'S MURDER.

When the college was in a flourishing condition under Dr. Chapman twenty years ago, Mrs. Chapman and a young man named Minor became enamored of each other. Feeling that the doctor was an obstruction to the free enjoyment of their love, they accomplished his death by aid of arsenic. In trying to obliterate traces of the crime, some of the arsenic was thrown into the yard, where some of the ducks ate it and died. The death of the ducks in such a manner led to an investigation, resulting in the arrest of both Mrs. Chapman and young Minor. Minor was hanged. Mrs. Chapman escaped the law.

Since that time the house has had the reputation of being haunted. Persons in that neighborhood say they saw lights in the house for years, and few of them would pass it after dark. After the murder the college proved a failure, and no one could be found willing to occupy it. The owner of the premises had a portion of the building torn down and the remainder fitted up as a boarding house, but the unsavory reports concerning it prevented him from getting a tenant. Mr. Endicott finally offered to occupy the place and has now been living there for some months.

MR. ESHBACK'S STORY.

Horace W. Eshback said yesterday: "A friend of mine, John F. Endicott, resides in the old Andalusia College, and the other day he invited me over to pay him a visit. Of course I accepted the invitation, taking with me Frank Tygh, a cigar dealer of this city. The weather was none of the best in the morning, and by afternoon a wind and rain storm arose which lasted until early the next morning. We had intended to return to the city on one of the late afternoon trains, but as the storm raged without promise of early abatement we decided to remain over. It must have been near midnight when we went to bed.

"We were shown to the 'spare room.' This apartment was very large, with three deep windows, two doors and a fireplace. The old college has about twenty rooms, the larger number of which are unoccupied, and Tygh, who is a short, fleshy man and much given to the subject of spooks, shuddered as we walked down the hall and muttered something about its being an elegant night for ghosts to play football. We entered the room and Tygh thought someone was yelling, but he grew more composed when I told him it was only the wind. The wind was really howling as if the very imps of iniquity were frenzied in the delights of a free night. With the wind whistling through the tall cedar trees it was almost impossible to sleep. Anyhow, I could not compose myself to sleep and lay listening to the noises outside and to the snoring of my roommate.

A GHOSTLY SLUGGER.

"Suddenly a light spread through the room, a light like that produced by a candle. In the surprise or rather astonishment of the moment I turned and sat up in bed. I tell you, what I saw made me feel sick and wish I was almost anywhere else. Before me was what appeared to be the bust of a man, perhaps forty-five years of age, the shoulders covered with a mantle. The face had a perfectly natural appearance, only it lacked mobility, and the whole seemed to be resting on a cloud of snow. The terrible apparition was moving about the room, and I thought it might be a robber, but I noticed that there were no lower limbs, but that it glided around like a balloon. Now I am not a believer in spirits, but I was frightened. 'What do you want?' I asked, hardly aware of what I was saying. The sound of my voice awakened Tygh. He said bolt upright in bed, gave one glance and tumbled over on the floor and began to pray. Tygh is not a religious man. The answer I received from the ghost was something unlooked for, being in the form of a severe blow on the mouth, cutting my lips badly and stretching me at full length on the bed.

THE GHOST EXPLODES.

"Almost simultaneously with the blow the figure noiselessly exploded and seemed to go straight up through the wall. The light did not go out for some time, but gradually died away, leaving us in darkness. I jumped up and lighted a lamp and found Tygh doubled up in a heap on the floor, almost insensible. I looked around the room and found the windows closed, the doors locked and everything in the condition as it was when we retired. I will admit that I was frightened, and the quickness with which I dressed myself and hauled Tygh downstairs was something wonderful. It is perhaps unnecessary to say that we spend the remainder of the night before a glowing fire in the sitting room.

"When Endicott saw me in the morning he laughed and wanted to know where I got my thick lips. I did not care to tell him the truth, so I replied that I had struck it on the bedpost in getting into bed. Now, as I said before, I do not believe in ghosts or anything of the sort, but I'm going to investigate that matter and capture whatever it is, that is, providing it is anything human."

Mr. Tygh solemnly swears that he saw the whole business and relates a story exactly similar to that of Mr. Eshback. He says he knows there is a ghost in the old building and money could not hire him to pass another night there.

Evening Star (Washington, DC), Dec. 11, 1886
Reprinted from *Philadelphia Times* (Pennsylvania)

THE GHOST OF SAMUEL KOHN.
The Old Hide House in South St. Louis the Place of Strange Scenes.
NO DOUBTING OF THE FACTS.
Jerry Pagels' Victim Comes Back in Spirit to Haunt the Place of the Murder—
The Stories of the Terrified Witnesses.

The people of South St. Louis are awe-stricken in the presence of the exciting demonstrations of the ghost of a murdered man, whose slayer is to be hanged this month by due process of law. When the ghost had a corporeal existence on earth it was known as Samuel Kohn, and its business was to buy hides and fat from the butchers of the city for the firm of Norman Brown & Co. The firm was doing a good business, and its city buyer, who was an active and popular young man, temperate in his habits and honest and straightforward in his dealings, was one of their most valued employees. He made friends rapidly, and in the fall of 1885, he was the best agent of a hide-buying house in the city and was widely known among the butchers.

Then he was murdered by a drunken, dissolute wretch, Jerry Pagels. Pagels was the city buyer of hides and fat for E.S. Brooks, a business competitor of Norman Brown. He had been a good business man but had fallen into dissipated habits, and as his craving for liquor grew upon him, his work was neglected, and his slipshod business methods became unsatisfactory to his employers and objectionable to the butchers who were selling him their hides. He continued to drink, and the butchers began to carry their wares to Kohn, whose manner pleased them and whose settlements were prompt and accurate. As Pagels lost his clients he drank more deeply, and discovering that Kohn was getting his trade, he swore vengeance against his innocent rival. His threats against the life of Kohn were publically made and came to the ears of the young hide-buyer himself, who paid no attention to them. They were mere vaporings of a drunken brain for a long time, but continuous absorption of liquor finally brought Pagels to the verge of delirium tremens, and in an alcoholic frenzy he carried his wicked intention into effect.

THE CRIME.

November 10, 1885, had been a busy day for Kohn. He had been employed from the early morning until late in the afternoon, receiving hides in the warehouse, in the alley, and weighing them on a huge pair of platform scales in the room. At 5 o'clock he had finished with the butchers and was sitting on the scales, running over the figures in the little memorandum book in which he kept his accounts, when a little boy ran up the alley to the open warehouse door and put in his head as he called:

"Mr. Kohn, there's a man out here wants to see you."

"All right, I'm coming," replied Kohn, thinking another butcher was waiting outside with a load of hides. These were his last words. As he appeared at the door, Pagels, who was waiting in the alley by the doorway, raised a double-barreled shotgun to his shoulder. "Sam, — — you, I want to see you!" he called, and fired.

The buckshot pierced the abdomen of Kohn, and he fell across the threshold of the door fatally wounded. Pagels looked down at him a moment and then ran down the street. The murder had been seen, and

85

the police were in the alley a few minutes later. Kohn died in two days, and Pagels was arrested while hiding on the day after. He was tried, convicted and sentenced to death, and unless the governor interferes, he will be hanged on the morning of August 13. He has been sullen, unrepentant and defiant in jail, and has not once shown any sign that he regretted his cowardly crime.

FIRST APPEARANCE OF THE GHOST.

Kohn's place after his death was given to Albert Brown, the brother of Kohn's employer, and he found it necessary soon after taking charge of the large business which had been built up by the murdered man to employ an assistant, George Knecht. Both had been intimate friends of the murdered man and frequently talked of his death and the fate of his murderer. Both are clear-headed businessmen, and neither is a spiritualist, a member of any society of psychical research, a theosophist, or any other kind of an investigator or discoverer of occult phenomena. Until Thursday night all they knew about ghosts was that they were unpleasant creatures to have about the house. That night they learned something more.

They had been detained in the hide warehouse by some late purchases beyond their wont, and 11 o'clock found them sorting the hides into piles. They worked by a dim lamp, which they moved about with them as they threw the hides into heaps and which cast long, quivering shadows down along the floor and up among the beams of the roof. In one corner the long scales, on which Kohn had sat a few minutes before he was murdered, threw out an uncertain form on the wall, its arms and body making a long, slim shadow and a broader one underneath, strongly suggestive of a gallows. It may have been this, or the strange influences of the hour, or the unusual silence that made the two men fall to talking about Kohn and his murder, and they had been on the subject but a minute or two when a tall bale of hides, just outside the circle of bright light made by the lamp, toppled over and fell to the floor, sending the echoes rolling through the building. Both men straightened up from their stooping position and stared at each other with their hearts beating rapidly.

ACCOUNTING FOR THE EVENT.

"Must have been overbalanced," suggested Brown.

"Yes, but it scared me at first," assented Knecht with a half laugh full of nervousness.

As he spoke there came a clang and clatter from the scales in the corner, like the noise made by one rolling something to be weighted on them and tossing the weights on the bar. Brown grasped the lamp and held it above his head, dispelling the shadows on the wall and

86

illuminating clearly the corner where the scales stood. They were not moving and no weights were on the bar, but as the two men looked there came another series of metallic noises from them, a rattle of weights and clashing of the parts together, and at the same time the thumps of bales of hides being rolled about were heard in every part of the building with the simultaneous sound of the moving of the fat barrels, unmistakable to the ears of the experienced men who heard them. The noises continued for some minutes while the two men stood rooted to the floor, seeing nothing and hearing all around them sounds they knew were supernatural.

"Let's go home," Brown at last proposed.

The two put on their coats and went to their homes, agreeing before they parted to avoid ridicule by telling no one of their fright. Friday they both went through the building and examined it in broad daylight. They saw nothing ghostly, and their fears of the night before appeared absurd. They resolved to investigate the mystery, however, and Friday night they remained in the warehouse again.

A SECOND MANIFESTATION.

Exactly at 12:30 o'clock a barrel of fat fell over on its side and rolled up against the scales, and then all the noises they had heard the night before were repeated. When they went up and stood on the scales the clatter of the weights continued, although there appeared to be no way of producing the sounds. The noise of hides and barrels moving was as plain as it had been, but after the first warning that they were about to begin, nothing was heard. Brown and Knecht at last took themselves out of the warehouse, not so much frightened this time as puzzled, and over a glass of beer in the neighboring saloon discussed the mystery with the saloonkeeper.

"It's Kohn's ghost," said that individual positively, "and you can't lay it until Pagels is hanged."

The story spread over all that part of the city Saturday, and Brown and Knecht were besieged all day by inquiries. They were laughed at by some and believed by others, but the theory that Kohn's ghost was haunting the scene of the murder became a popular one.

NO DOUBTING OF FACTS.

Saturday night Brown and Knecht took a number of butchers into the warerooms, and they came over to the saloon about midnight more serious than butchers generally are, and ready to maintain all the two hide buyers had told of their two nights' experiences. They had heard all the noises of the moving barrels and bales of hides, and had carefully examined the phenomenon of the active scales, but the inexplicable sounds continued and the business-like ring and creaking of the scales

87

had gone on, even when three butchers got on it. As on the other nights, the ghostly signal for the beginning of the uncanny proceedings was given by the falling over of a bale of hides in plain sight of all, but after that the sources of none of the noises were seen.

SOLVING THE MYSTERY.

Yesterday the people living in the vicinity of the warehouse had plenty of food for gossip, and by nightfall the alley was filled with men talking in a whisper and listening. Nobody went into the warehouse last night, and the two buyers, Knecht and Brown, stayed at home. The ghost hunters, however, stood on the street or in the alley until after midnight, expecting to see or hear something startling, and when they went away, two police officers, anxious for distinction as ghost detectives, took up the watch. Another party of investigators will occupy the warehouse tonight.

Omaha Daily Bee (Nebraska), Aug. 9, 1887

The ghost of Volkavitch,[3] who was executed April 3, seems to be wandering around the corridors of the jail to the great alarm of some of the more timid and superstitious inmates. About ten o'clock last night, while Warden Brockway and Deputy Smith were sitting in the main office, they were suddenly surprised by loud cries from the corridor in which the long term prisoners are kept. Upon arriving in the corridor the discovery was made that a prisoner named John Jones was nearly crazed with fright over the alleged visitation of murderer Volkavitch's ghost at the door of his cell. Not long after, Watchman McDonald was again aroused by alarming cries proceeding from Jones' new quarters. He went to him and found the cold beads of perspiration standing out on this forehead and his limbs quaking violently. The wretched prisoner was evidently frightened nearly out of his wits when the jailer appeared. He asserted that Volkavitch's ghost appeared to him. He was taken into another cell with his brother who is confined in the jail.

In the meantime his companion in the first cell called for McDonald, and with his face showing signs of alarm he said that he had been disturbed by mysterious noises and the rising up and down of the cover of the little table in his quarters. Another man also testified to having seen the ghost. All the prisoners were more or less excited over

---

[3] Adam Volkavitch was hanged in Wilkes-Barre, Pennsylvania, for the murder of Stanislaus Bioski.

the event, and but few of them slept after the disturbances occurred. They believed they had seen a real ghost.

Iola Register (Kansas), June 22, 1888
Reprinted from *Philadelphia Press* (Pennsylvania)

PRELLER'S GHOST
Said to Be Haunting
the Southern Hotel, St. Louis.

St. Louis, Jan. 25.—The tragedy enacted on April 5, 1885, in Room 144 of the Southern Hotel is revived by the strange experience of the guests who have recently occupied the apartment. It was in Room 144 that Maxwell chloroformed Preller to death, robbed the remains and then packed them in a trunk.[4] The room was not occupied for many months afterward, and such a horror was developed in the traveling public's mind that the hotel found it impossible to utilize the room, and in order to remove the ghastly dread of "144," the number was changed to "133." The nerves of several drummers[5] were tested, and only two exhibited signs of collapse the next morning. The experience of one guest was told Monday. The gentleman is a prominent commercial traveler, of well-balanced mind, sound intellect and good, broad commonsense. This is his remarkable story, given in his own language:

"I knew nothing at all about the room when I took it—in fact, the Maxwell-Preller incident had wholly escaped me. I went to bed at my usual hour and was awakened with a start by hearing a strange tapping against the head of the bed. Tap, tap-tap was the order in which they came, one disconnected tap and then two in quick succession. I was aroused in an instant, but heard nothing more and concluded the tapping was caused by the cracking of the glue. The same tapping

---

[4] On April 18, 1885, Kentucky's *Milan Exchange* reported that a maid at St. Louis's Southern Hotel smelled a horrible odor in the trunk of a guest who had registered as "Wallace H. Lennox Maxwell, M.D. London, England." The hotel porters carried the trunk, which dripped blood, from Room 144 to the street. Inside it, they discovered a body "in an advanced state of decomposition," later identified as that of C. Arthur Preller from Rochester, New York, who had also been staying at the hotel. There was also a paper in the trunk that read: "SO END ALL TRAITORS TO THE GREAT CAUSE." On June 12, 1886, the same journal reported that a jury had found Maxwell, who had several aliases, guilty of the crime.

[5] Travelling sales representatives.

89

occurred several other times during the night, but I dismissed it on the comfortable theory I have just mentioned. The next evening I noticed the drawers of the bureau would always open however often I closed them. I pushed them in whenever I passed near the bureau, but they would invariably open again as though forced out by some unseen agency. Still I was not alarmed.

"The most startling occurrence and the one which finally decided me to leave the room came on the third night. I had noticed that the chambermaid had entirely cleared the hearth of debris, and not so much as a scrap of paper was left in it. I was thrown from deep slumber into absolute wakefulness about 1 o'clock by an explosion on the hearth that sounded like the explosion of a big firecracker. I was scared, you can bet. A second explosion, a little louder followed, and then came a third, which capped the climax. It was terribly violent, and the detonation was fearful. I arose, dressed, lighted the gas, and looked at the hearth. It was completely filled with a slaty substance that looked like ore of some kind, and one of the large cubes that made up the mass was torn from the brickwork or tiling. Pieces of slate were thrown across the room. I went downstairs and told the night clerk to come right to the room and see what had happened. He refused with a sickly smile.

"I returned to the room, passed a sleepless night and changed my room the next day. I then learned from a friend the history of the room, and one or two things that hitherto had been inexplicable to me then became painfully clear. I noticed the bellboys would get out of the room as quickly as they could, not waiting for the occasional tip which I held to them, nor could I get an answer when I rang the bell after 10 o'clock at night. I found out that at that hour the lights in the hall were turned out and the bellboys would not go through the corridor after that time at any price. I give these facts for what they are worth, without comment or explanation. I am not a spiritualist or a believer in their doctrines. I was absolutely sober, too, as I seldom take a drink."

The manager of the hotel, Mr. Lewis, had nothing to say when the story was told him, nor could he suggest any explanation.

Evening Bulletin (Maysville, Kentucky), Jan. 25, 1889

A Ghost Tolled the Bells.

Before the earthquake shook it down, the old guard house or police station was just across the street, in front of the church. Every night for years an old policeman, who had grown old and decrepit in the service of his country and lastly of his city, kept watch at the door. He had seen many strange sights, and he always said that the strangest he had ever seen was the dead man ringing the chimes from the belfry of old St. Michael's. [6] He had seen the shrouded figure, time and again, climb up to the bells and, not touching the ropes, which had been pulled so often by living hands, swing the heavy iron tongues against the sides of the bells and clash out a fearful melody which thrilled while it horrified the listener.

He would tell you, if you cared to listen to his story, how the ghost had been murdered, for in its normal state it had been murdered by the thrust of an Italian stiletto in Elliot Street. The spirit was "to walk the earth," "revisit the glimpses of the moon," ring the old chimes, and do other horrible things, until the murderer was captured.

A few minutes before midnight the old watchman would see this spectral chimer enter the church doors, forgetting to open them, swiftly and in a ghostly way glide up the steps of the winding stair, pause under the bells by the ropes where Gadsden[7] rings them, climb on into the gloomy belfry and stop beneath the open mouths of the bells. They yawned down upon it, as if striving to swallow up the restless spirit. Suddenly, as if the inspiration had come, the shrouded hand would move silently and rapidly from iron tongue, and the wild eldritch music would swell the air.

Wahpeton Times (North Dakota), June 27, 1889
Reprinted from *Atlanta Journal* (Georgia)

---

[6] On Aug. 31, 1886, an earthquake hit Charleston, South Carolina, the strongest ever recorded in the southeastern U.S. It was purported to have been felt as far away as Boston and Chicago. Death estimates range from 60 to over 100. A police station, called the "Guard House," was deemed unsalvageable after the quake. Nearby, though, St. Michael's Church suffered less damage and remains standing today.

[7] According to *Beesley's Illustrated Guide to St. Michael's Church, Charleston, So. Ca.* (1898), by Charles Norbury Beesley, a man named Washington McLean Gadsden had served as the church's bell-ringer for 61 years. It also notes that the very first time those bells were tolled was for a funeral in 1764.

A HAUNTED COURTHOUSE.
RESTLESS SPOOKS IN A
TENNESSEE COUNTY BUILDING.
Workmen Refuse to Tear the Old House Down
to Make Room for a New One.
The Stories Are Told in Explanation
of the Popular Belief.

Workmen refuse to tear down the old courthouse building at Washington, Tenn, on account of a mystery which has surrounded the structure for nearly thirty years and which is vouched for by the representative citizens of the county. The county seat of Rhea County was recently removed from Washington to Dayton, and the courthouse, which has stood for over fifty years, has become so out of repair that it is deemed advisable to tear it down and especially so as the county has no further use for it. The ground which it occupies is wanted for the purpose of erecting a poorhouse, but it now appears impossible to obtain workmen who are willing to tear down the old building, as it has been known for years as the "haunted courthouse."

"JIMMY LONESOME."

It has been nearly thirty years since the supposed spirits took possession of it, and they have remained there ever since. The courtroom and county offices occupy the first floor, while the second story has always been vacant except one end, which was once occupied as a lodge room, and a small room in the corner of the building, which was formerly used as a doctor's office. In this room a skeleton was kept which was universally known as "Jimmy Lonesome," some of whose bones are still there. This skeleton was there when the strange phenomena which have since given the building widespread notoriety first began.

About the same time a man named Peterson was shot and killed in this room by an unknown hand. Soon after this tragedy occurred Judge Frank Locke, who was the clerk and master and circuit court clerk of the county, heard strange noises in the upper room every night. His office was directly underneath the small room in which Jimmy Lonesome kept guard, and he would hear footsteps start from the skeleton's corner and walk across the floor. Sometimes the object would fall heavily. Judge Locke was noted for his bravery, and he determined to find the intruder and eject him. Night after night he would go upstairs immediately after hearing the object fall, but nothing could be seen. He himself stated that he had gone up there at least a hundred times between the years of 1865 and 1885, but he never saw any form whatever.

Nearly twenty years ago Col. T.M. Burkett, now of Atkins and one of the leading members of the East Tennessee bar, was starting in the practice of law at Washington. He was poor at the time and, in order to save money, obtained permission to sleep in the haunted room, which he did. The first night he heard the walking plainly, but could see nothing. The object would walk up and down the room and then was seen to stand by his cot. He is a man of unusual nerve and bravery, and returned the next night determined to solve the mystery. Soon after he retired he again heard the walking, when suddenly a hand seized him and jerked him out of the bed. He could see no one, and trembling with fear, he hastily left the building and nothing could ever induce him to return.

WHY THEY DON'T STAY.

About ten years ago Mr. W.S. Shirley, an attorney living at Spring City, had been in the upper room of the courthouse during the day and had left a book there. After supper he went after the book, coming back on a run and never stopping until he had left the courthouse far behind him. When questioned, he said that, as he stooped for the book, the form of a man leaned over him with lighted blue candles about its head. He didn't remain to cultivate an acquaintance with the gentleman.

One night, a few years ago, T.J. Howard, now chief of police at Chattanooga, was sitting in the courtroom with a friend. They had built a fire in the stove which ignited a piece of cloth that had in some way come in contact with the stovepipe on the second floor. Howard went upstairs, taking some matches to light his way and succeeded in putting out the fire. Not knowing where the stovepipe went, he climbed into the cupola to satisfy himself that the fire was out. As he descended the ladder leading from the cupola, his matches became exhausted and he had to grope his way in the dark. When he reached the bottom of the ladder, a voice said: "Is the fire all out?" Howard supposed it was his friend whom he had left downstairs and answered without fear or surprise: "I think it is." He felt a sudden chill pass over him because he could neither see anyone nor hear footsteps, although the voice was directly in front of him.

When he reached the lower room, he said to his friend, who was sitting by the fire where he had left him: "How did you get down here!"

"Why," said the friend, "I haven't moved from this chair since you left."

Chief Howard says he wouldn't have gone upstairs again for any price, although he is far from superstitious.

93

The man, or apparition, whichever it is, has been seen through the window a few times, but he is not often visible, although he can be heard walking the floor almost every night. The character and standing of the witnesses give the courthouse widespread notoriety as being haunted. There are three theories extant. One that it is the spirit of the murdered man, Peterson, haunting the place; another that Jimmy Lonesome is responsible for the disturbance; and a third that the room has been occupied all these years by a man who for some reason has exiled himself from the world and has constructed a hole or place of some kind where he can disappear when the room is searched. The mystery would probably be solved by the tearing down of the building, but the people have become so superstitious concerning it that it will probably be impossible to utilize it as a poorhouse, as is now intended.

Wichita Eagle (Kansas), Oct. 10, 1889
Reprinted from *Chattanooga Telegram* (Tennessee)

THEY FEAR A GHOST.
Specters Haunt the Scene of an Awful Crime.
BROOKLYN POLICE TERRORIZED.
A Station House Where the Members
of the Force Do Not Like to Sleep.
A Decidedly Uncanny Place if the Testimony
of the Officers Is to be Believed.

New York, Nov. 23.—One would naturally imagine that the very last place in Brooklyn in which to look for a ghost would be a police station and, more especially, in the Second Precinct, located as it is in the noisiest quarter of the city. And yet, from Captain John Eason, its gallant army veteran commander, down to its latest enrolled patrolman, each and every one firmly believes that the station is haunted. Not only that, but all are willing to submit evidence on the subject.

In order to bring the ghost into prominent relief and give a reason for its existence, it is necessary to go a little into ancient history.

The station building, which comprises Nos. 29 and 51 Fulton Street, was formerly a bank and had for janitor John Kemlo. Mr. Kemlo occupied apartments on the fourth, or top, floor, overlooking Fulton Street. His son, the Rev. Mr. Kemlo, boarded with him, as did also his son's wife, and a partition separated the old man's rooms from those of his son and daughter-in-law, the latter occupying those to the west of the dividing line and the clergyman and his wife the eastern wing of the

94

floor. One night, about ten years ago, the young clergyman, while temporarily insane, cut his wife's throat and then, jumping from the open window of his father's bedroom to the sidewalk, fractured his skull and died at once.

This fourth floor is now used as a dormitory by sixteen officers of the station, and Patrolman Barney Malone sleeps, when he gets a chance, in a bed immediately under what is termed the "parson's window," by which is meant the one through which Kemlo jumped to his death. A week or so ago, in the silent watches of the night, Officer Malone was awakened by the touch of cold hands on his feet, which he felt were dragging him from the bed. Although the light in the big room burned low, there was still sufficient there for him to see—nothing. And yet he felt himself drawn down by an invisible power, and he yelled as loudly as he could and stretched his right hand to the spot under his pillow where rested his official revolver. Under ordinary circumstances Officer Malone's comrades, who raised their heads to inquire what he was raising such a row about, would have concluded merely that he had eaten a hearty dinner, but knowing the history of the room, Officer Hugh McLaughlin, acting as spokesman for the others, contented himself with saying: "Oh, boys, go to sleep; it is only that infernal spook at one of his tricks. Let us go to sleep, and Barney, please don't make such an awful clamor."

The fact is that they all had been annoyed before in the same manner, and they took the whole thing as a matter of course. Even Officer Malone drew himself up toward his pillow, turned over on the other side and resumed his slumber as if nothing unusual had occurred.

This midnight episode may appear grotesque, if not humorous, reading to most people, but the men compelled to sleep in that room take it very seriously indeed. And it would seem if they had cause, for there is something more tragic than cold ghostly hands connected with those apartments. It is a fact well known in police circles that the Second Station shows more deaths among its members by far than any other in Brooklyn, and though the medical man may be able to assign sanitary causes for such mortality, the officers of the Second persistently maintain that it arises from superhuman influences.

Anyone entering the room for the first time cannot fail to be struck with a vacant space between two bedcots right in front of him on the Fulton Street side. There is space for one more cot, but no cot is there, and no man in the station would lie on one placed there for one night, if by so doing he was to earn $100. As a matter of fact, Hugh McLaughlin, above mentioned, who is a philosopher in his way, has a standing offer of $25 to any man who will occupy the vacant space for one night. Up to this he had found no takers. The space is under the west window, and it was there the crazy clergyman committed the deed for which he died a moment later of his own volition.

The force belonging to the station is composed of fifty-five men. Since the tragedy of ten years ago, many have died, and of that number, five in succession used to sleep on a cot in that space. Their names were Richard Halpin, Edward Acker, Richard Colton, Patrolman Gardner and John Costello. Costello, the last victim, died seven weeks ago. A sixth man went crazy and was sent to the hospital. He recovered and was transferred to another precinct, where he does duty cheerfully and intelligently.

Officer McLaughlin, the philosopher, who knows more about the spook and its ways, and is more interested in its movements than anyone else, says regarding it: "People may laugh and jest about such things, but after all, will anyone assign a cause for the noises we hear and the things we see in this dormitory apart from the supernatural? The officers of the station, though I say it myself, are as brave and intelligent as any in Brooklyn. Owing to the peculiar locality they have to do duty in, they are inured to danger, and yet you cannot get one of them to occupy that space. Even John McCahan and John McKenna, two men remarkable for courage, who sleep on either side of it, are nervous and wakeful half the night.

"Would I sleep there? No, I guess not. I do believe in ghosts, but did not take any stock in them until I came here. The most unearthly shrieks are heard in this room at night, and though the captain says they are caused by the reverberations of the elevated railroad, we have our own opinion on the matter. Shrieks are heard when the trains are not running, and besides reverberations are not accustomed to pull big, strong men like Barney Malone out of bed.

"Have I ever seen the spook? I cannot say that I have, but other officers assert that they have seen the bloody drama of ten years since reenacted before their eyes; seen the woman struggling for life on the bed and the madman jump once more through the window. The men who have died are said to have been among the number who saw the gruesome sights."

For a long time the officers tried hard to treat the whole affair as a joke, but it was a dismal failure. Officer McLaughlin, pretending to "lay" it, used to stand between McCahan and McKenna's cots every night before retiring and read from Burns' poem "Man Was Made to Mourn" right through, and he reads it still sometimes, but his hearers no longer laugh. They think of Costello, the last victim, and they shudder and request the philosopher to leave off.

"What do you think of the ghost business?" asked the reporter of Captain Eason.

"I really don't know what to think," was the reply. "I don't like to encourage such a belief; but honestly I would not sleep there for Officer McLaughlin's $25."

Sergeant Corrougher, who was on the desk last night said in response to the same question: "There are more things in heaven and earth than are dreamt of in our philosophy."[8]

Wheeling Daily Intelligencer (West Virginia), Nov. 24, 1891

Henry Woods, lighthouse keeper at the Soo, disappeared a year ago, and his body was recovered only a week ago. Unfounded suspicions of murder were rife at one time. It is said Woods' ghost perambulated the lighthouse much to the terror of the successor.[9]

True Northerner (Paw Paw, Michigan), June 15, 1894

GHOSTS HAUNT MARIN'S MORGUE.
Deputy Coroner Even Startled by
Uncanny Noises Issuing from Coffins.

San Rafael, Cal., May 14.—Deputy Coroner William Eden is willing to take his oath that there are "spooks" in the Marin County Morgue. The spook craze has apparently struck San Rafael with as much force as has the prize-fighting fever, for the story about the morgue being infested with uncanny creatures follows closely upon the tales told by prisoners confined in the "haunted" chamber in the Marin County Jail.

Deputy Coroner William Eden is a son of Coroner Eden and well known in San Rafael, where he has lived all his life.

---

[8] *Hamlet* 1.5.167-8.

[9] The Soo is a nickname for Sault Ste. Marie, a city in Michigan's Upper Peninsula. Readers intrigued by a hunt for a haunted lighthouse might find some clues in this notice published on the front page of the June 3, 1893, issue of a Michigan newspaper called the *L'Anse Sentinel*: "Henry Wood, the lighthouse tender at Point Aux Pins, has been missing since May 5. He left in the afternoon to attend to his duties, and was seen on his way from the Sault to the Point but did not arrive there. The light at the Point failed to burn for several nights and an investigation disclosed the fact that the man was missing. The woods near the Point have been scoured and the creeks dragged, but to no avail."

"Last Tuesday night," said he, "I was sitting in the front office of the morgue at about 11 o'clock, talking with a friend. Suddenly I heard a noise like an animal scratching the ground. This was followed by the noise of the moving of some object over the floor. The sounds came from the room just in back of the parlor, where we were sitting.

"Thinking that there might be some person in the room, I went back and, opening the door, stepped up to the gas jet and pulled the cord which lights the gas. In the room are a number of cases containing coffins. As I turned up the light I saw the cases move distinctly. There was a sudden flash, a noise, and that was all.

"I was frightened, for I could not make out what could possibly cause the disturbances. My courage returned and I set about to investigate. I looked over the entire establishment but could discover nothing amiss. I returned to my companion and told of what I had seen and heard, and he left immediately and has not since been back. The room was formerly used as the old morgue until we fixed up another in the rear, and it may have been the ghosts of some of the departed that returned.

"I might assign the strange experience to some other cause, but not a long time ago, the Coroner, my father, was putting on his coat in the rear office when suddenly some unseen power gave it a jerk, which almost pulled the garment out of his hands. He thought at the time that some of the boys were in the office and had done it for a joke, but when he inquired about it in the morning, none would confess that they had anything to do with it."

The Marin County morgue has been located on C Street between Fourth and Fifth for many years, and Coroner Eden has been in charge of it for over twenty years. Many bodies have been received and placed in the room where the Deputy Coroner saw and heard the strange sounds the other night, but now the room is used as a storeroom for coffins and ghosts.

San Francisco Call (California), May 15, 1897

GHOST HAUNTS THEATER.
Spirit of William Warren, an Actor,
Still Treading the Boards of a Boston House.

The ghost of William Warren, who 25 years ago was one of the most celebrated actors of America, haunts Boston Museum, according to the firm belief of Frank Cauley, the stenographer in the box office, the treasurer and several other attachés of the theater. For some years there have been stories of the ghost of Warren being seen in the place where he scored most of his celebrated triumphs, and these have been so persistent that a good many people have come to credit them.

A couple of years ago Frank Currier, an actor, spent the night in the foyer to escape a constable who was looking for him with a bill and a writ. He had heard of the ghost of Warren, but had no faith in such yarns. He undertook to sleep on a couch in the foyer, and in the morning the theater attachés found him pacing the promenade, his hair on end, his eyes red and bloodshot, and his mind and body almost a wreck. He told the story of his experience. He had heard fearful noises and seen fearful things, and there was never any doubt about the ghost of Warren being a real if intangible thing.

Off and on since then people who have been about the interior of the theater at night have reported seeing the ghost, and one night recently Cauley is certain it made a manifestation to him and to the treasurer. They were alone in the box office about midnight counting the receipts when footsteps approached the private door. Cauley looked out, but saw no one. Thrice this was repeated. Cauley is absolutely certain he heard the steps and equally certain no living person made them. He says it was the ghost of William Warren.

Mower County Transcript (Austin, Minnesota), Dec. 27, 1899

Abandoned Schoolhouse to a Ghost.

A ghost has received official recognition in the action of Trustee Jesse Martin, of Jackson Township, of Carroll County, Ind., when he gave a contract for the erection of a new school building in the Walnut Grove district.

Several years ago Amer Green was lynched by a mob for the murder of his sweetheart, Luella Mabbitt, the hanging taking place at a walnut tree in the Walnut Grove schoolyard. Since then the children have been filled with superstitious terror in regard to the place, and the once large school dwindled to two pupils last winter, and after a few weeks' effort to get others to attend, school was dismissed. Strange stories were told about the place. Green's ghost was reported to have been seen, and the teachers reported that they heard unexplainable sounds about the building. The walnut tree, before then a large and thrifty one, never bore foliage after the lynching and stood a bleak reminder of the tragedy.

No teacher could be found to accept the school for next winter, and in response to the insistent demands of the patrons, a new building will be erected a short distance away, the old site being abandoned.

The New Enterprise (Madison, Florida), Sept. 26, 1901
Reprinted from *Indianapolis Journal* (Indiana)

GHOST IN THE JAIL.

Casper, Wyo., April 27.—Jim Adams, the lone prisoner in the county jail, whose sentence will expire next Oct., has asked the authorities to let him out before he becomes insane. Adams was in jail with Woodward during the time the murderer was confined there and the two got rather chummy. Adams now claims that Woodward's ghost appears in the jail every night and talk to him. Besides, it plays the mouth harp, sings and whistles, and otherwise disturbs his sleep. Last Sunday night the ghost visited Woodward's cell and searched for the dead man's clothes. [10]

Salt Lake Herald (Utah), April 28, 1902

GHOST HAUNTS THE COLLEGE LIBRARY
Watchman Declares Invisible Feet
Are Heard in Corridors at Night.

Parkersburg, W.Va., July 28.—The library of the West Virginia university is haunted: ghostly visitations and spiritual manifestations have become so frequent of late that in the opinion of many staid residents of the vicinity there is no use trying to conceal the fact any longer.

---

[10] Charles Woodward was a rancher in Wyoming's Rattlesnake Mountains. He was arrested for stealing provisions from a neighboring ranch. He broke out of jail. Upon returning to his ranch, he discovered Sheriff William Ricker lying in wait. Woodward shot and killed the sheriff, even pistol-whipping and stealing $45 dollars from the corpse. A posse then re-apprehended the outlaw. He confessed to the murder and was sentenced to be hanged. The case was to be reviewed by a higher court, though—a delay that provoked a lynch mob to storm the jailhouse, drag Woodward to the gallows, and put the rope around his head. In an attempt to escape death, the murderer leapt and wound up hanging himself. One of the best accounts of the tale is told on the front page of the March 28, 1902, issue of the *Minneapolis Journal* (Minnesota).

The library is built on the site of an old cemetery, the bones and dust of former occupants having been removed to another resting place. There is a tradition among the old citizens that years ago a Frenchman named Jean Mareschal lived in that vicinity and, after dying mysteriously, had been buried in the old cemetery. It is said that he had been banished from France by Marie Antoinette, and it is a fact that a certain volume on the French Revolution, once owned by the dead man, has shown marks of much usage lately, its pages and binding being found on more than one occasion damp in the mornings with fingerprints stained with clay upon the leaves, as though but recently handled, and many persons believe that old Jean Mareschal's spirit is now haunting the library built over his grave.

Many persons have heard strange sounds and have seen strange sights during the midnight hour, but have heretofore been diffident to describe their experiences for fear of public derision, but H. Hoffman, the night watchman, who weighs 250 pounds, has not been afraid to tell what he has seen and heard. His first knowledge that the library was being visited at unusual hours was gained about two weeks ago, when about midnight he heard the noise of footsteps ascending the stairs. He listened, opened the door and followed. The footsteps receded toward the basement and Hoffman hurried after them and turned on the light, but although he made a thorough search, he could find nothing. Neither could he find a place through which anyone could make his escape.

He heard the noise a number of times, the sound of footsteps, rustling as of paper and such a sound as would be made by the dropping of a book, but although all the doors were locked and the windows fastened down, he was unable to make the slightest discovery.

One night Hoffman heard the same sort of noise in the next room and rushed in to catch the mysterious visitor. He saw a face gazing at him from behind a pillar and ran toward it, but it disappeared, seemingly in the direction of the door and down the steps leading to the basement. The pursuer closed the door behind him and followed. Around the basement fled the nimble feet and up the stairs. Again Hoffman saw the pale face and shadowy form. Carefully guarding the narrow passageway, he advanced. Near the door the face turned full upon him, a low moan was heard, and all was silent. Nothing could be found on the stairway.

On another night Hoffman was startled by the sound of voices singing in the basement of the library. There seemed to him to be a hundred singers singing with musical precision the measures of an old hymn. The notes and the time seemed familiar at the time, but afterward he was unable to give the hymn a name. The singing stopped

101

when Hoffman entered the basement, but began again when he stood still, and on listening intently he distinguished the words and tones of a man praying.

Hoffman's inexplicable experience is backed up by the experience of quite a number of persons, none of whom can explain the mystery except on the theory that old Jean Mareschal is haunting the library.

Saint Paul Globe (Minnesota), July 30, 1903

Ghost Conductor Haunts Station; Calls for Fares

New York, Feb. 14.—Flatbush residents who use the Woodruff Avenue station on the Brighton Beach division of the B.R.T.[11] now have a nickel in hand late o' nights as a talisman against a phantom conductor who is credited with haunting the station.

The story goes that the spook has terrified two pretty station agents, who requested that they be transferred to other stations. It is certain that the transfers have been made, although it is not on record that the phantom conductor was the cause.

He's a perfectly harmless ghost, and all that is necessary to make him vanish is to display a nickel. Flatbushites who boast of having seen him say that he appears at the outside of the station window and, if a belated passenger approaches, murmurs:

"Fares!"

If a nickel is displayed, he is appeased and disappears. The window at which he watches overlooks the "cut" through which the trains pass after leaving the Park Place station on their way to Brighton Beach. Some go so far as to say that they have recognized the conductor as one whom inspectors worried into his grave. Fear that a fare would escape him and that his error would be detected caused his demise. So his astral self is now ruled by the passion for vigilance.

And it doesn't cost the B.R.T. a cent for this ghostly espionage.

Washington Times (DC), Feb. 14, 1908

---

[11] Brooklyn Rapid Transit.

GHOST STALKS IN THE LAW LIBRARY
COLUMBIA UNIVERSITY SPECTER
FRIGHTENS THE WOMAN LIBRARIAN.
SEEN CRAWLING UP THE WALL.
Spook Is Discovered by Index Boy
Who Shuns Gallery after Six P.M.—
Students of Occult Watching for It.

New York.—Columbia University holds that ghost stories may be dismissed with a laugh, until an educated, nice, old gentlemanly ghost gets to hovering 'round Columbia's library building of nights. In other words, there is an undeniable ghost in Columbia's law library, and as the undergraduates say: "What d'ye know about that?"

Three weeks ago the Century Club, of Forty-Third Street, borrowed four portraits of the Columbia law library to hang in a portrait exhibition. They were the portraits of Chancellor Robert E. Livingston; Chancellor Kent; Theodore Dwight, Columbia's old law professor; and Charles M. De Costa, lovingly remembered at the university for a wad of money he bequeathed it.

All four came back about two weeks ago in good condition except the De Costa picture, which had a check or two on its varnish. The Century Club, being notified, took the canvas to a restorer, leaving where of old the portrait used to hang a bright green spot on the otherwise faded green burlap wall.

Three days ago, at 6 p.m., John Henry, the library's card index boy, rushed from the library gibbering. Miss Cox, the assistant librarian, captured him.

"Not again," wailed John though his chattering teeth. "I don't go in there no more: there's a man crawlin' on the wall where the picture was. I don't go back for no money."

Miss Cox entered the library full of scornful unbelief and turned on the electrics. All was as it should be—a bright green oblong on a faded green ground with a book gallery running below it and—

Suddenly a peal of laughter broke in the room and two cases of books on either side of the picture spot emptied their contents with a crash.

When Miss Cox found herself in the outer hall, John Henry had gone.

In the morning a watchman reported to Dean Kirchwey that "a kind of a glow" had been visible through the glass doors of the room all night.

103

Only a few summer and "conditioned" students haunt the library these days. That evening at six (as before) one of them, prowling for a book in the half light of an upper gallery, heard the scratch of a pen writing, writing.

He traced it to the olive green oblong on the blank wall and marched over at once. The pen scratching ceased, but as he stood before the picture spot there rose from the floor a prodigious hollow sigh. The student ran.

With a classmate he returned to the library on tiptoe. The room was vacant, but on the haunted picture spot there glowed an outline of the features that once adorned it, rimmed with a phosphorescent frame. As the youths stared, the face and frame dissolved and the bent figure of a man came out upon the gallery, scurried to the furthest wall and blended with the books. As he vanished they heard a sigh.

The apparition picture, the fleeting figure in the galleries and the hollow sigh have become commonplace now. Even John Henry, the card index autocrat, enters the library without fear—in the daytime. For scholarly Columbia is taking its ghost in a cold, scholastic spirit and already has his nightly walk scheduled for six o'clock evenings, from which hour the ghost has not deviated an iota.

Prof. Hyslop,[12] it is understood, is on the job with other students of the occult and will conduct a series of experiments with the ghost and the ghost's picture. Possibly, it is said, he may endow science with a pamphlet.

In the meantime in the daytime, last year's "canned" students continue to work off conditions, John Henry shuffles the index cards and Miss Cox enters names against missing law books.

Barbour County Index (Medicine Lodge, Kansas), July 22, 1908

NEW JERSEY'S HAUNTED MILL.
Spooks Can't Be Evicted,
so Ancient Building Will Be Torn Down.

Wilburtha, N.J.—Superstition, which peoples the ancient structure with mysterious and terrifying occupants who weep, wail, laugh weirdly, dance and even fight at different times, threatens the further existence of one of the oldest buildings in New Jersey. Situated near

[12] James H. Hyslop (1854-1920) taught ethics and logic at Columbia. He is probably better remembered for his contributions to psychical research, investigating séances and writing a series of books on the spirit world from the perspective of a converted believer.

this place, the structure is a deserted Colonial grist mill, standing near a macadam road much frequented by automobilists. Historical societies and persons interested in the preservation of the ancient landmarks are trying to save the old mill, but it is likely that it will be torn down within a few days.

The reputation of the place as being haunted is not confined to the residents of the neighborhood. Persons who have passed the scene at night in automobiles have told strange stories of gruesome sights and sounds as they passed by the old building. Some of those who have had the experience once now go miles out of their way rather than pass by it late at night.

Among the countless legends which have clustered about the "haunted mill" is one concerning a young man of the neighborhood who went to investigate the place alone about fifteen years ago. The mill, even at that time, had acquired a doubtful reputation and the young man, a farmer, said he was determined to find out for himself just what was inside. He went in, but no one but him ever knew what he saw, for he was a raving maniac when he emerged from the old grist mill and he remained in that condition until his death.

The tradition upon which the reputation of the "haunted mill" as a resort for unearthly visitors is based tells the story of a young man who lured his betrothed into the building more than half a century ago. They were to be married the next day. According to the story, the youth slew the girl and afterward took his own life.

Stories are told how at least four other persons have committed suicide in the old mill, and how two or three other persons have been murdered there.

Such is the ill repute of the mill that even if the municipal authorities decide to tear it down, it is expected to be extremely difficult to get men to do the work.

Shawnee Daily Herald (Oklahoma), Sept. 25, 1910
Reprinted from *New York Evening Telegram* (New York)

**A Nice, Gentlemanly Ghost Inhabits
the Library.**

From "GHOST STALKS IN THE LAW LIBRARY," page 103.

HAUNTED GROUNDS & WATERS

Even a ghost likes to get away from the dank or dusty indoors every now and then. Some spirits, rather than clinging to a particular building, linger around a woods, a cemetery, or a stretch of river. There's a certain understandable psychology behind a phantom remaining near the spot where its bodily host met a tragic, often violent, death, and occasionally this inconsolable trauma occurs out of doors. But other phantoms prefer to remain close to that bodily host after its burial in a cemetery (and, perhaps, in the company of others laid to rest).

The added headroom and roaming space of haunting an outdoor setting allows for some intriguing variations on how ghosts are said to manifest. There are the unnaturally tall ghosts you'll meet in this chapter, such as the ten-foot ghost in Ohio or the eight-foot one in Indiana. Then there's the weird entity encountered in remote Minnesota—part specter, part demon, and part werewolf—that seems particularly well-suited to its forest setting. A few cases of glowing ghostly orbs illuminate this chapter, too. Such ghost lights, also known as "will-o'-the-wisp," are generally encountered in marshy regions (and often explained as the phosphorescent reaction of swirling swamp gasses).

It's time now for a field trip. Pack a sandwich, and wear waterproof hiking boots. Luckily, where we're going, you won't need sunblock.

A GHOST STORY.
A Mysterious "Woman in White"
Flitting Around in Prospect Hill Cemetery.

It has not been long since the report that the house standing at the northwest corner of Thirteenth Street and Capitol Avenue was haunted, excited considerable curiosity among the superstitious. This morning, however, we were told a reliable story that puts the haunted house way in the shade. The scene of this strange and true narrative is Prospect Hill Cemetery, adjoining which Mr. H.P. Stanwood, the well-known sculptor, has a small dwelling and a marble cutting shop, in which several hands are employed.

On Tuesday night, shortly after dark, one of two brothers, who sleep in the shop, happened to step out of doors before retiring, and looking out over the silent city of the dead, a vision—a ghost—a "woman in white"—the invariable costume of ghosts—met his astonished gaze. The mysterious being was slowly flitting towards the building, when he ran in and brought his brother out to view the strange sight. Both became scared, and hastening out of the backdoor, just as the ghost came in the front door and blew out the light, they ran over to Mr. Stanwood's residence to inform him of what had happened.

Mr. Stanwood and the men went out to see what was the matter, and sure enough they saw before them the ghost, who hit Mr. Stanwood on the back and asked where her children were—if they were buried in that tomb. The ghost then flitted into the house, blew out the light, and entering a bedroom, so scaring the occupant that he jumped out of the window and ran away. One of the two brothers mentioned above, having pulled out his revolver, deliberately took aim and fired twice at the ghost, but without effect. She then took her departure into the cemetery, followed by the men to a certain grave, where she vanished.

On Wednesday night the mysterious ghost again made appearance, and so frightened the two brothers that they came downtown to sleep during that night and the next night.

The above is a true statement of the facts, as related to us by a gentleman of veracity.

Mr. Stanwood himself is not a superstitious man and has no faith in ghosts, but our informant assures us that he substantiates the above statement.

Omaha Daily Bee (Nebraska), July 18, 1874

GHOST GUARDING TREASURE
Spectres Light as Air and Thin as a Shadow
Watching Over the Sunken British Frigate Hussar.
A Phantom-Ship in Midair—
An Iron Chest that Vanished
Before an Affrighted Lady's Eyes—
Ghostly Visitants.

That staid old Harford (Conn.) *Times,* which claims to be one of the most reliable papers in the country, has asserted that ghosts and hobgoblins haunt the locality at Port Morris, Westchester County, on which place the British frigate Hussar was sunk nearly one hundred years ago. Ghost stories, as a general thing, are mere bosh, but it was deemed of sufficient importance to send a *Mercury* reporter to Port Morris to investigate the alleged facts concerning the Hussar phantoms. It is thought that the ghosts frequent the locality all the more now because active measures are being taken to secure the millions of British gold and silver which went down with the Hussar when the vessel was wrecked.

THE GHOSTLY VISITORS.

The Port Morris ghosts are a remarkable set of supernatural creatures, and, according to the statements of the residents of that locality, cut up some queer nocturnal pranks, well calculated to make the hair of the ordinary mortal stand on end. There are people on both the Westchester and Long Island shores of that part of the sound, which terminates in the East River, who claim that they have beheld things which partake of a decidedly supernatural nature. When the frigate Hussar sunk, a part of her crew and seventy American prisoners who were onboard went down with her and found a watery grave. From the time of the disaster up to the present time luminous forms have trod the waters opposite Fort Morris. The luminous forms wear manacles, which clink as the prisoners walk.

One old gentleman relates how he witnessed a ghostly reenactment of the Hussar disaster. He was sleeping in an upper room in his house a short time ago, when he was awakened by shrieks and groans which seemed to fill the air outside. He jumped from his bed and rushed out of doors. He saw the phantom Hussar enter Hell Gate in the moonlight, heard the thud as she struck the rock, saw her head for Port Morris, and then beheld the vessel sink in the waters, while the air all around was filled with the shrieks of the drowning men. The poor wretches who struggled in the water called in horrible sepulchral tones for help, and beat the waves with skeleton hands, and glared through the night with awful, ghostly eyes.

WHAT AN OLD RESIDENT SAYS.

The reporter found an old resident of Port Morris at his place of business, and interrogated him about the ghosts. "Why," said he, "there is nothing about these ghosts that every man, woman and child in this place cannot tell you. The stories of supernatural phantoms are at the tongue's end of every person. A great many can tell of strange sights they have seen with their own eyes in the dead of the night. A neighbor of mine told me that Mrs. LaFarge, his sister-in-law, who resides in Michigan, came on two years ago to see his wife, who was sick. Mrs. LaFarge sat up watching the invalid several nights. One night she heard a noise as of a mighty rushing wind outside. Thinking that a storm was blowing up, she went to the door to take a look at the clouds. Her surprise was great to find that there was no storm coming at all. It was a calm, moonlight night. There was not breeze enough to stir the leaves of the trees. The lady looked at her watch and saw that it was just twelve o'clock. She was just about stepping back into the house and closing the door, when her attention was attracted by half a dozen or more lights, which seemed to be carried by men on the shore. 'Someone has fallen into the water,' she thought, 'and the men were trying to get him out.' Much alarmed, she called her brother-in-law. He was dilatory in responding, as he was in bed and had to get up and dress. It was fully ten minutes before he joined his sister-in-law, who remained standing in the door."

A SPECTRAL HOST.

Mrs. LaFarge said that while waiting for him to join her she saw the lights approach to within a dozen rods of the house. The lights were carried by ghosts, while other ghosts carried, evidently with much labor, what seemed to be a large iron money chest, such as was used a century ago. The lady called lustily on her companion to hasten and see the strange sight, but that gentlemen was so slow that, when he joined the lady, the phantoms with the chest had vanished into thin air. The lady said that there were at least forty or fifty specters in the group.

A SHIP IN MIDAIR.

He also related a yarn about a young man who was nearly frightened out of his seven senses by seeing a phantom-frigate suspended in midair over the water off Port Morris. Whether this strange sight was witnessed in the day or nighttime the reporter could not learn, but it is supposed it must have been on a moonlight night, as the Port Morris spooks seldom come in the daytime. The young man, who was a sailor and familiar with the build or shape of all kinds of

110

vessels of the present day, says the spectral craft was evidently old-fashioned in build. Credulous people believe that the phantom ship was none other than the ghost of the ill-fated Hussar.

A DIVER FRIGHTENED.

Several years ago a diver employed by the "Hussar wrecking company," a corporation organized under an act of the legislature of the State of New York, saw, as he alleged, a queer sight down in the water walking around the wreck of the sunken frigate, where he found several skeletons of human beings. The bones were not ghosts. They were real and tangible, and were the remains of the poor wretches who perished when the vessel sank. The diver collected the bones in a pile, and was about to fix a "scoop grapple" to them so as to have them hoisted to the surface of the water when he saw a skeleton walking toward him in the water. The animated skeleton waved its long, bony arms, and with impatient gestures motioned the diver to leave the bones alone. The frightened diver nearly fainted, but he had presence of mind enough to pull the signal cord, and have himself drawn up to the surface of the water. When he related his strange adventure to his fellow workmen, they laughed at him and said he was either fibbing or the victim of a vivid imagination. Another diver went down, but he did not see any animated ghost.

TWO BOYS DROWNED.

Ten or fifteen years ago two boys, living in Port Morris, went out on the Sound in a rowboat. It was early in the evening, and the boys were fishing, when the boat capsized. They screamed for help, but some men who were on shore thought the screams came from the ghosts of the victims of the Hussar wreck, and did not dare to go to the rescue of the boys. The poor lads were drowned. The next morning their bodies were washed ashore.

OTHER GHOST STORIES.

Said Mr. Palnekel: "A Port Morris preacher once delivered a sermon on ghosts, in which he said that no good Christian would believe the people who claimed to see ghosts. The preacher followed his sermon with a prayer that God would remove superstition from the minds of believers in ghosts. It is not strange that believers in the supernatural have circulated many weird tales, which have often been connected with hidden treasure, and in this case the material for superstitious stories is temptingly abundant. But the stories most current bear chiefly on superstitious searches for the sunken gold, and the recovery of much of it by parties who dived and grappled for it by night, before the place was so closely watched as it is now. These stories bear a close relationship to those concerning the quest for the hidden treasure of Captain Kidd, which, tradition says, is buried on the Long Island shores."

Memphis Daily Appeal (Tennessee), Sept. 10, 1876
Reprinted from *New York Mercury* (New York)

AN OLD MAN'S GHOST.
An Apparition that Is
Startling a Neighborhood.

Ulster County seems to be a favored neighbor for ghostly visitations, and other things of a marvelous nature. The widespread excitement last winter regarding the Dunn dwelling, which for a long while was believed by many credulous persons to be haunted, has already been followed by another singular sensation. Unlike that of old man McDonald, the prevailing ghost does not confine itself to a particular dwelling or spot, but haunts a whole neighborhood. The locality visited by this ghost is a thinly inhabited farming region, situated at the foot of the Shawangunk Mountains, in a remote part of the town of Rochester, and called Logtown.

In this neighborhood lives a family by the name of Rose, the head of which, Louis Rose, died some months since. "Old Man Rose," as his neighbors called him, was a remarkably eccentric character. A scoffer at the Christian religion and a blasphemer in no small degree, he despised all religious instruction up to the day of his death, and entertained a contempt for ministers of the Gospel which he could ill conceal. He repeatedly informed his family that he did not want a preacher to officiate at his funeral. He looked upon eternal punishment as the penalty of his disobedience and impiety with anything but fear. He was an illiterate old fellow, intellectually incapable of indulging in philosophical speculations on any subject. But there was one fear that constantly haunted Rose, and which, in spite of his fearless and stoical nature, he could not conquer, and that was a terror of being buried alive.

About a year ago Rose was seized with his last illness. On his deathbed he raved and cursed, but became calm in his last moments and called his wife to his bedside and said: "Wife, I'm goin' to die. Satan is after me. I hear the rattling of his chains. But I will promise you if I can break away from him I will come back." Still haunted with the fear of premature burial, he concluded with the request that his body be kept eight days before being buried, and he desired to have it thrown out on the fields after that length of time to be eaten by the crows. This request his friends regarded to a certain extent, strange as it was, but having no means to preserve the body, decomposition set in almost immediately after death, and the turgid and discolored corpse, which emitted a stench that it was scarcely possible to bear, was interred on the fifth day.

The promise of Rose to come back if he could break the chains of Satan was known only to himself and family for a long while, and certainly nothing was more unlooked for than its fulfillment, for as much given to superstitious notions as the people of remote neighborhoods usually are, none doubted that Rose had been taken care of, and so not a thought was given the matter. But that he has come back is very generally believed in the community. His ghost first appeared, it seems, one night recently, when it was met on the open highway by a member of the Independent Order of Oddfellows. The ghost, he affirms, was standing with his face toward him, not ten feet away, and as there was bright moonlight at the time, he is positive that he could not have been laboring under a delusion. Besides, he had been acquainted with Rose for years, and the personal appearance of the deceased was such as to make his identity certain under almost any circumstances. He did not speak to the apparition because it vanished before he had an opportunity to do so. On a subsequent occasion Rose appeared to another resident of the community and, he avers, spoke to him. At another time a lady living in the adjoining neighborhood asserts that the ghost of the departed was seen in her house, and she is willing to testify so under oath. Altogether the apparition has been seen on five different occasions by as many different persons.

Cincinnati Daily Star (Ohio), July 8, 1878
Reprinted from *New York Times* (New York)

GHOSTS IN THE WOODS.
A Murderer's Spirit Thought to Be Wandering about the Spot Where the Criminal Was Lynched— Terrible Sounds and Sights.

Carnesville, Ga., Dec. 21.—A well-authenticated report has reached a local newspaper office that an apparition has been seen several times lately near where Frank Sanders, the murderer, was lynched. It is said that there are heard strange noises and the most awful groans that mortal man ever heard in the woods, and they are unaccounted for by any line of human reasoning. A short while ago an apparently large fire was seen at a distance in the woods, and a large crowd of small children was seen dancing and playing around and having a merry time.

The fire appeared to be some 200 yards from the road, and when those who saw it attempted to go to it, it would appear to make a retreat through the woods, and the pursuer could never get nearer than when he started to it. The children appeared to be having a perfect jubilee, as they were dancing and playing like so many fairies, and having a picnic in the woods by firelight. After making the chase for some time it was abandoned, and the light was left burning and the children dancing in their merry glee.

It is said that hooting owls are heard near the spot at all times of night, and there is one heard almost nightly that has a different voice from any of the others, and one who once hears it is impressed with the idea that it is a warning of danger. Several colored people have passed the place recently who have seen something that had the appearance of a gallows and a victim upon the scaffold upon his knees making a confession, and several ministers around offering up prayers for the culprit.

J.A. Hilley, who rented Dr. Freeman's place last year, near the place of the execution, left it on account of himself and family having seen things for which they couldn't account, and which they thought were supernatural, and its present tenant, J.E. Crawford, has also heard things near the place that are shrouded in mystery to him. These reports have become so general, and are so much believed by the colored people, that those who came from up that road to town always leave in time to pass the place of the execution before nightfall.

Pittsburgh Dispatch (Pennsylvania), Dec. 22, 1889

A TEN-FOOT GHOST
NOW MAKING ITS HOME
IN A BUCKEYE CEMETERY
A Bold Young Man Attempts to Brave
the Spirit, but Retreats in Confusion—
He Will Not Go Outdoors After Sunset Since.

Hamilton, O., July 27.—What is claimed to be a genuine ghost has made its appearance here. The apparition has been seen in the Boudinot burying ground, in the First Ward, by a number of parties. About a year ago the grounds were put into the hands of the City Council and an effort made to convert them into a park. The grand old trees that had stood for a century and shaded the tombs were cut down, and the grave-mounds were leveled to the earth, the stones being carried away. The grave was robbed of its once solemn beauty, and the hallowed associations of years disregarded. Day after day the graves were torn open by the plow and the rotting bones thrown promiscuously upon the ground. A few days ago the plowshare turned up a tombstone bearing the inscription: "Charley, aged 12, son of Herman and Anna Carter."

Soon after this rumors that were calculated to keep the immediate residents in the house after night were circulated, and some superstitious ones declared that in the old cemetery there were ghosts. A few evenings since Joseph Myers, who resides on Boudinot Street, had a strange experience. While he was sitting in his doorway shortly before retiring, he looked in the direction of the park and saw a queer-looking object appear. From the deserted Carter tomb arose a shrouded figure. It was about ten feet in height, and carried a torch in its outstretched hand, making at times quite a brilliant light. In a short space of time the figure seemed to rise and glide toward the street. Myers was somewhat nervous for a short time. He arose, however, and walked across the street, and pursued it for the purpose of investigation, but before he could approach the mysterious figure it suddenly disappeared.

It is claimed that the spirits of the bodies that belong to these graves which have been disturbed nightly promenade the grounds. A young man residing on Park Street boldly asserted that he had no fear of any such thing as a ghost, and that he would fathom the mystery of the apparition. Last Friday night he took a seat in the extreme eastern portion of the cemetery to carry out his design. About midnight the ghost arose before him, and he became so badly frightened that he started at a breakneck speed in an easterly direction, and on the following day was discovered hidden in a blackberry patch near Reily, some 12 miles distant from the corporate limits of Hamilton. Since this adventure he cannot be persuaded to go outdoors after sunset.

Pittsburgh Dispatch (Pennsylvania), July 28, 1890

ITS BONES RATTLE.
An Old-Fashioned Spook Terrifies
the Inhabitants of an Eastern Village.

Westerly, R.I., Nov. 26.—The quiet little Rhode Island hamlet of Saylesville has had a real, old-fashioned spook this winter. The ghost frequents a wooded strip of land leading from Crossman Street to Pagley Street, appears nightly, glides over the ground with a fantastic, graveyard gait, and some people that have met the spook and whose hearing is acute think they heard its bones rattle in its white habiliments. The citizens of obscure and lonesome Saylesville avoid the ghost's walk and take a short footpath around the Crossman wood after dark.

The spook has appeared to more than half a dozen people, but most of them were too scared to let it come very near to them and see how it looks; but the other night the Rev. Mr. Calvin, with his two daughters, strolling nonchalantly through the haunted wood, saw the ghost at short range. A figure clad in white suddenly rose up out of the brush or ground and flashed with the quickness and elusiveness of a firefly past them. The young ladies were very much frightened, but as the apparition disappeared almost instantly they regained their courage, and the party went home. All three persons had a good look at the phantom, and aver it is a genuine ghost. They have told the story of the encounter to a hundred people. Some of the brave young fellows of Saylesville propose to lie in wait for the ghost at night.

Pittsburgh Dispatch (Pennsylvania), Nov. 27, 1890

A MURDERED MAN'S GHOST.
A Startling Sight Witnessed
by a Party of Campers.

Burlington, Iowa, Sept. 15.—An evening paper prints a sensational story to the effect that five Burlington fishermen camping out on Big Island, below the city, saw the ghost of Robert Rankin, the murdered stockman of Monmouth, Ill., wandering around the island. The story goes that one of the campers, awakened by a noise, saw the form of Rankin leaning against a tree in the firelight. His uncovered head showed a ghastly wound, the scalp hanging down over his forehead, blood streaming over his body to the ground.

The horrified spectators saw the body reel and fall to the ground with a thud, while out among the trees could be heard retreating footsteps. The ghost rose slowly to its feet, moaned and shivered, and then stalked through the crowd of paralyzed campers away into the darkness of the woods. The paper claims its informants to be reputable persons. There is still great interest in the whereabouts of the body of

Rankin, who was murdered over a year ago, and it is believed to have been buried on Big Island.

Arizona Republican (Phoenix), Sept. 16, 1893
Credited to the Associated Press

THE GIRL IN WHITE
MYSTERIOUS DISAPPEARANCE OF
LIZZIE CLARK TWENTY YEARS AGO
The Tragedy of a Little Illinois Town—
Murder or Suicide—The Ghost that Is
Seen by Hunters and River Men—
It Is Always Arrayed in a White Gown.

Fully 20 years have passed since Lizzie Clark, an orphan with a heritage, disappeared from a hotel in Dallas City, Ills., as completely as if the earth had swallowed her up. In all that western country there has never been a stranger case than the disappearance of that girl, and there has never been a greater ghost mystery than has been and still is occasioned by the evidently disembodied spirit of the girl.

The story of Lizzie Clark has been county history. She was an orphan and had some property and money. A guardian had been appointed, and Lizzie, being ambitious to add to her little store, set about to work in a hotel hard by the river's edge. Through the dining room of this hotel runs the line between Hancock and Henderson Counties, so that often a guest reached from Hancock into Henderson County when after butter. A country swain and his lass, if seated opposite each other at this board, are in different counties. Many a man wanted for some offense in Hancock county has sat at this table in Henderson County and grinned at the sheriff of Hancock County.

It was one afternoon about 20 years ago that Lizzie Clark, who had been washing dishes in the kitchen, stepped out into the yard of the hotel. She was seen to leave the kitchen by several working around the house, who paid no attention to the girl, but that was the last ever seen of her. Those who saw her step out into the yard heard no scream, no stifled moan, no struggling, but there are people yet living who believe that the girl was suddenly seized, strangled, concealed in the house until dark and then cast into the dark river. Be that as it may, the murderers, if they remained in the same locality long, have been amply tormented since.

It is said that the murderers did not leave the locality for some time thereafter, and yet again, others say the girl was never murdered, but drowned herself, and that her ghost is not one of a murdered person's, but one of a suicide. All one can gain from the different stories and theories is that the girl was dealt with foully in some manner, and that her ghost still haunts the locality. Of course every effort was made to ferret out the mystery. Detectives hunted high and low, money was spent to no purpose, and finally the guardian of the girl's estate turned her money and property over to the county authorities, in whose hand it remains to this day because there is no kith or kin to claim it.

The girl's ghost was first seen in Dec., 1887, when a party of duck hunters were returning to Dallas City from the islands. An excursion steamer had become disabled late in the season and was lying on the bank of the island across the bay. She was in a rather bad fix. It was expected to leave her there during the winter. As the hunters neared the craft, a form in white was seen to run out upon the upper deck. It was a young girl's figure, and she was evidently being pursued, for from across the water came screams and then the following words: "Leave me alone, leave me alone, or I will drown myself!" With that the specter flung itself into the river. There was a splash, and the cold waters closed over the white body. Several times during that winter the ghost of Lizzie Clark was seen at night and at early candle light around the disabled steamer. When the steamer was taken away the next spring, workmen and steamboat men heard pitiful screams from the willows on shore as the boat moved away. The spirit did not leave the island, and it is believed now that she was buried on the island after the murder.

Of later years, however, the girl's ghost has been seen in a skiff at night, and it was only a few evenings ago that one of the St. Louis and St. Paul fast steamers ran into the spectral thing. The pilot did not see the ghostly craft until too late. He says he saw a boat of white that looked more like floating fleece than anything else. In the boat was a young girl in white raiment, but there were blood clots on the white dress. "She was rowing swiftly. When the prow of the steamer struck this frail craft, it cut through it like mist. The ghostly occupant only laughed a sort of uncanny laugh—a half scream—and when we had passed I saw the spectral craft dancing on the waves behind. I doubt if an ordinary skiff could have lived in the waves of our steamer, right under the paddles." Thus spoke the pilot, and he is a man of few words and sterling integrity.

"Have you seen Lizzie Clark's boat?" is now the question that goes from one mouth to another during the summer season. The question is not asked so often in winter from the fact that the poor girl's spirit does not seem to roam so much. Hunters have come into Dallas shaking with fright and calling for a dram to brace their nerves, saying that while coming down from the islands above the ice, they had met Lizzie Clark walking rapidly toward them. She always wears that white dress, and the blood stains on the neck are plain. The girl's eyes are always staring wide open, as if she were being suffocated. Her spirit has been known to step out from behind a clump of dead trees at the head of the island and face passersby. She will give them a terrible look and then scream piteously. In an instant more, the spirit has disappeared.

Democratic Northwest and Henry County News
(Napoleon, Ohio), Oct. 18, 1894
Reprinted from *Chicago Times* (Illinois)

A GHOST EIGHT FEET TALL.
IT HAUNTS AN INDIANA TOWNSHIP
AND WILL NOT DOWN.
Carries an Awful Club and Travels with a Roar like a Summer Thunder Storm in a Forest— Heeds Neither Buckshot Nor Rifle Bullets— Brave Men Terrified.

Benton, Ind., July 26.—Wearing a long white beard and robe, and carrying a huge club, a real ghost, eight feet high, is abroad in Benton Township, Elkhart County. Night after night it has been seen for the last week, and night after night searching parties of farmers have fired at the fearful object with shotguns. But that it is a real ghost is proved by the fact the shot whistled harmlessly through the ghost, and it disappeared only to reappear in a different place, waving its long white arms and shaking its club at pursuers.

It has been seen by hundreds, it has been fired at by terrified searching parties, and it has each time vanished and then flashed its fearsome presence in another place.

Last Tuesday night it made its first appearance. On that evening John W. French and his good wife made a call at a neighbor's some miles away from their farm. The evening was spent in storytelling and jollity, and it was well along toward midnight when Farmer French helped his wife into his big farm wagon and climbed up beside her to start home. A few miles along the lonely country road over which they had to travel is an old church, moss grown and weather beaten, and beside it is a graveyard well filled with the bones of those who once tilled the soil in this locality. Ten years ago an aged man who lived alone not far from the old church and who visited the graveyard almost daily to pray over the resting place of some relative, was foully murdered for the store of gold he was supposed to have hidden about his hermit abode. The robbers and murderers escaped justice and the luckless greybeard was buried in the graveyard where he spent so much time.

And just as the lumbering wagon of Farmer French drew within sight of the white headstones in the churchyard the horses reared back on their haunches and snorted in terror. French was alarmed, and suspecting highwaymen had been scented by the horses, he reached for a shotgun which lay in the bottom of the wagon for just such an emergency. But before his hand touched it he was startled by a scream from his wife. Clutching his arm she pointed straight ahead and gasped: "Look, John, look!"

Far down the road, just beside the glimmering monuments of the old graveyard, he saw an apparition. It was that of a man with a long white beard sweeping over his breast. The figure appeared to be eight feet in height, and in one hand it carried a club, such as the brains of the old man had been beaten out with ten years before. Slowly raising one arm the ghost with a majestic sweep beckoned French to come ahead. He was too startled to do anything except try to restrain the prancing horses, which were straining at the harness in attempts to break away and run. A cold sweat started out all over the body of the farmer as he realized that he was at last looking at a ghost, and then the sound of his wife's voice came to him begging him to return the way they had come and escape the doom which seemed impending. French was still too much scared and excited to control the horses, and as he gazed steadfastly at the fearful white object in the road it slowly began to move toward the wagon. The club was now raised to its shoulder, as a soldier carries a rifle, and it seemed to move forward without touching the ground, like a winged thing.

Then the farmer recovered his faculties, and whirling his team around, he lashed the horses into a run and began the trip to the house of the friend he had just left. As he did so a great roaring noise as of thunder filled all the air and maddened the frightened horses, so that they ran over the road like wild creatures. The noise came from the ghost, which followed close behind the wagon. Though fainting with fear Mrs. French could not resist the temptation to look behind and see whether the spook was following. She saw it about ten feet behind the wagon, and as she screamed, it vanished.

A few minutes later French drove into the barnyard of his friend and told his tale to the frightened people. No ghost could then be seen, and some of those in the house were inclined to doubt the story and laid it to imagination. But Mrs. French could not be induced to pass the graveyard again that night, and the couple stayed for the night with their friends. The next day the story was repeated over the countryside, and by night everyone from Millersburg to New Paris had heard of the Benton ghost. The old church and graveyard were visited during the daytime by hundreds, but no trace of the ghost could be found. Parties of boys and young men boldly ventured to stay in the graveyard all night and watch for the apparition, but as the shades of night drew on and the shadows of the headstones began to lengthen across the grass most of the watchers left the place under various excuses. A peculiar, creepy feeling, common to those who ever pass a cemetery at night, took possession of those who remained, and it soon amounted almost to a panic, so that every man in the crowd left for home and vowed the ghost could do as it pleased.

Night came on with the great wall of blackness which shuts down over everything in the country at night. The moon at times struggled through the clouds which overspread the heavens and shed a faint radiance on the tombstones in the lonely graveyard and the long rank grass which flourishes in the city of the dead. Absolute silence reigned when Milton Moon, a farmer of Benton township, strode sturdily along the highway which passes the graveyard and over which Farmer French's team went flying the night before. Moon had not heard of the ghost, or if he had it did not scare him. He was perfectly familiar with the lonely road, for he had traveled it for years. He knew just where the old church was, for he had spent many hours in its shadow, and he felt no qualms about passing the deserted graveyard which he had so often passed after dark. Moon walked boldly ahead, his thoughts on a business venture which he contemplated, when suddenly he heard a wild roar and rumble like 10,000 bolts of thunder. Stopping in amazement he looked up, and the sight which met his eyes turned him sick and giddy. All the blood in his body seemed turned to ice and his brain reeled.

Fifty feet before him he saw a ghost, a figure over eight feet tall, with flowing white robes and a patriarchal beard which reached its waist. As he gazed, stupefied and almost insane, Moon observed that the figure was transparent, and through it he could still see the dim outline of the old church looming up in the darkness. In its right hand the awful apparition grabbed a club, murderous, fearful. And as it swept toward Moon, as though borne on the wings of the wind, and the thunderous roar continued, he sank to the earth and knew no more until he awoke in the farmer's house surrounded by his friends and with a doctor bending over him. In broken words Moon told the awful story of his fright and of the ghost which had almost bereft him of reason, and when the narrative was done he again swooned at the memory of the fearful object. Ever since he has been under the constant care of a physician, and his condition is grave.

When this tale was spread broadcast throughout the neighborhood, the countryside seemed to flame with a desire to trace the mystery to its source and discover the cause of the apparitions, which had so terrified French and Moon. Meetings were hurriedly held and posses organized to hunt down the spectral creature with the long white beard and menacing club. Many farmers and hired men positively refused to join the expedition when they had learned of the fate of Moon, but enough brave men were found to make a goodly showing and armed with shotguns and rifles they set out Friday night to hunt down the ghost. A leader was chosen, and he divided the men into squads of three and four, posting them at various places along the road near the old churchyard. Each squad was ordered to challenge the ghost should it appear and, on its failure to halt, to fire directly at it. With these instructions well understood, the men separated and waited for developments, which they felt sure would come.

When the main party was thus divided some of the watchers were not so bold as they had been at the outset. The little groups kept close together and whiled away the anxious hours telling ghost stories and weird tales of apparitions of bygone years. The history of the luckless old man, whose ghost they thought they were awaiting, was recounted by those who had known him, and the horrible story of his murder by robbers was retold. That he had come to haunt the neighborhood where once he toiled and suffered all were agreed, and the fact that the tall ghost carried a club was taken to indicate that he was to be revenged upon the countryside for his sudden taking off. While these stories were causing shudders to chase up and down the spines of the more timorous in the party, John Martin, a farmhand, startled one of the groups with a cry, "There it is!"

Less than twenty feet away stood the ghost, evidently looking directly at the watchers. Its long arms hung motionless and in one hand was grasped the club. It did not attempt to approach the group of men huddled there in the darkness with hands tightly clutching their shotguns and hearts beating so loudly they could almost be heard. Martin was the first to recover himself. Raising his shotgun to his shoulder he called in a loud voice: "Who stands there? Speak, or I fire." No answer came from the spectre, but instead one of the long arms slowly raised and the figure began an almost imperceptible advance. This was enough for Martin and his friends. Four shotguns rang out at once and four loads of buckshot passed through the white figure and rattled among the tree trunks behind it. In a flash the figure disappeared and darkness, more intense than before, supervened.

The noise of the guns aroused the other watchers in distant spots, and their lanterns could be seen flashing among the trees as they approached where the ghost had been seen. A meeting was held, and Martin and his friends related their adventure. Extra caution was ordered, and all through the long watches of the night the men lay around in the darkness near the deserted churchyard watching for the ghost, which did not come.

The next night the party was again reorganized and under the same directions watched once more, and once more the awful apparition was seen. It was further away than on the first night, and as it approached the thunderous roar which Moon and French had described was plainly heard. A volley of shots was sent through the spectre when it came within firing distance, but they whistled through it as harmlessly as on the previous night, and at the same instant the ghost disappeared.

The stories told by the members of the posse when they returned to their homes created intense excitement. Women refused to go out of doors at night, and half the country people are sitting up all night to watch for the coming of the tall ghost with the big club. It appears in various places, but usually somewhere near the graveyard or the old church where the murdered man lies buried. Each night searching parties go out to run down the specter, and each night they return with the same tale. The ghost of Benton is talked of at night in country homes and wayside villages and still it stalks abroad, spreading terror and dismay in its wake.

The Sun (New York, New York), Aug. 2, 1896
Reprinted from *Cleveland Plain Dealer* (Ohio)

MAINE'S HAUNTED TOWN.
Nearly Every Other House in Easton
Has a Ghost of Some Kind.

It is doubtful if any town in all New England has more ghosts and haunted houses than Easton, Me. It may well be called a haunted town. Although the citizens are sensible and well-to-do farmers, with all sincerity and almost to a man they vouch for the truth of many tales of remarkable and startling supernatural visitations.

For years one of the houses in the center of the town has stood vacant. Several attempts have been made to occupy it, but no one has ever succeeded in remaining within the fated walls for any length of time. One brave and skeptical youth recently determined upon an investigation, and as he is the scion of one of the first families and tells his story openly, it is believed in implicitly by all Easton people.

The first night after he had gone to bed, leaving the light burning, the shade of a great dog came into the room right through the closed door. Advancing to the bedside, the canine specter regarded him savagely. He started up, and the phantom dissolved into thin air.

But the courage of the investigator failed him not, and he determined to brave it out. Before he could get to sleep, however, a woman all in white, with disordered black hair hanging over her face, made her appearance, weeping and wringing her hands. This vivid apparition was accompanied by still more gruesome signs from below. The heavy clanking of a chain reverberated through the still house, and soon deep groans were heard from various points. By this time he was thoroughly frightened, and getting out of bed he went down to the dining room, where he remained the rest of the night listening to the noises made by his ghostly companions. The house has never been entered since.

Another Easton man of undoubted veracity claims to have seen a phantom woman in broad daylight, when the sun was shining brightly and no thoughts of the ghostly were in his mind. It was in his own home, too, where all were cheerful and nothing existed to put him in a morbid state. She had a remarkably white face, luminous dark eyes, and masses of dark hair hung in wild disorder about her face. He raised his eyes and saw this phantom advancing toward him. So real did it seem that he thought she was a mortal woman. He rose and stepped toward her, when she gave him one long, searching look and vanished into empty space. The piercing glance of those eyes, which, he says, seemed to penetrate his very soul, haunts him still, although he never has had a repetition of the ghostly visitant.

Copper Country Evening News
(Calumet, Michigan), Feb. 19, 1898
Reprinted from *San Francisco Examiner* (California)

GLEAMING
Balls Seen Where Girl Drowned.

Vincennes, Ind., Aug 22.—The little town of Decker and the surrounding country is in a fever of excitement over the report that the ghost of Nora Fiers, who was drowned in the White River last week, has appeared in their midst and has been seen hovering along the banks of the river. The apparition, it is claimed, takes the form of two gleaming balls of fire and wanders up and down the route taken by the girl the time she was drowned.

Marietta Daily Leader (Ohio), Aug. 24, 1901

SNAPSHOT OF GHOST.
Ohio Doctor Says He Has Photograph of an Apparition.
Ghastly Midnight Visitor Broke Up a Pretty Honeymoon by Rappings, Groans and Other Strange Doings.

According to a Bucyrus (O.) correspondent of the *New York World,* the northern part of Crawford County is trying to solve a mystery which surrounds a little cottage on the farm of Horace Burger. The cottage, which was built as a bridal present to his daughter by Mr. Burger, is small but comfortable. It is only 50 feet from one of the most traveled roads in the country, with a pretty grove of native forest trees at the rear. In this wood, before the house was built, a wandering workman named J.G. Klinghardt took his life by hanging himself.

After their wedding the young couple took up their residence under most auspicious circumstances. A week had not passed when their nights were disturbed by strange tappings on the windows and at the doors. Moans and groans came from nowhere in particular. Later on the figure of the suicide could be plainly seen about the house and woods, and though the windows and doors were securely fastened, he could enter the house and wander aimlessly from room to room, his coming being heralded by a dim phosphorescent light, a damp draught and weary, sighing groans.

The young couple supposed at first that some of their friends were making them the target of a practical joke, but two weeks of such a honeymoon convinced them that life at the old family home, amid friends, would be more congenial, and they gave over the cottage to the ghost.

Burger volunteered to prove the fallacy of their story, and the next night went to sleep in the cottage. He was awakened suddenly about midnight by a cold breath, and, sitting boldly upright, he saw the well-known form of Klinghardt wandering about the room. Burger threw a stick of wood at the apparition. Though his aim was true, the stick seemed to go through the misty form without result. Burger lighted a lamp, but the ghost had gone. He returned to bed, and the ghost reappeared. This was enough, and he went home to acknowledge that he did not understand the matter.

Night after night a new candidate came forward to prove the foolishness of his neighbors, but none will consent to spend a second night in the place.

Parties have been made up to explode the fallacy, but they have invariably ended in making a larger number of mystified people, all of whom would gladly welcome proof that they were victims of hallucination rather than the observers of a real ghost in its weary journey from the grave to the scene of its departure from life. John Wilford, George Burger, John Strohm, Philip Cramer, R.D. Whisler and Tony Herzer are all referred to as being able to corroborate the stories of the reality of the ghost.

So notorious had the affairs of the Burger neighborhood become that they attracted attention in the neighboring village of New Washington. Dr. Miller with Editor Lautz of the village paper; J.B. Ledman, superintendent of the Sycamore schools; and Undertaker John Geiger went to investigate. All had been present when the body of Klinghardt had been cut down.

Speaking of the matter, Dr. Miller says that when he determined to investigate he kept the matter quiet, so as not to apprise anyone who might be the cause of the joke. He took along his camera, determined to get the only photograph of a real ghost ever taken.[1] He waited until a few minutes before midnight and then went down to the grove where the dead man had been found hanging. The doctor knew the way to the sapling and intended to go to it in the moonlight, and from there to the grave. He had gone but a short distance when he perceived a form ahead of him leading the way. He was surprised, but not frightened. For the moment he forgot his camera, but just before reaching the woods he remembered it and quickly made an exposure. The photo shows plainly the apparition in the woods. The trip to the tree was continued under the supernatural guidance, and also the visit to the grave. Being convinced that what he saw was the ghost and not desiring any further acquaintance, the doctor went home.

---

[1] This is a revealing glimpse of the popular view of "spirit photography," which had existed for about four decades when this article appeared. William Mumler (1832–1884) is typically credited with having launched the practice in the 1860s. It grew and lasted well into the 1900s, but such photographers were repeatedly charged with fakery. It would be interesting to see the photograph that, as this article reports, Dr. Miller managed to take.

He has expressed himself as fully convinced that the Burgers and their friends are sincere in their belief, and he cannot explain the matter.

Perrysburg Journal (Ohio), May 29, 1903

Interesting Ghost.
New York Letter in Philadelphia Press.

His nerves shattered by a famous "ghost" of Van Antwerp's woods, near the Westchester Country Club, Robert Fuller is suffering from hysteria and under the care of physicians at his home on Eastern Boulevard. Charles Willis and his wife, neighbors of the Fullers, also say they saw the "ghost," and it was not until daylight yesterday morning that they turned out the lights in their house and sought repose.

Fuller and his wife and Mr. and Mrs. Willis were sitting on the porch of the Fuller home Thursday night when they say the "ghost" appeared. It had the form of a woman, and they say its outline was distinct and ghastly.

Mrs. Fuller screamed and her husband, completely unnerved by the apparition, jumped from the porch, ran to the back of the house and, entering the backdoor, fell fainting in the kitchen. The Willises hurried to their home, lit every light in the house and sat up until daylight. Both were terrified by the apparition. Mrs. Johanna Quinlan, who formerly lived in the house now occupied by the Willises, saw the "ghost" five years ago and was made insane. She is now in a sanitarium.

Westchester tradition has it that the ghost is that of a woman servant who was employed by the Van Antwerp family twenty-five years ago. She was returning to the house late at night when she stumbled and nearly fell into a sunken well. She cursed the well, which was said to possess remarkable properties. A few days later she disappeared, and the story has since survived that she was murdered and her body thrown into a pond near the well.

Indianapolis Journal (Indiana), June 24, 1903

FOUR-LEGGED GHOST IN FROG HOLLOW CEMETERY

MANCHESTER, Conn., Nov. 6.—Consternation reigns in Frog Hollow over a four-legged ghost which has been repeatedly seen in St. James' cemetery by persons who cut across the burial grounds to reach the village.

Miss Mable Willis, who saw the ghost, has not been able to leave the house since her experience. Matthew Moriarty placed little credence on the story, and last night when it became dark he told his friends in the village grocery story that he was going through the cemetery.

As Moriarty reached the center of the cemetery he heard a noise like that made by horses' hoofs, accompanied by the clashing of chains. He was terror stricken. The clattering came from one of the roads in the cemetery and continued until it reached a spot near the receiving vault.

Moriarty saw a white object emerge from the vault, and as it came toward him, he noticed it had four legs. He started on a dead run and never looked behind him until he had reached the store.

Los Angeles Herald (California), Nov. 7, 1906

FIREMAN FLEES FROM
GRAVEYARD GHOSTS
ALONE IN A CEMETERY AT MIDNIGHT
HE SEES WEIRD SPECTERS
AND RUNS AWAY.

St. Louis.—Lost for an hour among the tombstones of Calvary cemetery at midnight, fleeing till out of breath from mysterious white figures that seemed to rise up from among the graves, William Carpenter, a fireman, had an experience which he hopes will never be repeated.

Members of his fire company, still talking about Carpenter's experience, look on the whole affair as a joke. He is not quite convinced that the white-garbed figures were not ghosts.

Late at night, about half-past ten o'clock, the Baden firemen were aroused by an alarm turned in from a box at Calvary and Florissant Avenues. Their shortest route to the fire was through Calvary cemetery. At the big iron gates on the Broadway side of the cemetery Capt. Ammon and Fireman Carpenter left the hose reel. Ammon opened the gates and then sprang to his post on the wagon. Carpenter was left behind to close the gates after the engine.

When he had closed the gates, the hose reel and engine were a hundred feet ahead of him, dashing rapidly up the hill. Carpenter ran after the wagon, shouting loudly.

He saw the lights of the engine disappear in the distance and started to find his way out of the cemetery.

"I kept on running," he said to a reporter in telling of his experience, "wishing every minute I could get out."

"All around me were white tombstones. I heard a noise in another direction and then I saw a white thing. It seemed to rise out of the ground. My hair went up, too, I think.

"Then I did run. I'll admit I was dead afraid. I just wanted to get out of that place of horrors. I think I prayed. I was damp all over with a cold, clammy sort of sweat."

Carpenter wiped his forehead with his handkerchief in memory of the event before he went on.

"I thought all the time that I was heading for Calvary Avenue. After a time I saw the light of a street car in the distance and it sort of kept me company. I followed the light, and the next thing I knew I had stumbled and fallen, and there looking at me was another white thing. It wasn't as bad as the first, though. I was getting used to the spooks a little.

"I got up again and ran until I came to a barbwire fence. I got over the fence without a scratch and found I was in Walnut Park, north of the cemetery. All the time I had thought I was going south.

"A policeman told me where I was, and how to get back to the engine-house. He said we had made a run on a false alarm. I had been in the cemetery an hour."

Spanish Fork Press (Utah), April 18, 1907

SEES GHOST IN THE WOODS.
Beautiful Woman Robed in White
Follows and Beckons to Him.

Coleraine, Minn.—Polish settlers in the country east of here are in a state of excitement over the alleged discovery of a "wehr wolf," which takes the shape of a beautiful woman garbed in a long white robe and whom the superstitious believe is seeking men's souls.

Milan Prevosko, a homesteader, says that while he was walking to his claim through the woods recently, a woman dressed in a long white robe appeared. She followed him about ten paces in the rear and constantly beckoned to him. When he stopped, the woman also stood motionless and when, terror-stricken, he took to his heels, the wehr wolf kept close behind him. At last in desperation he stopped and hurled a huge stone at the mysterious form which instantly vanished.

He describes the woman as about the ordinary height, with long, raven-black hair, which hung down over her shoulders, reaching below the waist line. The face, which was intensely pale, nevertheless was beautiful, and eyes that seemed like liquid fire.

Some of the settlers who listened to Prevorsko's tale were inclined to disbelieve it, but he has found many others who have implicit faith in his tale. Those who have doubted the story have traveled the path at all hours of the night without encountering the weird spectacle.

Richmond Planet (Virginia), June 1, 1907

WHOLE TOWN HUNTS GHOST
Agile Spook Climbs Trees and Hills
Near Worcester, Mass.,
Then Hides in Pond.

Worcester, Mass.—Northbridge has a ghost, or a ghost has Northbridge, residents of the heretofore peaceful village are uncertain which. For several nights at about the same hour a mysterious light, varying in size from a small bulb to that of a bushel measure, has appeared and performed queer antics on the high ledge near Wayside.

First treated as a joke, continued nightly repetitions have caused the phenomenon to become a serious reality, and the village and its neighborhood are discussing the affair, while scores of children are seriously frightened. At least three families are packing up their household goods with the announced intention of moving out of town.

About eight o'clock fully 200 persons assembled in the vicinity of the ledge, but when the light appeared many women screamed and hurried home, evincing no desire to continue the investigation. Half a dozen armed men had the temerity to go to the top of the ledge, and, in close formation, shoulder to shoulder, tried to catch up with the light. Like a will-o'-the-wisp, the light zigzagged along the ledge, climbed up the trunk of a tall pine tree, from which point it was visible for a considerable distance, descended rapidly within a few yards of the watchers and, mounting the crest of the hill, disappeared in the nearby pond.

Bisbee Daily Review (Arizona), Sept. 11, 1909

GHOST OF A TRAPPER
HAUNTING A CANYON
Weird Figure of Bear's Victim
Seen by Arizona Boys—
Horses Enchanted.

Williams, Ariz.—In Wilson Canyon, southeast of Williams, is an uncanny spot wherein horses shy and bolt from terrors heretofore invisible to the human eye. At least three wagons have been wrecked there by runaways that started without apparent cause. But at last a veritable ghost has been materialized on the unshaken testimony of two young residents of the locality, Wright Clark and "Tex" Ownby.

They say that on a recent Sunday evening about dusk they were riding down the Wilson Canyon trail when their horses became frightened, snorting and prancing in terror. The boys looked to the right and saw, emerging from behind a juniper tree, the form of a man at least six feet in height, with long gray hair and beard, clad in buckskin and dragging an old-fashioned gun about as long as himself. Boys and horses stood as through enchanted, while the apparition circled them noiselessly, though the rifle was seen to strike the rocks. The circle about complete, the figure stopped and, still without sound, dropped the butt of the gun to the ground. Then it was the boys departed without delay to pull up their foaming and trembling steeds a couple of miles away and determine it had not been a dream.

Pioneer residents declare the description of the ghost exactly fits that of an old trapper named Wilson, after whom the canyon was named. Eighteen years ago, one summer day, he wounded a bear and chased it into the canyon. The beast turned back upon him, and as he had no charge in his muzzle-loaded rifle, he climbed into a juniper tree, but not to safety, for the bear followed, dragged him by the foot to the ground and killed him.

Madison Journal (Tallulah, Louisiana), March 28, 1914

HOB-GOBLINS INFEST
BENTON HILL AGAIN[2]
Elmer Clifton and Party Are
Panic Stricken by Ghost Apparition.

Benton Hill, which until comparatively recently was famous as a loafing spot for hob-goblins, spooks and mysterious night-prowling lights, has come into its own, and Wednesday night a party of young women who were motoring over the hill were frightened almost into hysterics by an apparition, the exact character of which all were too scared ever to ascertain.

The young women were motoring with Elmer Clifton in his car when they perceived the apparition.

The road at Benton Hill follows a course that is particularly well adapted for the operation of spooks. It is banked on one side by a heavy, deep wood and at the time the hill was famous as a resort for goblins, it was a common thing for motorists to see mysterious lights flit back and forth behind the trees several yards back from the roadside.

Persons became accustomed to the presence of lights, and on several occasions, men had stopped to endeavor to follow one of the lights. It was a will-o'-the-wisp sort of a chase that got them nowhere.

The lights became so common that they were known as jack o'lanterns.

For some reason or other, the attention of the members of Mr. Clifton's party was directed toward the heavy woods Wednesday evening as they passed down Benton Hill, and they were startled by the unusual sight of a bright light that flickered and flitted, danced and skipped about the trunks of trees.

This particular light kept even with the machine, and as the end of the wooded stretch approached, the jack o'lantern came down to the road and its weird presence threw the members of the party, who watched it fascinated, into a panic.

The women screamed and more gas was fed to the motor of the car in an effort to leave the spook in the rear. As the car drew away from the jack o'lantern's stamping ground, the lights withdrew to the darkness of the woods.

Weekly Tribune and the Cape County Herald
(Cape Giradeau, Missouri), July 7, 1916

---

[2] See the report titled "A GHOST EIGHT FEET TALL" on page 119 in this chapter.

The Ghosts Appeared on Every Side.

From "FIREMAN FLEES GRAVEYARD GHOSTS," page 128.

HAUNTED ROADS

Hitchhiking ghosts. Crybaby bridges. Haunted tunnels. For centuries, stretches of roadway have been spots where the living cross paths with spectral manifestations. Be they rural or urban, trampled dirt or steel rail, roads serve as a fitting metaphor for the journey away from life and toward the Hereafter. And, of course, one can turn back on a road even if it's marked "ONE WAY."

Curiously, my research led to only a few reports of ghostly bridges or tunnels, despite the eerie imagery that goes with them. Railroad ghosts clearly dominate the articles I found about such hauntings. This makes sense, considering the first trans-continental track in the U.S. was completed in 1869. The iron horse was a new technology of bewitching power and speed, a tantalizing yet deadly innovation, and railroad ghosts are often traced to someone killed on the tracks. In an interview about a psychological—not supernatural—haunting, a railroad man explains that his train had been unable to stop soon enough to avoid crushing a baby carriage and the infant within it. "Every time I pass that crossing," he says, "I see the little white face and the 'broidered dress all stained with red. Even the old engine seems to tremble as she wheels over the spot. . . . Other engineers have their wicked rails further out of town."[1] The railroads introduced a very ghastly form of death.

Other kinds of specters traverse this chapter, though. Some are on horseback. In one case, the spirit itself walks four-legged. And there's a cop who didn't let being murdered stop him from strolling his appointed beat. Let's take a little road trip now. Be sure to bring something warm. There might be a chill or two along the way.

---

[1] *Wichita Eagle* (Kansas), Jan. 20, 1887.

Goblins—Wheeling is Frightened— A Railroad Haunted by a Murdered Man— The Mystery Insoluble.

Haunted houses having become too common, the Wheeling (West Virginia) *Intelligencer* occupies over a column in telling a story of a haunted tunnel near the city on the Hempfield road. After laying the ground work of the story by reciting the number of murders that have been committed in the tunnel, the *Intelligencer* proceeds to relate the experience of four men who passed through the tunnel on last Thursday evening, about six o'clock, as follows:—

The darkness of the cavern had set into an appalling storm, but still they held their way. Soon groans and supplications for mercy fell upon their startled ears. The usual cavernous echo was doubly apparent, as the tone of the voice was unnatural and sepulchral—the men stood transfixed with horror and fright; the atmosphere was close and stifling. All at once issuing from the solid rock which forms the ceiling, directly over the spot where the murderer slaughtered his victim, a ghastly form appeared. All around, as we have said, was impenetrable darkness, but the spectacle itself was as clearly visible as in the noonday. It descended feet first till it reached a place about equidistant from the floor and ceiling of the tunnel, where it stopped and remained for a few seconds. Although covered with the slime and earth of the grave, the features of the ghastly spectre were distinctly visible, clad in the habiliments of the tomb. Its appearance was horrible in the extreme. With one arm extended, and the bloody fingers of the hand hanging half-severed from their stems, with the forefinger of the other hand, it pointed to a gaping wound in its temple. The wound seemed fresh, but the drops of blood seemed clotted and stood out in bold relief on the face of the ill-starred wretch. Without a movement of the lips, a voice, apparently issuing from the throat of the ghost, exclaimed in a tone so unnatural as to be totally indescribable, "Let the dead rest."

The horror-stricken witnesses of this appalling spectacle rushed from the scene. At the mouth of the tunnel they met other parties whose credulity was not sufficient to believe the story of the witnesses. They therefore obtained a lantern and returned to the spot where the apparition was first seen. They were not long waiting when the spirit appeared in the same place, repeated the words he had before used, in, if possible, a more horrifying tone, and glided rapidly through the air towards the western mouth of the tunnel. The individuals thus made sure of the authenticity of the apparition, were deprived of the power of speech for some hours, and even after intervention of days their fearful recollections are so vivid as to render them almost afraid of speaking on the subject.

The persons who witnessed this appalling spectacle in the tunnel being men of respectable and truthful characters, their statements created a widespread and profound sensation in the eastern part of the city where they reside. This was intensified by facts which were disclosed yesterday morning by a gentleman who lives a couple of miles east of the city, and which are related as follows:

He was coming into the city afoot, by way of the railroad, late in the evening, and was approaching the tunnel on the east, and had noticed a couple of persons walking about a hundred yards ahead. He was a short distance this side of the school house, walking on the track and looking down to guard his steps, when he suddenly felt a strange shiver and sensation of horror, and looking up saw a man standing a few yards ahead, directly over the stone culvert (where Ulrich's body was hidden).[2] His arms were held up above his head as if guarded against apprehended blows, and the blood was streaming down his face and neck. There was an awful stony glare in the eyes, which rooted the beholder to the ground. His first thought was that it was one of the men who had been walking ahead of him who had been assaulted by the other; but before he had time to follow out the thought he glanced past the horrid spectacle, and saw the two men just about to pass into the tunnel. At that instant, the man, spectre, or whatever it was, vanished, and was nowhere to be seen. Utterly confounded, the frightened and horror-stricken beholder stood gazing at the vacant air, trying to comprehend what he had seen.

In a moment or two he had recovered sufficiently to think connectedly. He looked carefully around. Nothing whatever was to be seen, though it was still light enough to see objects with perfect distinctness. He says he thought at one moment of running forward and telling the men who were ahead, and asking them if they had seen anything, but he reflected that of course the apparition was not there when they passed, and remembered that he had been looking forward over the very spot where it stood, in the alternations between looking ahead and down at the track. Besides, he felt sure he would be ridiculed and called a fool for his fright. He found it impossible, however, to go

---

[2] On July 8, 1867, the *Wheeling Daily Register* reported that a murder victim had been found near the Hempsted railroad tunnel. The mangled body was later identified as Aloysius Ulrich. On January 10, 1868, the same journal reported that John Schaffer had confessed to that murder—and two more.

forward over the spot, and turning about he returned home (we judge with a good deal of precipitancy). Yesterday morning he came into the city by the pike, and hearing of the appearance in the tunnel, told one or two friends in confidence what he had witnessed. He is an intelligent person, and not given to credulity, but he expresses himself unable to explain the mystery. His account of the appearance of the apparition corresponds substantially with that of the murdered man Ulrich.

Weekly North Carolina Standard (Raleigh), July 28, 1869

A Phantom Train on the Kansas Pacific

Edwardsville is twelve miles west of Kansas City, on the K.P. road, and has a haunted house, and has been the theater of many mysterious sights and sounds. But the following which occurred in daylight, and to which there are a dozen eyewitnesses, is one of the most remarkable occurrences on record. Mr. Timmons, our informant, is one of the most substantial farmers and reliable men in Wyandotte County:

Edwardsville, July 31, 1878.—Last Tuesday morning the section men on the K.P. road on my farm, seeing the storm coming up very fast, got their hand-car on the track and started full speed for Edwardsville. They had run but a little ways when the entire crowd at the same time, saw coming around the curve east of Edwardsville, what they supposed to be a locomotive at full speed. They jumped down and took their car off the track as fast as possible, when they saw it was not a locomotive. Whatever it was came down the track giving off a volume of dense smoke with occasional flashes resembling a headlight in the center of the smoke. It came three-fourths of a mile from where they first saw it, then turned off the track at a pile of cordwood, went around it once, then went off in a southwesterly direction, through a thick wood. The section men came running to my house evidently much frightened, and bewildered by what they saw. What was it? J.F. Timmons.

Leavenworth Weekly Times (Kansas), Aug. 8, 1878
Reprinted from *Kansas City Pioneer* (Kansas)

The Ghost of Smoky Hill

Smoky Hill on the Kansas Pacific railroad, is haunted by a ghost. Some years ago—before the railroad was built—an emigrant family was murdered there by Indians. This is the unadorned legend out of which the romance has grown. Whether the uneasy spirit is one of the nameless victims of the savage atrocity years ago, of course we are unable to tell, but the engineers say that, crowning the summit of Smoky Hill of moonlit nights, a female form often startles the engineer of approaching trains. Sometimes it comes walking down the long reach of track, to all appearances a veritable woman in flesh and blood, but when the train is almost upon her, and the engineer's hair is standing on end with terror, and he "down brakes" to avoid a tragedy, the form disappears in mist, and nothing more is seen of it. As all this happens on a treeless plain—miles away from any habitation—and the phantom invariably disappears in the full blaze of moonlight, it must be confessed that the thing looks as if it was referable to the inexplicable agencies of the world of spirits. In conversation with an engineer of the division haunted by the uneasy spirit, the question was asked:

"Have you ever seen the phantom?"

"Often!"

"What does it look like?"

"I can give you a better idea of it by relating my first experience with it. I had heard a good deal about the ghost of Smoky Hill before I ever made the run, and of course believed it was all moonshine, so when my turn came to make a trip over the haunted track, I felt very little concern about it. But about midnight, when we were running at full speed, and the moon was shining clear and brilliant, I saw a woman coming down the track towards the train. Of course the first thought that occurred to me was the ghost. But the woman looked so lifelike and was heading towards the train in such a confident way that I concluded it must be a living creature. By this time the train was nearly upon her and seeing no evidences of an intention to leave the track, I whistled "down brakes," and made every exertion to stop the train. But when it seemed almost impossible for her to escape being killed, she seemed to me to spring up in the air, and disappear in a cloud-like mist."

"Are you sure of that?"

"Why man, I saw it with my own eyes, and have seen it acted over again a dozen times since."

"How do you account for the strange phenomenon?"

"I don't account for it at all. I don't undertake to do it. All I know is, there's a ghost on Smoky Hill, and it's about the most weird and unsatisfactory ghost I ever heard of in my life" was the energetic and conscientious reply of the stalwart engineer. "When a person sees a thing, he's not likely to be deceived about it."

"Surely—and you saw it?"

"I did, and others have seen it too."

"And looking always the same?"

"Always the same."

Juanita Sentinel and Republican
(Mifflintown, Pennsylvania), June 11, 1879

A Pike County Ghost

The latest sensation in the neighborhood of Milford, Pike County, Pennsylvania: Fifty-two years ago a man named John Goble was found lying in a pool of blood on the road leading from Milford to Dingman's Ferry. A large gash was found in the side of his head, and it was supposed that the old man had been murdered and robbed. He was buried immediately after the Coroner's inquest, and in a few years entirely forgotten. About three weeks ago the stage driver who carries the Philadelphia mail between Milford and the Delaware Water Gap, while passing the spot where Goble was murdered, saw an object clothed in white start up from the ground and walk in the road just in front of the horses. The driver urged his team on, but the "ghost" still kept a little in advance. After trotting his horses some distance, the driver stopped, and as he dismounted from the stage the ghost sank into the ground and disappeared. This was repeated two or three evenings, and the mail-carrier at last became alarmed and armed himself with a six-shooter. Since that time he has seen the ghost at a distance several times, but he has not shot at it.

The mail carrier's name is Searles, and he told his story in Milford, where it spread like wildfire. Parties were organized to search for the wandering spirit, and one party saw it at a short distance. They fired several shots at the object, and it disappeared. A party of young ladies, accompanied by a gentleman, a day or two ago visited the place where the ghost is usually seen. About a hundred yards from the spot is an old deserted house, and one of the young ladies, who was more courageous than the rest, started to walk around this old house in search of the "spook." When about halfway around the building she heard a groan, and turning around, she saw, standing just behind her, an object about six feet tall, clothed in white. She screamed and fainted, but before the remainder of the party reached her the "ghost" had vanished. The "spirit" has since been seen twice, and on each occasion it was pursued, but it always vanished after reaching a certain place in the woods. It is supposed by many that the ghost is a man, dressed up in a sheet to create a sensation. Others, who are more superstitious, believe it is the spirit of John Goble, searching for his murderer. Whatever it is, it certainly succeeded in creating a decided sensation.

News and Herald (Winnsboro, South Carolina), Dec. 30, 1879

Queer Pranks of a Ghost.
AN INTANGIBLE THING
THAT BOTHERS AND BAFFLES
READING RAILROAD ENGINEERS.

A ghost, who looks big enough and is presumably old enough to know better, spends his evenings on the tracks of the Reading railroad, just below Port Kennedy station, scaring the life out of the engineers and trainmen who may happen to pass. He has been shot twice, is run over several times nightly, and has been struck on the head with a bludgeon once. This kind of thing doesn't disturb him, however, for he swallows the bullets without fear of indigestion and plays roley-poley with the heavy car-wheels as they are crushing and mangling his intangible body.

Ten years ago a vagrant was run over just near the spot which is now haunted, under circumstances which implied negligence on the part of the man in charge of the locomotive. Immediately ghosts began to make their appearance by the dozen, until the fall of 1880, after which time it was thought their wrath was appeased, as they came no more. On Christmas night, however, an apparition of unusual size attacked the 9 o'clock freight train, which is managed by Engineer Charles Welch. This was the signal for a general onslaught, and every evening since then phantoms have flitted across the line and otherwise made themselves felt. In consequence a great many of the trains which leave the Callowhill Street depot after dark are loaded with missiles and weapons for use against bogies wherever they may be found at large.

Brakeman George Nelson, on the train which leaves Philadelphia at a quarter to 8 in the evening, claims to have had a thrilling experience with the ghost. It ran away with his cap. On New Year's night he was standing on the front platform of the first car to get a whiff of fresh air, with the train steaming thirty-five miles an hour. When within fifty yards of the usual spot, the headlight's rays piercing the darkness rested on what seemed to be the figure of a man standing out in bold relief.

141

Although it could not have been more than a few seconds before the train reached it, the time seemed prolonged to minutes. Nelson excitedly seized the bell-rope, pulled it violently, and in addition shrieked out to the engineer to pull up. Although he laid hold of the cord at once, he says that it was not until the apparition was passed that the gong struck. Gradually the train neared the person, who seemed to be standing with one of his hands shading his face and the other pointing to the throbbing engine, straining to mow him down. There was a sudden blankness, a cold blast of air which carried off his hat, and Nelson did not know what happened till the conductor opened the door and told him he would catch cold. He was certain that what he had seen was not flesh and blood. On the succeeding evening, however, he had a clean shot at it, and a passenger on the train, who had been told of the bogie, joined him and fired two barrels of a revolver in his face, all without effect.

The most interesting experience, however, was reserved for Engineer Charles Welch, who has been mentioned as having heralded the ghost's first appearance this season. On last Saturday night he spied it as usual ahead, but it looked so different from what it did on the previous occasion that he thought it was a real individual and not an artificial one. In a few seconds, with great presence of mind, he had the brakes down, the steam whistle blowing, and the bell ringing. He shuddered perceptibly as the train slid over the figure and then came to a dead stop. He had not had sufficient notice to stop the train in time.

"We've killed someone, Jim," said Welch, sorrowfully, to the conductor, "and we had better go back and pick up the pieces." A mournful procession proceeded to hunt for the required items, but not a scrap could they find. Welch all at once remembered about the ghost, and the train sped on.

Daily Dispatch (Richmond, Virginia), Jan. 12, 1883
Reprinted from *Philadelphia Times* (Pennsylvania)

A GHOST IN SULLIVAN COUNTY
Appearing in the Form of a Woman and Frightening People

Shohola, April 7.—One night last week Charles Gillett, of Barryville, N.Y., across the Delaware river from this village, rushed into Quick's store with a blanched face, and presenting other evidences of fright.

"I've seen a ghost!" he said. "I was coming down the Berme side of the canal, and when I approached the upper-lock bridge I saw a woman standing there, all in white. I thought it strange that she be out dressed in that way on a cold night, and as the bridge is very narrow, I stopped to let her step off before I stepped on. She turned toward me, but I could not see her face. She did not move either way. I advanced to the bridge to pass her, but when I put my foot on it the woman had disappeared. My first thought was that she had jumped into the lock, and I looked carefully all through it, but she wasn't there. I tried the lock shanty and found that it was closed up tight. By that time I began to feel that I had seen a ghost, and I became so frightened that it was all that I could do to get to the store."

Gillett is a reputable and respected citizen of Barryville. Since his declaration that he has seen a ghost, other persons report having seen it also.

Mrs. Watson, who lives on the Berme bank of the canal, says she has seen the apparition, just as it was described by Mr. Gillett, at three different times. Every time the ghostly figure stood close to the edge of the canal, and once raised its arms, and then pointed down into the canal. It always disappeared suddenly, as if fading away.

A report comes from Brodhead's mill pond that a similar apparition has been seen hovering about the borders of the pond, and that it once flitted across the road in front of a teamster between Barryville and Brodhead's.

The non-believers in ghosts in the vicinity have failed to satisfactorily explain to the superstitious the appearance of the mysterious visitor, and it is the opinion of those who believe in its ghostly character that its appearance conveys a warning of some evil or misfortune that is to befall the neighborhood.

San Antonio Light (Texas), April 25, 1885

A QUEER GHOST IN CHICAGO
It Wears the Usual Garments,
but Walks on All Fours

Chicago, Jan. 18.—People who live on State Street, between Forty-Fifth and Forty-Ninth Streets, declare that a ghost patrols that district at midnight every night. The specter is described as being dressed in white, flowing garments, and as walking on all fours. The conductors and drivers of the street cars on Forty-First Street are greatly alarmed. Two of them refused to take their cars out last night.

Hyde Park policemen saw the apparition about midnight last night, and pursued it, firing their revolvers as they ran. When the spook reached the Grand Boulevard it suddenly disappeared. The officers reported their adventure to Captain Hunt. Tonight several officers were detailed to lay in ambush for the ghost.

Pittsburgh Dispatch (Pennsylvania), Jan. 19, 1889

An Uncanny Visitor

Kansas City, Mo., Oct. 2.—Kansas City, Kan., now comes to the front with a regulation ghost story. It is not one of the common, ordinary ghosts which prowl around deserted houses, but a full-fledged ghost of a policeman, uniform and all.

Two years ago a Policeman Henry James was on the beat leading toward the Southwest Boulevard, and was very regular in passing such points, so much so, in fact, that the people used him in place of a clock, for they knew that when James passed it was a certain hour of the night or day, as the case may be.

One morning James was found lying dead on the sidewalk with an ugly hole in the back of his head.

He had been struck with a pickaxe, which was afterwards found nearby, covered with hair and blood. Not the slightest clue was ever found which would point to the perpetrator of the deed, and after a time the matter was relegated to the annals of mysteries.

It seems, however, that James did not rest easy in his grave, and it is now said that his form can be seen on a moonlight night patrolling the beat just as he did in former days when he was in the flesh.

The people living on the beat say that he can be heard walking with the same measured tread as formerly and he appears as plainly as if he were alive.

He is never seen from the street, but always from the windows of the houses. When the people try to get nearer and see what it is, the form vanishes out of sight and appears no more that night.

It is difficult to find anyone who has seen the ghost, but all can tell what their neighbor saw and what they heard. They say that James walks along every night at the same hour and disappears at the spot where his body was found.

The appearance is at 1:20 o'clock in the morning, and it is supposed that he was murdered at that hour.

Laurens Advertiser (South Carolina), Oct. 13, 1891

CUPERTINO'S SPOOKS.
Five Mounted Wraiths En Cavalcade
on the County Road.

Lately Cupertino has been visited by some spooks, or ghosts, or specter, or something of that sort. At least, several reputable citizens so declare. On their first appearance your correspondent was in San Francisco, and, of course, when told of the apparition, not having convincing proof, remained silent, but on Saturday evening he saw with his own eyes the apparitions, for, being perfectly sober at the time, it was no optical illusion, and this is what he saw:

Five figures dash by on horseback at a mad pace; two were females and three were males. One of the males, who evidently was the leader, was a giant in size, and was mounted on an immense charger. He was dressed in martial array and of a commanding mien. His companions I did not notice so closely, but they were all mounted on Indian ponies, and, as near as I could tell, his male companions wore no uniforms. The females had their long hair flying wildly about their faces, but what glimpses I did get I would say they were Indians or Mexicans. Several others saw them, and some say they gave unearthly yells or war whoops whenever they saw anyone. This is their second visit, and as yet no one is able to explain the mystery.

Joe Kelly, an old settler who resides on Stevens Creek, tells a legend about an American soldier who was lured to his death by a beautiful Indian maiden, the daughter of a chief of a tribe which once owned the country around Cupertino. Mr. Kelly claims that those apparitions were often seen around here in the forties and early fifties, and says their present activity is caused by their resting place being disturbed by some of the buildings that have lately been erected. In the fight that took place when the soldier found he was betrayed, before the Indians killed him, two braves, his treacherous sweetheart and another Indian maiden met their doom, hence the five specters that are now disturbing our peace.

Morning Call (San Francisco, California), Feb. 22, 1892
Reprinted from *San Jose Mercury* (California)

GHOST ON A SPREE
PETER COOLEY MEETS WITH
AN INVISIBLE SCORCHER[3]
Bike Goes Like Mad but the Rider is Unseen—
The Bell Tinkles without the Aid of Visible Hands—
It Goes Through a Cow While Green Balls of Fire
Drop from the Tips of Her Horns—
The Wheel Makes a Perfect Figure Eight
in the Middle of the Road—
Strange Phenomenon.

The good people of East Central Avenue, beyond Chisholm Creek, are now in a fever of excitement over a most mysterious, invisible scorcher, and not a mother's son or daughter of them will stir out of doors after the chickens go to roost.

Central Avenue is the public highway to the cities of the dead. It is the path of mortality—the highway through which every Wichitaian passes to his last resting place after he has kicked the bucket and shuffled off his mortal coil.

It has always been more or less haunted, or supposed to be haunted, but until recently no one could ever be found who could positively testify to having seen anything strange. Many and many have been found who are willing to swear that as they wended their way along the avenue they felt a creeping sensation come over them and looked in fright over their shoulders expecting to see a ghost ready to pounce upon their backs.

Peter Cooley of 2502, the street mentioned, has seen what others have felt.

Peter is an Englishman, and the evening the war news was chalked on the *Eagle* bulletin board[4] he felt that it was necessary for him to get up a little artificial enthusiasm. He and Barney Ross, the well-known Scotchman, went down to Jim Donavan's place, and they found another friend or two who had no serious objections to taking a drink of spirits. Mr. Cooley ordered four whiskies and one brandy, and after drinking them the five began to talk about the great battles of history. Barney

---

[3] A "scorcher" is a bicyclist who rides with reckless speed.

[4] The U.S. didn't officially declare its involvement in the war between Cuban revolutionaries and Spanish colonial powers until April of 1898, starting the Spanish-American War. However, newspapers such as the *Eagle* were publishing reports of U.S. support for the independence movement in Cuba since early 1895.

Ross then set 'em up twice in succession, and Mr. Cooley ordered another round. The man who drank the brandy seemed to have the best of the argument, and when the next round was ordered Mr. Cooley took brandy, too. About 10 o'clock they started for home, but when they reached Emporia Avenue one of the unmentioned two gentlemen said, "Well, boys, if the war breaks out, times will be pretty good, and I think I can afford to set 'em up once." "That's right," said Mr. Cooley; "I don't mind if I have a night cap before going home." At this place they ran across some pale ale, and Mr. Cooley dabbled in that. To make a long story short they stayed there until Officer Sutton stuck his head in through the door and in a minor key suggested that it was getting late. The party disbanded, and all left for their separate homes.

When Mr. Cooley crossed the Chisolm Creek bridge on Central Avenue, the court house clock struck midnight. As if to verify the clock Jack Richardson's rooster lent his clarion voice to convince Mr. Cooley that it had reached that bewitching hour when graveyards yawn and give up their dead. Mr. Cooley hastened his stride, expecting to be able to reach his home from the west before the ghosts could reach it from the direction of the cemetery. His calculations were all right so far as pedestrian ghosts were concerned, but he did not take into consideration the possibility of ghosts using bicycles.

He was just half a block from his home. He could see the lamp light shine from his parlor windows so powerfully that he knew Mrs. Cooley was awaiting his arrival, and he then began to have more dread of family curtain lectures than he had of the peaceful dead.

As he was reaching down into his vest pocket for another clove, he saw something pass through the beam of light, and his heart jumped to his mouth. Every hair in his head began to move, and his bald spot felt as if it was under the current of a static machine. He wiped his eyes and looked again, and there before him, twenty feet away, he saw a bicycle scorching down the road towards him. The little bell tinkled, he jumped aside with a yell, and whiz went the bicycle past him. He shivered and trembled, and big beads of perspiration stood upon his brow.

Even at midnight it is nothing to meet a bicycle on the road, but great scott, what a strange thing it is to meet a bicycle traveling at the rate of twenty miles an hour without a rider. That is just what Mr. Cooley saw. That bicycle was spinning and scorching along without a rider.

Mr. Cooley, when he found the energy of his legs, ran like a coyote and dashed in through the door of his home with such force that his affrighted wife fainted and the dog came within an ace of eating him up.

The poor old man was deluged with perspiration, and his face was as pale as the moon at her zenith. His daughter came screaming downstairs like one released from a horrible nightmare, and she, too, nearly fainted. She applied the usual restoratives to her mother, and in time all of them went to bed but not to sleep.

Mr. Cooley, after a sober second thought, concluded the riderless bicycle was simply the result of mixed drinks, and he never explained his strange conduct either to the wife of his bosom or the daughter of his heart.

As he peaceably read the bible the next night, his good wife frequently looked at him over her glasses and then pegged away at her knitting again. The fact is she thought her husband became temporarily insane the previous night, and she was very uneasy over it.

Wednesday night, about 3 o'clock or a little later, Mr. Cooley heard his dog Duffer barking violently, and having read in the *Eagle* about chicken thieves he took his revolver from under his pillow and went to the back door. As he opened it he saw his fine Jersey cow kicking her heels in the air like mad and making for the street. He jumped into his trousers, then into his shoes, a la Jerry Simpson,[5] then into his coat, hat and overcoat, and away he went after the cow. He was guided after his Jersey by the light of the Milky Way and now and then by the glimmer of Ed Goldberg's blinkers. He gained steadily on the cow and finally caught the end of her rope at the foot of College Hill. He was not afraid of ghosts anymore for it was long after the hour when he saw the riderless bicycle the previous Monday night. "Ghosts ain't going to town this hour," said Mr. Cooley to himself, but he never for a moment thought about ghosts coming back from town.

All at once his Jersey pulled on the rope, and looking over his shoulder he saw a wonderful blueish green light in her eyes, and she was trembling from head to foot and so scared that she was losing her milk in the middle of the road. She wouldn't go another step with him. The cow's eyes wobbled in her head, and as they did so their color would change from blue and green to yellow and red. Little green balls of fire fell from the tips of her horns, and Mr. Cooley thought it the strangest

---

[5] Jeremiah "Sockless Jerry" Simpson (1842-1905) was a People's Party member who was twice elected to represent Kansas in the U.S. Congress. His reputation for being sockless resulted when he accused a political rival of being too pampered by wealth—down to his silken hosiery—to represent the farmers of Kansas. That rival replied that it was better to have silk socks than none at all. Simpson used the insult to his advantage, gaining votes by playing the homespun hick. Simpson is now buried in Wichita.

phenomenon he had ever seen. All at once the road became almost as light as day from some strange new energy being put into the stars, and looking down towards the house he saw the riderless bicycle scorching towards him, going like mad but wobbling fearfully. If it had a rider Mr. Cooley would swear he went into town to go on a bender, but it had not. He was terribly scared, and he could hear the cow's heart beating up against her ribs, and she was panting fearfully.

About twenty or thirty feet away from him the riderless bicycle made a few fancy cuts and then described a complete and perfect figure 8 in the middle of the road. After that it dashed towards him, and its bell was ringing like fury. He got out of the way himself all right, but the cow would not budge an inch, but the green balls of fire kept falling thicker and faster from the tips of her horns. Instead of the bicycle turning to one side it went straight through the middle of the cow, and as she bellowed and kicked, the dull distant tinkle of the bell could be heard inside her.

After the bicycle left the cow's body it seemed to have lost some of its motive power for it wobbled fearfully for a few seconds. It then left the road, dashed through a hedge fence, scorched over the stubble field, then through a wire fence and pulled out across lots for the cemetery at such a fearful rate of speed that it would seem the very devil was riding it. In five minutes the voice of a vigilant cock was heard bidding salutation to the approaching dawn and then Mr. Cooley knew why the bicycle was in such a hurry to get to the cemetery.

When Mr. Cooley got up in the morning and went to milk, he found the cow dead in the stable and Duffer, the dog, with his head laying on her neck.

Mr. Cooley never did believe in ghosts before, but he believes in them now. He has no doubt in the world but what the bicycle was ridden by the ghost, and he was over in town yesterday getting some spirit believers interested enough in his story to go out there some night and investigate.

Wichita Daily Eagle (Kansas), Jan. 24, 1896

Mollie McGruder's Ghost

The ghost of Mollie McGruder, who was killed near Seventh and Tracy Streets, about a year ago, by William McCoy, still appears to frighten those who have to pass along that way in the early morning hours, writes a Kansas City correspondent.

As stated in these dispatches two weeks ago, the woman first appeared to the keeper of a saloon on the corner of Independence and Lydia Avenues, and appeared to be asking for a bucket of beer. She then appealed to several passersby and to a policeman, who, since that time, has never had occasion to get near the spot where the murder was committed.

The publication in a morning paper here of the fact that such an apparition had been seen caused a number of people to go in that neighborhood on such nights as they happened to be out late, in the hope of being able to see the spirit. The result is that there are now not less than seven people who declare that they saw the ghost of the murdered woman, and, while she invariably has the appearance of wanting to reveal something, no one has yet had nerve enough to stay to hear her story.

The latest tale is from a man who had heard nothing about the ghost, and who had occasion to cut across Lydia Avenue about 2 o'clock one morning recently. The gentleman was hurrying through the dark street, when his attention was attracted to a woman who was standing perfectly erect near a telegraph pole about ten feet from a street lamp. She stood so still and looked at him so intently that he thought she might be a man who was dressed as a woman for the purpose of robbery, and drawing his revolver, he approached her with the intention of asking what she was doing there at that time of night.

She was in full view, but as the man got near to the telegraph pole the woman seemed to dissolve in thin air, and left no trace behind her. The gentleman thought it strange, and it was only when he related his story next morning that he found he had approached Mollie McGruder's ghost.

Banner-Democrat (Lake Providence, Louisiana), April 17, 1897

HAUNTED.
River Styx Bridge.
Fearful Sights Witnessed at the Place Where Engineer Logan Lost His Life.
Phantom Train Dashes Down Steep Grade.
Frightful Wreck Re-enacted Every Night— Strange Story.

The ill-fated train, on which Engineer Alex. W. Logan lost his life, is said to haunt the bridge over the River Styx near Rittman.

It was at this place that he went to his heroic death last spring. The frightful wreck caused great excitement in this city. There were a large number of Akron people on No. 5 that morning. Local citizens recall the circumstances surrounding the brave sacrifice made by Engineer Logan, whose steady nerve saved the passengers behind him.

That which follows is taken from the *Wadsworth Banner* of Friday:

Several Rittman people are very much excited at what has occurred at the Styx bridge over the Erie at that place during the past week, and what they term was the appearance of a phantom train.

The first appearance of this awe-inspiring, marvelous apparition, was on Saturday night and was witnessed by Dr. Faber and a companion. The doctor had been out east to visit a patient and was leisurely driving along about 11 o'clock when his attention was attracted by the noise of a swiftly moving train. He casually watched the train and saw its glaring headlight and dense clouds of smoke rolling up from the smokestack.

No particular attention was taken of the train, but just before it reached the bridge the shrill whistle of the engine caused the men to glance back. On came the train with the speed of wind as it swept down the grade, throwing out great streaks of fire from the wheels. Just then was heard the "chuck, chuck" of the engine, as if she had been reversed. On further investigation a frightful sight met their gaze. The train was enveloped in great clouds of dust and smoke, and huge flames of fire shot up in every direction, and immense volumes of steam making a terrific noise shot up from the engine, and breaking iron bars were plainly heard, but above all came the shrieks of those pinioned beneath the wreckage. The noise was plainly heard by a number of others. Spellbound at the sight before them, Faber and his companion started immediately for the railroad, thinking that a frightful wreck had occurred. Imagine their surprise when they reached the bridge and found everything perfectly quiet, no sign of a wrecked train and not even a ripple upon the placid surface of the Styx.

The men hurried to town and related their experience, but could not induce anyone else to visit this spot, so strong is the belief down there that this place is haunted or that some evil spirit lingers about this bridge. Near there the ill-fated train 5 jumped the track last spring and the engineer was killed, ever since which time many people have been afraid to pass over this stretch of track after night.

Akron Daily Democrat (Ohio), Oct. 28, 1899

LONG ISLANDERS ARE STARTLED BY SPOOK.
Midnight Prowler Appears as Woman in White and Wears String of Blue Beads.

New York, Oct. 10.—A ghost in the form of "a woman in white" is about Bellport, and the countryside is alarmed to an extent that the terrified refuse to venture out late at night.

Many prominent New York families have their summer places in Bellport, among them Frank A. Otis, Frederick Edey, Mr. John L.B. Mort and Walter Cook, the architect.

It is in Mr. Cook's picturesque stable that the apparition appears at midnight, taking the form of a tall "woman in white" with a long string of blue beads encircling her neck. Like the specter in one of Wilkie Collins's tales,[6] the woman appears and seems to float away as one watches it.

Mr. Cook's country place in Bellport extends for acres from the shores of the Great South Bay to the old South Road. Through the property there winds a broad drive. On the east side of this drive is a deep hollow. The haunted barn is a vine-covered building in which are the coachman's quarters occupied since spring by Jim, Mr. Cook's gardener.

Up to several days ago he saw nothing to disturb his peaceful slumbers. Then at about midnight, with the inky darkness all around, there appeared in the carriage room a tall, white apparition that floated in and out of the carriages, finally disappearing into a stall, where it patted the horse "Dan" before fading into space.

Since then this "woman in white" appears and disappears every dark night, always around this spot. Those who have seen the ghost say it is extremely tall and floats in space (or appears to), encircled by a glow of light, and fades away as one approaches it.

The ghost discloses its form to few persons. Many reputable Bellport and Brookhaven men have formed watching parties for the object of finding out the mystery, but so far only a few have caught a glimpse of the spook.

The apparition appeared to Jim and "Gene" Barnes of Brookhaven, floating through the closed doors of the carriage house, and its appearance was so unexpected and sudden that the men did not have time to shoot.

---

[6] Along with spooky short stories such as "Mrs. Zant and the Ghost" and "A Terribly Strange Bed," Wilkie Collins (1824-1889) authored a mystery novel titled *The Woman in White*.

The "ghost's walk" in *Bleak House*[7] could not have been more weird and quaint than the shaded drive from his ivy-covered barn to Mr. Cook's picturesque residence on the high hill overlooking the waters.

Along this drive, like the ocean mist, the ghost is said to float about the trees, frightening the servants and anyone who happens along about midnight. The hounds baying in the kennels and the old windmill with its uncanny creaks make a fit place for ghostly meetings.

The more skeptical think it may be some insane person or evildoer up to some mischief, as the Cook family are not here, and there are some valuable horses in his stable, among them being Golden Bronze Maid, the best trotting mare about this section, the property of Mr. Gardiner Murdock, Mr. Cook's overseer.

The ghost was also seen on the old South Road at Mott's Bridge by one of Bellport's most respected businessmen.

Saint Louis Republic (Missouri), Oct. 11, 1903

TOWN HAUNTED BY HEADLESS GHOST
SPECTER WHICH HAS STARLED
PEOPLE OF FLAHERTY, IND.
APPARITION WALKS TRACK
Appears in Attitude of Switchman
Flagging a Train with a Dinner Pail—
Attempt Made to Capture It.

Laporie, Ind.—Ranked among the impossible spirit stories of tradition and of poetry is the one that keeps the residents in the vicinity of Flaherty in constant fear and trembling. They are not afraid during the daytime, but their voices are lowered in a singular manner when they approach the little railroad station where the history of the ghost of Columbus Cole is being made.

Nightly, after the sun sets, Flaherty station is avoided, because there is no question about the possibility of the ghost's appearing. Headless and acting for all the world like an animate thing, the apparition occurs intermittently. Sometimes the elements appear to control its action, but more generally it makes its appearance, dinner pail in hand, on the platform and attempts to swing its arms as if it were

---

[7] A novel by Charles Dickens (1812-1870). The ghost's walk is referred to in Chapter 7.

flagging a passing train. Then it disappears, and its subsequent appearances are a matter of chance.

Hearing so much of the alleged spirit, a company of young men, accompanied by a newspaper correspondent, went to the station the other night and the previous night for the purpose of investigating the matter.

On the first night they sat near the depot, and amused themselves as best they could until daylight began to break, when they returned home without having their curiosity satisfied, but the next night they had a different experience.

Reaching the station early in the night, they prepared to take things easy, but had hardly made such a disposal of themselves as was satisfactory, when one of the boys raised his hand and cried: "Hist."

They all looked and saw the ghost—the ghost they had been told about—headless and carrying a dinner pail. It was no delusion of the eyesight. It was the real, clear outline of Columbus Cole as they had known him in life and the same eternal dinner pail. For five minutes or more they watched the apparition as the arms swung as if signaling a train, and then, spurred on by one united impulse, they rushed to the place where they had seen the figure. Nothing but vacancy greeted them when they reached the spot where the figure had been seen. Cole's spirit had entirely disappeared, and they stood and looked at the supernatural incident and no longer skeptics, but believers.

Unstrung from the shock of the manifestation—totally unexpected, by the way—they walked home in silence, firm adherents of the ghost theory.

Some of the good people who live in the neighborhood of Flaherty are anxious to do something to set the spirit at rest. They say that something is troubling it. The generally accepted theory is that Cole wanted to do something before he died—that the something remains undone and that the spirit will continue to wander until it comes in contact with a sympathetic spirit clothed in worldly clay to which it can communicate its desires.

Columbus Cole was a well-known and popular resident of the vicinity of Flaherty, who lost his life years ago in a boiler explosion. The top of his head was completely blown off by the accident. Soon after he died, the trouble with the ghost began, and the people have come to look at it in a matter-of-fact manner. They do not deny the story. They have got beyond that point, and many interesting incidents are related of the ghost's history.

Flaherty people swear by their "ghost." It is an interesting ghost, and it is more powerful in keeping the old and young within doors than all the curfews that ever sounded from city hall or church steeple. There is hardly a man living within three miles of Flaherty station who cannot entertain one for hours with stories of the ghost's doings. Meanwhile the people are anxious to locate the kindred spirit garbed with a human body to which the shade of Columbus Cole will tell its troubles.

Barbour County Index (Medicine Lodge, Kansas), Aug. 16, 1905

GHOST OF A GIRL GUARDS CROSSING
DEAD GIRL HAUNTS THE PLACE
WHERE SHE WAS KILLED.
MYSTERY OF VERMONT ROAD
Engineer of Limited Which Caused Her Death
Meets Fate in Collision near Spot
Where Fatal Accident Occurred.

Boston.—This is a story of a factory girl's ghost which has been haunting a matter-of-fact, superstition-hating New England community for two years. It is a ghost that many God-fearing folk swear they have seen and their reports of the shadowy shape have made the whole of commercially centered, unimaginative, cotton-manufacturing Lakeside, on the outskirts of Burlington, Vt., believe it.

It was in the spring two years ago that Josephine Ladue received employment in the Queen City Cotton Company's mill at Lakeside.

Whence the girl came nobody knew. From the beginning there was a shadow of mystery on Josephine Ladue. She had no relatives in Lakeside nor anywhere else so far as anybody was able to learn. She lived alone. She did not mix with the women and girls of the mill and none of them ever knew her to permit any man to press his attentions to her. She had a happy, carefree, sympathetic disposition, and she had a smile that rippled forth infectiously.

Josephine Ladue had been at the Queen City less than two months when she disappeared. Whither she went nobody knew, and when she took her place at the looms a few days later she didn't consider it necessary to enlighten anybody as to her movements. A week after that, the girl dropped out of sight again, and the whispering which had started with her first appearance grew in volume and point.

These mysterious comings and goings of Josephine Ladue continued with periods varying from two weeks to a month between them. Her qualities as a worker had been the thing that stood between her and being discharged. Finally her example began to bear fruit in the

155

ranks of her fellow workers in broken discipline and disregard for the regulations governing the employees of the Queen City mill. Josephine Ladue was warned that, if she ever went away again from the mill without being excused, she need not return.

It was only a week later that the girl, defying the warning she had received, disappeared. Three days later she was back and the foreman told her her place had been filled.

"You can't send me away," she threw at him. "I'm going to work at these looms and at seven o'clock tonight, when you have all gone home, I'll be at my looms."

The girl's words mystified the foreman. That evening as the village hall bell was ringing out seven o'clock, big Denis Mahoney, at the throttle of the Rutland railroad's Burlington flyer, reeled through Lakeside southward bound. He knew he was on time, but from force of habit he looked up from his cab window at the clock on the Queen City mill. For an instant his eyes were held by a girl in a window working deftly at a loom. The light in the mill was so bright that he saw every feature plainly. He saw that she was good looking and he noticed, too, that her lips were parted in laughter.

Mahoney brought his eyes back to the singing rails ahead and, in that moment, something happened—something that had happened to a good many engineers before him and to many since—something that had often been described to him, and he knew as he caught his breath what he had done. As the great machine had flung the thing it had killed aside, Mahoney caught the shape of it out of the tail of his eyes and he knew that it was a woman.

When the flyer's engineer brought her to a stop, he leaped from the cab and was the first to reach the dead. He picked up the poor little crushed corpse in his arms and carried it into a cottage beside the road. A woman brought a light to see if she knew who it was that the train had killed. Denis tried not to look, but something impelled him to bend over the face of the dead and he staggered back, shaking as one with the palsy. The dead girl was the girl he had seen at the looms in the cotton mill window. The woman told him it was Josephine Ladue.

Mahoney didn't take the flyer through Lakeside the next night, but the man who did took back to Denis a story that made him quake.

"The girl you killed that night," he told Denis, "was in the mill window when we came through. I saw her and others saw her and the mill watchman, they say, swears she was at the looms at midnight. When we struck the crossing where you hit her, the headlight went out. I don't like it, Denis."

Mahoney didn't take the flyer out for nearly a month, and when he did the tales that came to him of the headlight being extinguished every night at the crossing where he killed Josephine Ladue and of her being seen in the mill and by trainmen as they went by the Queen City took the sand out of him—the little that was left.

The first night Mahoney's headlight was blown out at the crossing and he saw the smiling face of Josephine Ladue at the mill window just as he had seen it on the night the flyer killed her. At the end of the run he spoke of it as "a fancy," but nevertheless he ordered a new headlight, which was the third that had been put on the flyer since the Lakeside killing. Other engineers had found fault with it, too.

But the next night the new headlight failed at the Lakeside crossing and Denis Mahoney saw Josephine Ladue in the mill window. He called the girl's face "a fancy" and cussed the headlight. The "fancy" was in the window every night, however, when he went by, and one day he laid off his run and went to Lakeside. It was the day he met William Dugan, the old watchman of the Queen City mill. Dugan had resigned. He told Mahoney that it was because he couldn't stand seeing Josephine Ladue at the looms at night when he knew that she was dead and buried.

A few weeks ago Denis Mahoney "got his," and his kind says, in a head-on collision only a few hundred feet from the spot where Josephine Ladue was killed by the Burlington Flyer and where his "fancy" sat in a mill window. He went out just as he had expected for a year that he would go—quick and violently. He had prayed against it, but it was of no use.

Since Mahoney's death an appeal has been made to the state board of railroad commissioners to change the grade crossing of the Rutland railroad. Those with whom the petition originated live near the railroad track and some of them accept the ghost as a matter of faith and others profess to have seen it, but whatever the motives of the petitioners as a whole may be, they are known as "the Lakeside ghost layers."

Richmond Planet (Virginia), Jan. 6, 1906

NEW JERSEY GHOST
PROOF AGAINST MURDEROUS CARS
Phantom is Run Down Twice by Trolley, Declare Truth-Tellers—
Quietly Strolls After Each Engagement.

NEW YORK, Jan 19.—This tale is solemnly sworn to by Mortorman Howard Hoffman and Conductor John Shaw, of the Bloomfield Avenue trolley line, who took their car out of Caldwell, N.J., for the last trip of the night to Newark at 12:00 o'clock yesterday morning.

There was one passenger, an employee of the Fairfield Dairy Company, bound for Montclair.

Hoffman rang his gong at the approach to Pompton Turnpike. The headlight illuminated the road, which was deserted. Hoffman peered back over his shoulder, and when he looked forward again he saw a man, with bowed head and hands in his pockets, plodding along not fifty feet ahead of his car. He slammed on the brakes, but the car ran over the man. Hoffman and Shaw and the passenger got off, but they did not find the mangled body they expected.

"It was all your imagination," said Shaw.

"There he is now. Is that my imagination or is that a man?" cried Hoffman, pointing down the tracks ahead of the car. They looked and saw the man Hoffman had seen, hands in pockets, his head bent and plodding slowly along. They ran after him. The figure swung ahead at the same distance, with no apparent effort of eluding them. The three men ran a hundred yards beyond an electric light, and the figure suddenly disappeared. They stared at each other foolishly.

"I am all gooseflesh," said Shaw. "I swear I saw a man."

The two others vowed it as solemnly. They turned around again, and they saw the man again. He was walking toward them, in the middle of the track. The three white-faced men stood still on the front platform of the car, speechless. As the man passed under the electric light, all sought a view of his face, but they could not distinguish his features. The man continued at his plodding pace, walking to the dashboard of the car and suddenly disappeared.

Washington Times (DC), Jan. 19, 1907

GHOST HAUNTS ROAD
MERRYMAKERS DISTURBED BY
INCONSIDERATE SPIRIT.
Apparition Wandering on Highway
between Butte and Rocker, Mont.,
Believed to Be That of
Recently Executed Murderer

Miles Fuller's ghost haunts the road between Butte and Rocker, and its first appearance was made as a party of merrymakers was on its way from Crystal Springs to Butte, says the *Anaconda Standard*. The night was a dreary one, and clouds cut off the little starlight that would otherwise have been in evidence. The time was just midnight, that popular hour when graves are supposed to yawn. The tally-ho[8] had just topped the little raise below Sunrise saloon, when the horses stopped, snorted in terror, for their eyes had caught the gleam of something white. An instant later it came out of the darkness, and the sight was so appalling that the passengers actually fell out of the carryall and fled shrieking toward Crystal Springs. The horses were petrified with terror for a moment and then fled panic-stricken through the darkness, the driver in his fright being unable to control them. The tally-ho was almost completely wrecked, and the driver and horses escaped serious injury only by a miracle.

As soon as the passengers arrived at the springs, they told of the frightful vision they had seen and the danger in which the driver had been placed. Immediately a party was formed to hunt up the driver and lay the ghost. The driver was found before going far, for he had swung the horses towards the springs and he still had control of them, although the wagon was wrecked. The poor brutes were actually wringing wet with sweat of terror and were trembling so their teeth rattled. "I have the horses all safe," said the driver. "Go up there and see what has frightened them," and the rescuers hurried on only to see a shadowy, phosphorescent object disappear over a hill towards Rocker.

One of the men who saw the ghost is positive it is that old Miles Fuller, who was hanged in Butte a few months ago. Fuller used to be a resident of that section of the country, and the people there say there is no doubt that his spirit is now haunting the road. "The sight was a terrible one," said one of the passengers. "When the driver stopped his horses, I looked out, and coming directly toward us were two people on horseback. One was a woman shrouded in white and riding a white

---

[8] A type of horse-drawn coach.

159

horse. She was leading a horse so black that he only made a faint shadow against the darkness, and upon his back was a figure bound in straps and with a black cap tied over his head. He sat on that horse like a soldier. We only took one look and then we fled, but we searched our souls for screams to tell how frightened we really were, and we were not content until we got into the shelter of the hotel at the springs."

Many of the residents of Rocker corroborate the truth of the ghost story. It may be that someone is playing a practical joke, but that is not believed by the superstitious, and a number of schemes are being planned whereby the ghost will be laid to rest again. Why Fuller's spirit should be accompanied by a woman is a mystery which his best friends cannot solve, as he was classed as a woman hater during all of the years he lived in Montana.

McCook Tribune (Nebraska), Jan. 25, 1907

A Galloping Ghost.

Ghosts on horseback are a novelty that make even the most intrepid citizen sit up and take notice. The horseback riding ghost is the very latest variety that has appeared in Bowdoinham, and he is a particular spirit, making visitations only at certain times. The hunter's ghost, they call him, and the big man on the big white horse who comes galloping down the Lisbon Road at the full o' the moon, right up to the side door of Sunny Crest Farm, strikes terror to the heart of the farmer folk as he raps smartly with his riding whip on the panels of the door. Whenever one appears in answer to the knock, the ghost, so they tell the story, wheels round and disappears at a gallop, turning into the old woods road much used in Revolutionary times by the soldiers of that stormy period. Ghost of the old cap'n, they call him, connecting this horseback riding spook with a certain officer of unsavory name, who once haunted the district of Maine. It is on the hunter's moon when the ghost rides abroad, and nervous people on the Lisbon Road are much disturbed by this galloping horseman.

Times-Dispatch (Richmond, Virginia), Oct. 19, 1908
Reprinted from *Lewiston Journal* (Maine)

Ghost Widow Terrifies

Sag Harbor is in the throes of a ghost scare, and Capt. Abe Selvers, who has sailed the Spanish Main and skirted the edge of the Sargasso Sea, is leading those who are hunting for the ghost in the hope of laying it. Seemingly, it is the ghost of a woman. It is draped heavily in black and wears a mask. Many women have seen it following them. They are terror-stricken and are afraid to go out of doors after 9 o'clock at night.

Capt. Selvers, who is a gallant tar, boasts his long experience as a sailor taught him not to be afraid of any woman nor the ghost of any woman. Therefore, if he can get within grabbing distance of the ghost, he thinks something will happen. The Sag Harbor women are praying earnestly the ghost may fall into his clutches, because until it is caught they cannot go out to quilting parties, carpet-rag sewings, and other social diversions. Many of the young women also complain bitterly that they are deprived of the excitement of going to the railroad station to see the evening express train come in.

"The ghost haunts Main Street, between Howard and Glover Streets," Capt. Selvers explains. "The first thing a person feels who walks along that section of the street is a cold, clammy sensation. That's the atmosphere the ghost carries around with it. When I first felt it I turned around and saw a tall, masked figure. It was in black from head to foot. I tipped my hat, stepped toward it, and it disappeared. Then I recalled that I had forgotten to put the spade in the smokehouse, and I started for home. It is wonderful what a longing for home a thing like that gives to a man. I guess I've seen ten women rushing for home from that section of Main Street in the past week. They all had seen the Ghost Widow."

Topeka State Journal (Kansas), Feb. 5, 1909
Reprinted from *New York Press* (New York)

SOLDIER GHOST
Crowds Gather to View Luminous Spectre
That Salutes With Transparent Arm

New Orleans, La.—Under the trees in Carrollton Avenue, between Maple and Burthe Streets, a ghastly, shimmering, half-tangible shape stood one night this week. The shadows around lent a weird, eerie atmosphere to the place. At times the shape moved slightly from its position, and then moved into the shadows again where it was only half discernable.

A half-luminous, half-transparent apparition dressed as a soldier, booted and hatted with a spectre rifle slung across its shoulders, it seemed a half-real, yet half-unnatural something that no mortal dare encounter.

A man came down the street, jauntily whistling. He was between Maple and Burthe Streets. Suddenly from its place beside a tree the ghost glided menacingly onto the banquette. It halted—stood silent. No sound did it utter; there was no rustle of cloth as one long arm went up in seeming salute to the barrel of the spectre rifle. It was just something that stood there, the man saw. He could not be mistaken. And before the spectre's arm had finished the half circle of its slow salute, the man was there no longer. The tap-tap of his fleeing feet quickly died away in the distance.

Then the news spread. A ghost was haunting Carrollton Avenue. Thomas Cleary, in front of whose house the spectre had taken up its stand, was notified by phone. Cleary came to his front porch and looked streetward. For a while he stared into the darkness. Then slowly, very slowly, seemingly growing out of the dark that lent a background to the somber thing, the shape reappeared. It looked as it had been described—the likeness of a soldier on guard, yet only half discernible and illusive, even as a shadow might seem if viewed with a dim light behind it.

In the unaccountable way that news travels, others heard of the apparition. Crowds of people who didn't generally pass that way at that time of night thronged the street cars going past. Crowds viewed the apparition in the shadow. The jitneys[9] did a big ghost-seeing business. Nevertheless, hundreds can give voice to the apparition's authenticity.

Further investigation will be made, and the findings submitted to the professor of physics at Tulane University. According to the tale told by one street car motorman, he saw the dim shape standing there at dusk, but thought possibly it was only a figment of his imagination as his car sped swiftly past.

It was not until nightfall that anything that might be construed as tangible was observed, and from then on, it was viewed by hundreds.

Charlevoix County Herald
(East Jordan, Michigan), Nov. 13, 1915

---

[9] Buses ridden for a low cost.

THE HEADLESS APPARITION.

From "TOWN HAUNTED BY HEADLESS GHOST," page 153.

HAUNTED PEOPLE

Like a strand of ectoplasm, the line between being haunted supernaturally and being haunted psychologically is diaphanous and—some would say—dubious. Guilt can act like a relentless ghost, as evidenced by the articles in this section about criminals who confess after being persecuted by the phantoms of their victims. Perhaps a society that keeps an open mind regarding ghosts has a more efficient criminal justice system.

But other manifestations aren't as easily attributed to a guilty conscience. Sometimes, it seems a ghost becomes fixed—not within a house or a graveyard—but upon an individual or a family. Moving to another location doesn't stop the spectral phenomena. Especially dreadful is that these haunted people are frequently children—which moves us toward the realm of poltergeists, since these noisy, object-throwing entities are frequently reported in homes where a child or adolescent lives.

Speaking of dreadful, some of the haunted people in this chapter were targeted by spirits intent upon extracting revenge, as in the article titled "A Malignant Ghost" or the one titled "A Malicious Ghost." Then there are the living who seem plagued less by ghosts—be they malignant or malicious—and more by curses or even demons, like the poor Busch family featured in "Ghost Building Fires."

Altogether, the people you'll meet in this chapter—from the guilty men to the innocent girls—suggest that no one is safe from being targeted by ghosts or darker spectral entities.

A Haunted House.—Strange noises are heard o' nights at the house of Mr. Graves, residing a little east of Quincy Center, usually in or about the sleeping room of his little son, about twelve years old. It has caused quite an excitement in the neighborhood, and many have been there to ascertain the cause, and some have continued their investigations during the night through which the noises were continued at intervals, but their precise location could not be ascertained—they seemed to be in different parts of the room—nor the cause satisfactorily ascertained. Some say it is the work of the spirits, as whenever the voices are heard, a nervous twitching of the boy's muscles are observed, whether sleeping or waking.

Occasionally, when the boy goes out, stones are thrown at him by invisible persons, which fall near to him, sometimes hitting the house but not him. No one seems to be present at such times except such as are there for the purpose of detecting the trick; yet, strange to say, no one has yet been seen to throw one of those stones, which seem flying at or towards the boy at all times of the day when he walks out, and many of them have been picked up and preserved in a pile, but no one has as yet hit him.

Baltimore Daily Commercial (Maryland), Oct. 9, 1865
Reprinted from *Coldwater Sentinel* (Michigan)

A girl in San Jose is possessed of a devil in the shape of a bushwhacker's ghost. The spirit, on being questioned, replied through the mouth of the girl: "I was what you call a bushwhacker, and was killed by this girl's father, and, as I still feel a spirit of revenge against him, I have taken control of her to further my designs; I have nothing against the girl, and intend to do her no harm." Apparently, the evil spirit went on to tell many things which had happened between himself and the girl's relatives (all of which was true), and finally told them that there was a letter on the way to them, giving information of the severe sickness of a little sister of the girl whom he was using for his evil purpose. The letter alluded to arrived in a few days, confirming the truth of what had been foretold.

The relatives of the girl, with whom she was living, thinking that the child might be insane, sent her to a private asylum in Alameda County a few days ago, and have learned that she is not disturbed any longer by the revengeful monster. The spirit had told them before that he would leave the girl when she should be removed from her relatives, but he would enter into some other member of the family. A day or so ago a letter was received from Missouri, stating that the father of the girl was afflicted in a manner which exactly corresponds with the former disorders of the child. The story comes from the parties directly connected with the strange affair, who are upright, honorable people.

Daily Phoenix (Columbia, South Carolina), Oct. 22, 1870

STRANGE PHENOMENA

At this age of the world the public is not expected to give credence to every ghost story and haunted house report in circulation; but we have just received from a reliable source the details of some very singular manifestations that have been witnessed for some time past in the neighborhood of Mill Creek, about four miles north from York, Illinois. Those who are inclined to doubt the truth of these statements have only to consult fifteen or twenty families in that vicinity, or open a correspondence with some of the parties named, for additional proof of the validity of this story.

The manifestations of this chain of supernatural events took place several days ago, at the house of John Haddox, and after strange and apparently impossible phenomena had been witnessed, a series of like performances was opened at the residence of the widow Haddox, a sister-in-law and neighbor of John Haddox. Tables, chairs, beds and articles of furniture were tumbled about in the most reckless manner. Dishes, fruit-jars, and all articles capable of being moved, were misplaced and often broken and destroyed. Members of the family frequently received blows from flying articles, and everything was kept in a constant state of agitation. On one occasion the head of a little boy terminated the flight of a small article, which inflicted a very severe and painful wound. Knives and forks flew out of the cupboard drawer, the drawer remaining closed. Rocks, clubs, pieces of mud, and all kinds of moveable articles, were hurled about by some unseen and mysterious power. Some parties carried away the marks of clubs and rocks, thrown by his (or her) ghostship. A lady's shawl was picked up in a remote part of the house, thrown into the fire and burned up. A number of eggs had been stored away in a small drawer for several days, and on opening the drawer were found to be all broken to pieces. Everything capable of being injured or removed is reported unsafe.

These are only a few of the results of these strange manifestations, which differ from those usually related in the fact that they have actually been seen in daylight, as is testified by numerous reliable witnesses. Persons from all parts of the country go to Mill Creek to see the "ghosts," and numerous efforts have been made to ascertain the causes of the wonderful phenomena, and a certain old lady of the neighborhood was at one time decided to be a witch and responsible for all the excitement. Certain parties talked of lynching and hanging the unfortunate creature, but she stoutly denied all knowledge of the disturbance, and was not molested. Further developments are feared, but more are especially desired.

It seems, according to reports current in the neighborhood, that the wife of John Haddox died about a year ago, and that on her deathbed she declared that she would return and haunt him, if spirits were permitted to return to earth, in case he ever employed a certain woman in the neighborhood to keep house for him. A few days since, he took this woman to his house, and then the strange performances mentioned above began.

Idaho World (Idaho City), June 1, 1871
Reprinted from *Terre Haute Mail* (Indiana)

Ghost Building Fires.

Cleveland, April 28.—German residents of the Sixteenth Ward, in the vicinity of Lincoln and Lussenden Avenues, have been wrought up to a high pitch of excitement for several days on account of the strange happenings in the house and to the family of John Busch.

A short time ago Busch moved to the city from North Amherst, O., where he had been for a number of years in the employ of the Lake Shore & Michigan Southern Railroad Company. Busch had not been in his new home very long when he began to be troubled by fires breaking out in various parts of the house, for which no cause could be assigned, and he finally became so impressed with the belief that the house was haunted that he removed from 1177 Lincoln Avenue to 77 Lussenden Avenue. But his troubles did not end here. The affair had so mysterious an aspect, and created so much excitement in the neighborhood, that a *Gazette* man concluded to investigate as he did yesterday and today, with the following results:

The house which Busch occupied on Lincoln Avenue is a two-story frame, formerly used as a bakery, the oven still remaining in the back part of the house. The front room was occupied as a bedroom, and in it were three beds and a child's crib, side by side, with just room enough to pass between, the bed nearest the wall being close against it and shutting off entrance to a closet. A week ago Sunday, while the family and one or two friends were sitting in this room, smoke was seen issuing from the closet, which contained nothing but a suit of castoff clothing. This was discovered to be on fire, and was hastily put out, while the family was astounded as no one had been in the closet that day. A brother-in-law and one or two friends were told of the singular occurrence, but paid no attention to it until a child came running to tell him, Monday afternoon, that the fire had broken out again, this time in the pantry, where it had burned the paper off the shelves. The brother-in-law, who is an intelligent German, hastened to the house in company with some friends, and while they were in the kitchen discussing the event, the crib in the front room began smoking, and before they could put the fire out the tick was burned through. Monday afternoon seven fires occurred in various parts of the house. Tuesday afternoon a bed in the front room was destroyed; some wadding that was behind a door caught fire, and the contents of an old kettle in the kitchen suffered a similar fate.

This was too much for them, and the next morning, with what goods the fire left them, they moved out of the house and into a story-and-a-half frame building at No. 77 Lussenden Avenue. That night the eleven members of the family slept on the floor. A family living next door to the Lincoln Avenue house also took fright, and left the neighborhood. On the afternoon of Thursday the smell of smoke spread through the new house, and they rushed upstairs to find one of the beds, which had just been put up that morning, almost consumed. A chicken coop adjoins the shed kitchen, in which a hen's nest in a barrel took fire Friday. Saturday a coat hanging in the shed kitchen began burning in the middle of the back, and was ruined before it could be extinguished. Sunday was an exciting day for the poor people. A sister-in-law laid her hat on the bed while she went to speak to a neighbor at the gate, and while there the bed began smoking and destroyed the feather on her hat. The bed seemed hot, but there was no fire visible. In a short time the bed caught fire and was burned through before it could be put out. Monday the last straw bed was consumed. This left two feather pillows, a husk bolster, and a feather tick for eleven persons to sleep upon.

Tuesday forenoon the *Gazette* correspondent visited the house and found the family in a state bordering on frenzy. The mother, with twins at her breast, wandered aimlessly around a room, in which was a cookstove, two or three chairs, a feather bed, and two pillows. A few religious prints hung on the walls.

Two hours after your correspondent left, the husk bolster was consumed, and he returned again to the scene of the mysteries. There is now absolutely nothing left to burn.

In connection with this affair, the causes of which your correspondent does not pretend to understand, it may be said that the family are very superstitious, and one incident, which sounds more like fiction than fact, is vouched for by outsiders. Some person told them to look among the feathers and, if they found a wreath, to boil it and then burn the feathers of which it was composed, and the "spell" would be broken. They looked and found a wreath of feathers about two inches thick and eight inches in diameter. They boiled and burned it on Monday, but the fires continued Tuesday all the same. The father, who bears a good name for sobriety and industry, is completely broken down and unable to work, and the mother and daughter keep moving from room to room, in which are vessels filled with water, looking for incipient fires.

Anderson Intelligencer (South Carolina), May 20, 1880
Reprinted from *Cincinnati Gazette*

A MALIGNANT GHOST

In a tenement house on the estate of Mr. George Shannahan, near Royal Oak, there lived an old white man and wife named Jackson. On a different part of the estate, in another tenement house, lived a colored man named Jack Skinner. Jack belonged to Mr. Shannahan, but his wife and children were free born. Jack had a daughter named Nannie, after her mother. It was the delight of this girl to make mouths at and mock and torment old Jackson, always taking good care not to let the old man get hold of her. It made him so mad he swore that, when he died, he would come back and haunt her. The war between them was kept up for several years, until Jackson's death. Sometime afterwards, while the girl was sitting in her father's house, all of a sudden there came down the chimney a chunk of fire that fell and scattered over the floor, the coals hitting the girl. After that the house, when the girl would be in it, would be pelted with chunks of wood, clods of earth, brickbats, oyster shells, etc., and no one could see from whence they came, as no one on the premises was visible except the family, and they could find out nothing about it. They all believed and declared it was old Jackson's ghost.

The circumstance created the greatest excitement throughout the neighborhood, and indeed throughout the county, for persons came from a long distance to witness the phenomenon. We once heard a gentleman of unquestioned veracity say he went there determined to unravel the mystery, if possible. He took the girl alone out in the middle of a field, and, to his utter astonishment, she was pelted there with clods and sticks by some invisible agency, which he could never understand, as it was impossible for anyone to be in collusion with her. The mystery was never explained, and the throwing and tormenting of the girl continued until some of her relations came from Baltimore and took her with them to the city, when no further disturbance occurred. If it

170

was old Mr. Jackson's ghost it seemed to have been satisfied with driving her off the farm.

It is our recollection that the girl was never seriously hurt by any of the missiles hurled at her. If out of doors, she generally saw them coming before they hit and would dodge them; if in the house, they would strike the hearth, the walls or some article of furniture without hitting her. It was not a malicious ghost, but simply appeared to be full of deviltry; it was unceasing in its persecutions until it succeeded in driving her off the premises. There was an old woman in the neighborhood named Kattie Coburn, who had the reputation of being a witch, and some thought she was at the bottom of the devilment; but she lived some distance away, across a creek, and it is not likely that she could have had anything to do with it. The general belief at the time was that it was old Mr. Jackson's ghost inflicting on the girl just punishment for her impudence to him in his lifetime.

Sacramento Daily Record (California), March 12, 1881
Reprinted from *Easton Star* (Maryland)

SHASTA'S SPOOK.
INCIDENT AND FACTS
OF THE MYSTERIOUS AFFAIR.
Worse Than Table-Tipping and More of It—
Statements of Officials—Cavorting Spirits—Etc.

Some time since, an article appeared in a San Francisco paper in which were described certain mysterious phenomena said to have occurred on a farm nine miles from Millville, Shasta County. According to the article in question, stones were thrown into the house, doors opened, furniture moved, etc., and many other things done—all without visible cause. To ascertain if there was any foundation for the statements referred to, a letter was written to the Postmaster at Millville, asking if the statements as published were credited by the general public and requesting his own opinion on the subject. The gentleman replied as follows—the note being on file in the *Record-Union* office:

Millville, August 16, 1885.

The statement is supposed to be true by the general public. The family is in town, and the same things occur. Respectfully,

L.E. Baker, P.M.

ANOTHER OFFICIAL'S STATEMENT.

Another letter was directed to the Justice of the Peace, making similar inquires, and that official replied in the following letter:

Millville, August 18, 1885.

Yours of August 14th has been duly received. The newspaper article referred to the 10th inst. is substantially correct, but does not contain an account f one-half of the strange doings which have taken place at the Fisher ranch near this place. The manifestations stated were seen and witnessed by upwards of twenty persons of good standing in this neighborhood, and to doubt their statements would be very difficult. These statements are generally believed by the people of this neighborhood to have taken place, and more besides. I cannot doubt the veracity of the many persons who have stated to me personally that they saw those occurrences in open daylight. I therefore believe them to be true. Respectfully yours,

William Pullen,
Justice of the Peace.

THE MILLVILLE *TIMES* ACCOUNT.

The strange doings are described in detail in the *East-side Times* of August 8th, published at Millville, and in the following language:

Millville is just now the center of the sensation of the day, the cause being the supernatural exhibition which has been taking place for the past two weeks on the ranch of Peter Fisher, situated on the Tamarack Road, ten miles from town. It is a case without parallel in the annals of spirit manifestations heretofore known. We shall endeavor to clearly state the facts as they exist—facts to which many of our prominent people are ready to swear, having been witnesses to the strange manifestations.

We will premise by stating that the house is situated on a slight rise about 250 yards from Old Cow Creek; the nearest building is the barn, fifty yards away; no trees or shrubbery are nearer to the house than the orchard, which is at the bottom of the rise, some fifty yards away. The temporary cabin is on the opposite bank of the creek from the house.

Two weeks ago Thursday, while Mr. Fisher was away from home, Jim Fisher, the fifteen-year-old son, was fishing in the creek, when small rocks began falling around his line, scaring away the fish, which caused him to quit fishing and go up to the house. His mother took Jimmie to task when he got to the house for throwing rocks into the front room, which faces the creek, several rocks having been thrown in on the floor. The boy denied throwing the rocks; indeed, it would have been impossible for him to have thrown the distance from the creek. On the return of Fisher, the phenomenon continued in the shape of rocks

172

falling on the kitchen floor, the rocks appearing to come through a small opening where a windowpane was out, and were never seen until after they were heard to strike the floor. The fusillade kept up at intervals for two days before other manifestations appeared. The next doings were the moving of pictures, the opening of an umbrella on the front-room table, the throwing of the bedclothes and mattress off of a bed. Although a strict watch was kept, no forms of any kind were seen; and what made it still more mysterious, all the manifestations were made in the daytime.

Mr. Fisher, being afraid that some of the family might be hit by the flying stones, removed his family and household goods to a camp on the other side of the creek, 250 yards from the house, and built a temporary cabin. After the removal, the manifestations at the house continued when any of the members of the family were present. On one occasion Mr. Fisher and John Mears went to a bedroom door and, on trying to open it, found it locked; they turned the key in the lock, and even then could not open the door, and proposed to break it in; but, pending doing so, went down into the orchard, and on coming back in a few moments found the bedroom door not only unlocked but partly open. A clock had been placed in a satchel and the key left in the lock, but on a member of the family going to the satchel they found the key gone, and it was missing for three days, when suddenly the eleven-year-old daughter, Annie, felt something gliding down her back, and on investigation it was found to be the lost key; and on unlocking the satchel a string was found tied so tightly around the clock that it had to be cut to get it off. The windows had all been nailed down securely, when suddenly, while the family were all present, one of the windows shot up its full length, carrying the nails with it. Sticks as well as stones began to be thrown.

These strange acts continued until Tuesday afternoon without anyone being hit by the flying stones or sticks. On that afternoon D.P. and William March were present, and, while sitting on the back porch, heard six or seven rocks fall on the kitchen floor, the door of which opened on the porch, and the rocks could not have been thrown from the outside by mortal hands without their seeing them. The Marches went home, and about 6 o'clock the editor put in an appearance on the scene of action. We found the family in the orchard about forty yards from the house and down a short bank. Just as we arrived the first rock that struck anyone was thrown, striking the girl Annie, who was sitting under a tree, on the right ankle. It was a rock about the size of a large peach, and, although it seemed to come from a distance, it did not leave any mark on the ankle. From this time on all the manifestations seemed to center on or around this girl Annie, although nothing further occurred that evening. We went up to the Marches and stayed overnight, and the next morning returned with the whole March family, and were informed that that morning (Wednesday), before our arrival, the girl had been struck three times on the same right ankle, twice by stones and once by a stick; one of the stones seemed to come through a cooking stove, the girl having her feet under it at the time. These manifestations occurred at the cabin to which the family had removed. The family all came up to the house, and we remained there some three hours, when business compelled us to leave for home; during that time the house was struck three times by rocks, and the girl once in the ankle as usual. We then started for home, and shortly after our departure quite a fusillade of rocks fell in and about the house.

At 5 o'clock that (Wednesday) afternoon a delegation of Millvillites put in their appearance to down the spook. Soon after their arrival, while Arnold Graham was talking to the girl, a small rock the size of an egg fell between them. An adjournment was then had to the cabin for supper. The next new phenomenon then occurred. It was the taking of the girl's straw hat from her head twice and throwing it sixty feet, lighting crown down both times. While the girl was eating supper a half-gallon soap can, one-third full of soap, flew and struck her on the ankle, and no soap was spilled. After supper Annie was sitting, holding a willow stick about three feet long in her hands, when it was suddenly snatched from her grasp by unseen hands and thrown across the camp. A pitch-pine stick four feet long was also thrown across the camp.

The Millville delegation divided for the night, part sleeping at the camp and the remainder taking up quarters in the so-called haunted house. The night at the house was passed quietly, as none of the family were present; in fact as yet no manifestations had been made at night. At the cabin, however, a slight manifestation was noticed for the first time. David King, who is a brother-in-law of Fisher, was sleeping with the two little boys when he was awakened by the pulling of the bed clothes. He sat up in the bed and seemed to see a figure at the foot of the bed with outstretched hands. He edged towards the foot of the bed and finally grabbed twice at the apparition, but grasped only the air, the figure disappearing.

In the morning the manifestations again began, and Thursday was a regular field day for the spook. Rocks and sticks fell frequently, and on going to the neighborhood of the house the girl's hat was taken from her head four times and thrown from her; she then put on Abe Webb's hat, and it was treated in the same manner twice; she then took Arnold Graham's hat, and it received the same treatment once. The hats always went off in front of the girl, always went the same distance of sixty feet, and always lit crown down. On several occasions she had her hands crossed over the hat when it left her head; a light breeze was blowing, but it would even go against the wind in its flight. A close watch was kept to see the hat leave her head, but no one ever saw it start, although twice it was seen when about two feet from her head, and once it seemed to circle around in the air before alighting; on all the other occasions it was not seen until it struck the ground. The girl was struck once during the day by a stone, which was found to weigh eight pounds, one ounce.

Shortly after noon the Millville delegation started for home, and the family began to prepare to come to town; a perfect matinee took place for over one hour, one manifestation following close after another, the family having in the meantime returned to the cabin. A small satchel had been prepared to bring along and set against the wall; on going to look for it a moment later, it was found hanging on a nail in the rafters. It was taken down and was again missed, when it was found hid under a carpet sack in the corner of the room. A broom was thrown across the room. The little girl was sitting in a rocking chair alongside of her uncle, when the front slat of the rocker fell out, striking her on the inevitable ankle; it took all Dave's strength to spring the slat back in its place. The girl said, "Uncle Dave, it pinched me," and on taking down her stocking a small red mark was seen on the ankle. Fisher called Dave out to see where a pint bottle had been hid in a knife box and covered up with potatoes, the top potato having a string tied around it. On Dave's return to the cabin the rocking chair was found standing on the bed and firmly wedged between the bed and roof. Dave King and the girl then seated themselves in the cabin, and the next thing seen was that one of the pillows turned around in its place and started for the foot of the bed. Dave grabbed it and returned it to its place. Soon after Fisher brought in one of the children, who had gone to sleep, and placed the child on a pillow in the center of the bed. He had hardly done so before the pillow turned up on end, rolling the still sleeping child off onto the bed, and remained on end until laid down. The girl hung her hat on the bedpost, and it was soon missing and was found under the bedclothes. Dave King drank a glass of milk and set the glass on the table, looked away for a moment, and the glass was missing. It was found lying on the bed. Two butcher knives were lying on a bench, when all at once one was seen standing point down on the girl's shoulder. Soon after a fence board, eight feet long, was discovered laying across the back of the girl's neck.

Immediately after this last occurrence the family started for Millville, and the mother, daughter Annie and two younger children have since remained at the residence of David King. The father and son returned to the ranch, and we are informed that since the departure of the family no disturbance whatever has taken place. It seems as though all the manifestations centered around the girl Annie, and when she is not present nothing is observed.

Many seemed to doubt the truth of these occurrences at first, and attributed the first manifestations to human agencies, concocted by persons who wished to scare Fisher into selling; but the later acts, which have been witnessed by so many different persons, dispel any such theory. Among those who have, in addition to the Fisher family, witnessed some of these various manifestations, are the following: J.K. Mears, John Welch, D.P. March, Wm. March, L.W. Kidd, Lee March, Wm. Shules, Mrs. D.P. March, Bell March, Lily March, David King, Arnold Graham, Joe Connelly, Willard Welch, Wm. Williamson, Tom Harrington, Abe Welch and Ernest King, and any or all are willing to make affidavit to the truth of these facts as stated.

THE *TIMES* EDITORIAL SAYS:

The all-absorbing topic of conversation of the week has been the curious manifestations that have occurred at Peter Fisher's, in this township. It is evident that the acts are caused by supernatural causes; what they are, none have as yet been able to divine. In fact the local savants have given the matter up and do not try to explain the matter, but only state the facts as they are known to exist. Christians, Spiritualists, atheists and materialists have all been represented among those who have seen this wonderful phenomena, and those who have gone to scoff and declared that they would catch the spook, have come back convinced that it is beyond their comprehension. A curious fact is that, with all the queer and dangerous manifestations, the girl, who is the central point at all times, has never been injured in the slightest degree. She is a bright girl, 11 years old last month.

Sacramento Daily Record-Union (California), Aug. 29, 1885

Her Mother's Ghost.

A marriage, which was to have taken place at Campden the other night, was interrupted in an unexpected way. The contracting parties, Henry Brown and Miss Mary Morgan, stood before Rev. Mr. Clayton, preparatory to becoming man and wife. A portion of the service had been already read, about fifty witnesses being present, when the bride uttered a loud scream. All eyes were immediately fixed upon her. She was seen to raise her hand and point toward a corner of the church. The next moment she fell on the floor in a swoon and had to be carried out.

Physicians worked with her for nearly an hour before she was restored to consciousness. When fully recovered she gave a curious explanation of her conduct. Her mother, who died four months ago, was opposed to her marriage with Brown. The marriage was for a time delayed, but after Mrs. Morgan's death, arrangements for it were pushed. Miss Morgan says that just when she was about to pronounce the binding words she raised her eyes and saw her mother's ghost; then she fainted. The wedding was postponed for several days.

Princeton Union (Minnesota), March 12, 1891
Reprinted from *New York Journal* (New York)

Paralyzed by a Ghost.

Mr. and Mrs. Michael Shea, of St. Joseph, are having a series of strange experiences with a ghost. The other night, so the story goes, Mrs. Shea was awakened by a sense of suffocation. The night was very dark, but her eyes could distinguish an apparition standing by her bedside. She tried to scream, but could not. The ghost laid its cold, clammy hands upon her arm, and then disappeared. The next morning, to her surprise, she could not raise her arm, the one the ghost had touched, from her side. It was as if paralyzed.

That night Mr. Shea was awakened by a cold hand being laid on his forehead. He awoke with a start and noticed the strange phantom standing by his side. Mr. Shea was speechless with fright. The ghost continued to rub its icy hands upon the head of Mr. Shea, and finally touched him on both arms and disappeared. Great beads of perspiration stood out on the forehead of Mr. Shea. He tried to speak to his wife, but could make no sound. He thought how his wife had been affected, and tried to raise his arms. To his horror he could not do so. The next morning his arms were still paralyzed, and he ceased to laugh at his wife, nor was he able to work that day. The ghost appeared to both husband and wife again the following night.

Iron County Register (Ironton, Missouri), June 18, 1891

A MALICIOUS GHOST.
He Haunts and Worries a Farmer
Who Offered Him Work.

James W., a prominent farmer of this vicinity, has created quite a sensation by reporting himself the victim of the malicious spirit of a tramp who died on his place last summer. Mr. W. says that the ghost has killed his watch dogs, maimed his sheep and injured his horses, besides not permitting him to have a chicken or turkey about him. The tramp applied for supper and bed last August, when Mr. W., being short of hands, offered him work, when he refused very curtly, saying he was sick. He was then given a meal, but told he could not sleep on the premises, upon which he grew very violent in language and left vowing vengeance. As the man did look delicate and ailing, he was allowed to go, though it was feared that he would return and do some mischief; but the next morning he was found dead in an adjacent field and buried by the town, so nothing more was thought of the matter.

It was not many weeks, however, before the W's began to be persecuted by an invisible agent that emptied the milk pans, let the cattle out, broke the crockery and generally made itself a nuisance. Tiring of this and growing more vindictive, it began wringing the necks of the poultry, choking up the well and undermining the out-buildings. Mr. W., being skeptical in regard to supernatural interference, for a long time refused to admit these tricks to be aught but the mischief of some ill-disposed person, but was at last compelled to accept the manifestations as extraordinary. He would himself lock and guard his henhouse at night, only to hear the frightened fowls screaming and fluttering, though when he opened the door his lantern revealed the place to be empty, though the headless, still-living bodies were indisputable evidence that they had just been killed.

When the dogs were brought they showed the greatest reluctance to enter the house, whining piteously, shivered and cringed, though of fierce and game breed. Forced into the house, they were heard to give a sharp shriek, and the next moment their lifeless bodies were hurled by a powerful hand through the open door to their master's feet. Several of the most prominent and respected persons of the neighborhood vouch for this. The horses cannot be sufficiently guarded to keep the ghost from turning them out, and frequently the family is aroused by the clatter of hoofs past the house, when on looking out they see a horse fully saddled go tearing down the road as if ridden by some hard-pushed rider, though none is to be seen. The neighbors support this statement by declaring that it is no unusual sight to them, and that nothing can stop one of the W. horses when thus ridden. The poor creature, broken down and nearly dead, is often found many miles away, while several have died by such treatment.

Occasionally the ghost grows so aggressive that the family is obliged to leave the place, when it subsides for a time. Mr. W. says that he has frequently been attacked by it, and that once on entering the house in broad daylight he was knocked nearly senseless by a blow on the side of his head, while on another occasion he was crossing an unlighted hall, when he was pushed against the wall by a powerful hand holding his throat. He managed to gasp out a cry for help, when his wife came running with a lamp in her hand, which showed the hall to be empty, save for himself. Recently Mrs. W. heard her youngest child, an infant of a few months, crying in a room upstairs, and, running to it, could hear distinctly the sound of violent slaps, and on opening the door found the baby covered with welts and red from head to foot. It is believed that Annie W., aged three, can see the ghost, as she will frequently fix her eyes into space, saying, "Poor man, is you sick?" and she of all the family has escaped molestation from the malicious spirit.

St. Paul Daily Globe (Minnesota), Sept. 24, 1891
Reprinted from *De Kalb Special* (Mississippi)

HAUNTED BY A GHOST.
An Army Deserter Accuses Himself of the Crime of Murder.

GALESBURG, ILL., June 8.—Police authorities are exercised over a letter received in which the writer, Robert Isdale, now in the Fort Leavenworth military prison for desertion from the army, accuses himself of murder. A year ago last March a young man named Menifer was found dead in the Union Hotel in this city, and the coroner's jury returned a verdict of death by asphyxiation, as there seemed to be no suspicious circumstances.

Isdale, however, in his letter says that when Menifer asked him to get a glass of liquor he mixed with it a quantity of morphine, intending to put Menifer to sleep and then to take his money. The drink, however, killed Menifer, and Isdale, who was a porter in the hotel, left town. He now says that Menifer's ghost haunts him all the time, and asks that at the expiration of his time at Fort Leavenworth he be brought back here and punished.

Rock Island Argus (Illinois), June 8, 1894

179

CHIDED HER MOTHER'S SPIRT.
Practical Young Woman
Didn't Want to Be Aroused at Night.

Kansas City has a least one young married woman who takes a very prosaic view of ghosts and so-called spirit manifestations. She was forced to spend a night alone in a St. Louis hotel, her husband being detained elsewhere by business. In the dead of the night she was awakened out of a sound sleep by a tremendous noise in the wardrobe. It was such a sudden and unearthly uproar that the woman, sensible and practical through she was, was frightened. The noise ceased, then returned. The woman jumped up, lighted the gas, and made a thorough search both of the wardrobe and the room. There was nothing so far as the evidence of the senses went which could account for the racket. The woman put out the light and went back to bed. The noise was not repeated.

Six months afterward, however, the woman was in San Francisco, and for the first time in her life and solely out of curiosity, she attended a Spiritualistic meeting. Almost immediately the medium, a perfect stranger, turned to her and said: "The spirit of your mother is present, madam, and she says that six months ago (naming the precise date) she tried to communicate with you by means of the wardrobe in the Blank Hotel, St. Louis."

The woman's practical good sense did not desert her.

"Well, you just tell my mother," she said, "that the next time she wants to communicate with me not to make such an awful racket in the dead of night and frighten me half out of my senses."

Williston Graphic (North Dakota), July 29, 1898
Reprinted from *Chicago Chronicle* (Illinois)

KING OF HANGMEN HAUNTED
Executioner Pursued by the Spooks
of Eighty-eight Murderers He Has Hanged.

Springdale, Ark., June 11.—Haunted by the ghosts of eighty-eight murderers and unable to sleep on account of his uncanny tormentors, George Maledon, the king of hangmen, is ending his days in poverty and misery on a little farm two miles south of this place.

Maledon was for many years executioner at the Fort Smith Federal Court, where many of the most noted and desperate criminals that for years infested the Indian Territory were brought to trial before Judge Parker. In that capacity Maledon officiated at the hanging of eighty-eight men and won for himself the sobriquet of the King of Hangmen. He has hanged more men than any other officer in the history of the United States and, through his long experience, became an expert in his line. When the Indian Territory was given courts of its own Maledon started a grocery store at Fort Smith and accumulated some property. This he later disposed of and traveled over the country, exhibiting himself as the "King of Hangmen." The venture was not a financial success, and his money was soon all gone. Then he settled on a little farm near here and has at last fallen victim to superstition or insanity. Every night is made miserable to him by the imaginary visits of the ghosts of men he has hanged. To keep the ghosts away bright lights are kept burning at his house at night and friends guard his bedside.

Houston Daily Post (Texas), June 12, 1899

FATHER'S GHOST HAUNTS SON
Residents of Cumberland, Ill.,
Believe in the Apparition

In Cumberland County, Illinois, about three miles from the village of Montrose, there is an old log cabin that the people believe to be haunted. The house was formerly the home of Thomas Elliott, who before his death vowed to return in spirit and haunt his son, who had offended him. Many brave and honest men have spent the night in the cabin, and have told weird tales of the happenings. Chairs and other furniture would be moved about, strange noises would be heard, and all of the men would flee in terror. The son is no more able to explain the antics of the ghost than are his neighbors. Neither can he escape its visits. Once he moved to Mattoon, hoping to avoid the unpleasant visits, but the supposed ghost followed him. He moved again, but his change of location was no bar to his uncanny visitor. Finally, he gave up and went back to his old home. If he is in any way concerned with the ghostly apparitions his magic is so artful that no one has ever been able to detect it. One night last summer a party of thirty-five residents of that section went to spend the night in the house, but before morning all had been frightened away.

Lewiston Evening Teller (Idaho), Jan. 13, 1904

SPECTER DRIVES MAN FROM HOME.
GHOST OF FATHER-IN-LAW
CONSTANTLY HAUNTS
RETIRED INDIANA MERCHANT.
INHERITED PALATIAL PLACE.
Apparition of Deceased Relative Follows
New Owner Over Premises Continually,
Finally Forcing Him to Move.

Elkhart, Ind.—Harassed by the stalking specter of his aged father-in-law, John B. Garman, who died two years ago, John Otterson has abandoned a palatial suburban place which was bequeathed him by his deceased relative. Otterson is a wealthy retired merchant, having been in business in Elkhart for a number of years.

While Mr. Otterson is not prone to believe in ethereal materializations, he asserts that in spirit form his father-in-law haunted him. The apparition followed him over the premises, stood by him when he attempted to do light work about his country home, and frequently was his companion during the dead hours of night. That Mr. Otterson has an ordinary temperament and is not at all given to nervousness makes his story of the ghost all the more remarkable. He is a giant physically, and mentally, well-educated and well-read.

Otterson claims that he only escaped the apparition when away from the home and without the boundaries of the luxuriant gardens where his deceased relative spent the greater part of his four score years.

The aged Mr. Garman, one of the pioneers of Elkhart County, left a large estate. To his daughter, Mrs. Otterson, and her husband he bequeathed the greater part of it.

The eccentric old gentleman, who has come back from the spirit world to haunt the living, died from a broken heart, his only son having met a tragic death. Dating from that incident to the time of his demise, which occurred six months later, Mr. Garman walked sorrowfully about the premises lamenting through the long hours of the summer days his son's untimely death and refusing to be solaced. His grief was deep seated, and he virtually walked out his life on the familiar paths of the old homestead.

It is in the picturesque brick mansion about and around his favorite earthly retreats that the son-in-law in recent months has seen the ghostly form of John Garman. The specter first appeared a few months after the old gentleman's death.

Frequently while he was roaming over the fields or strolling through the groves or orchards, the mysterious, unreal and unnerving specter has sprung up beside him and, timing his pace to that of Mr. Otterson, has accompanied him about. It makes neither sign nor motion, looks neither to the right nor left, but with folded arms and bent head keeps up its noiseless tread with maddening precision.

Sometimes, asserts the haunted man, upon returning from a drive the unearthly vision appeared to him in the barnyard. As he unhitched and unharnessed his team the apparition watched his procedure with unseeing eyes. The expression of the face was always sorrowful—just as it had been in life during his days. The materialization to Mr. Otterson was full life size, the very image, he declares, of his father-in-law. No other person has seen the alleged ghost.

Mr. Otterson's experience with the specter but recently became public. He bore the ordeal silently, fearing the taunts and ridicule of his friends. Lately the annoyance became so great that he decided to remove from the place.

The Garman family was one of the most widely known in this city, being among the very early settlers of the county. The family, whose name was formerly spelled "German," came here from Pennsylvania, where John Garman's relatives settled and named the city Germantown. The Ottersons are equally well known. No one here doubts the veracity and sincerity of Mr. Otterson's statements concerning the specter which has haunted him, but all are at a loss to account for the strange incident.

Spanish Fork Press (Utah), March 21, 1907

GHOST FOLLOWS PAVIA FAMILY
Stone Showers and Dog
Drive It from Two Houses

Honolulu has another ghost. It does not appear to be such a lively apparition as the one which operated on Punchbowl some months ago,[1]

---

[1] A ghost in Honolulu's Punchbowl district was reported in Hawaiian newspapers during September of 1908. Though there were signs of poltergeist activity—unseen hands knocking down pictures, tossing kindling through *closed* windows, hurling kitchen items, even sticking a knife and corkscrew into a table—nothing indicated that the homeowners, Mr. and Mrs. Pecarick, were being targeted specifically. An investigation raised the possibility that the Pecarick's cleaning girl, Esperanza Gonzales, was a psychic medium and the channel through which the supernatural activity sprang. She denied it,

183

but what it lacks in variety in performance it makes up for in persistence. Unlike the Punchbowl ghost, which was purely local, confining its operations to the Boyd house, the new one is haunting a family, and has already followed it to three different places of residence. The police have been handling the matter for a couple of days, but have not as yet met with any success.

A Portuguese family, named Pavia, has been singled out by the spirit, and for a couple of months past, their lives have been made miserable by the phantom's pranks. All the members of the family, consisting of paterfamilias, his wife and several boys and girls, have seen the apparition and have witnessed its manifestations.

The ghost first made its appearance on the scene when the family lived on Kauluwela Lane, near School Street. It appeared in the form of a black dog, which would run up to the various members of the family and sniff at them. Then it would disappear, and a few minutes later a shower of stones would descend on the house, breaking the windows and flying into the rooms. The stones would keep coming for a few minutes; then there would be an interval of about half an hour, and then the fun would commence again. A weird feature about the thing was the fact that the manifestation took place only when the head of the house was awake. As soon as he went to sleep, it would cease.

This racket took place almost every night, and to escape it, the Pavias moved to another house at Waikahalulu. The ghost, however, was persistent, and again the family had to move, this time choosing its abode in a house on Chun Hoon Lane, makai of School Street.[2] Again the move failed to influence the ghost; the dog and stones came along with unfailing regularity, and finally the poor, haunted Portuguese took refuge with the police.

Last Tuesday night Chief of Detectives Kalakiela and his staff went to the scene. As they approached they heard a shower of stones striking the roof and walls of the house, but when they arrived, everything became quiet as the grave. All that night and the greater part of last night, Kalakiela and his band kept faithful watch, but neither ghost, dog nor stones made their appearance.

Evening Bulletin (Oahu, Hawaii), Jan. 21, 1909

---

insisting that such things never happened in any other house she cleaned and blaming the Devil for the disturbances. Journalists proclaimed the girl innocent, and the Pecaricks then revealed that neighbors told them earlier residents had experienced similar phenomena. As such, the Punchbowl ghost becomes yet another haunted house case.

[2] *Makai* is a Hawaiian word meaning seaward.

Coshocton.—Walter Carnes and wife left their home and are camping on the river bank for the rest of the summer because they declare Mrs. Carnes is being haunted by the ghost of her former husband, Simon Fisher. Five members of the family attest the weird story. Simon Fisher, much older than his wife, died last March and on his deathbed exacted a promise from her that she would not marry Carnes, who he cordially hated. In less than a month the woman married Carnes, and according to her story, her former husband has dogged her footsteps ever since. She and Carnes and her three children all declare that Fisher appeared before them attired in his grave clothes, pointed his long finger at her and then seemed to walk right through her and vanish.

Mahoning Dispatch (Canfield, Ohio), Aug. 4, 1911

MURDERED GIRL'S GHOST
HAUNTS PARENTS' HOME

Atlantic City, N.J., June 6,—There is a ghost scare here today. The persons who say they have seen the specter are members of the family of Jane Adams, an 18-year-old girl, who was murdered five years ago by being thrown from the Million Dollar Pier.[3]

The murderer was never found, nor has the reason for his act been learned. The mystery was deepened today by the appeal of the girl's family to the police to help them solve the appearances at their home of the ghost which, they assert, bears a strong resemblance to the murdered girl.

The Adams home is at 1815 Caspian Av., and on several occasions lately the family have startled the neighborhood by leaving their home and seeking protection with their neighbors, declaring the "ghost" or "spirit" was stealing about the house.

Mary, a sister of Jane, declares she has frequently seen a hand protrude from closet doors, has heard queer noises at night and has even observed the ghost's flight from a closet through the room. The whole neighborhood is having an attack of fidgets.

Seattle Star (Washington), June 6, 1913

---

[3] The pier still stands but is now called Playground Pier.

The Spectre Accompanied Him About.

From "SPECTER DRIVES MAN FROM HOME," page 182.

NATURAL EXPLANATIONS

In 1859, John Brown led an assault on the Federal arsenal in Harpers Ferry, Virginia. His goal was to ignite a widespread slave revolt, thereby ending slavery in the U.S. Though the nation took another step toward Civil War, the siege was promptly squelched and Brown was hanged for treason. Twelve days after his execution, newspaper readers learned that the martyr's ghost had been witnessed one night. Upon daylight examination, however, what had seemed like a supernatural apparition was given a natural explanation: a washerwoman had left some laundry—"one of those nether garments, peculiar to her sex"—on the line, where it had swayed in the starlight and "had been converted, by a disordered imagination, into the dreaded spectre."[1] The report served as a cautionary tale about being too quick to cry ghost.

Lest my own readers think that U.S. citizens after the Civil War had abandoned such caution, I end with ghost reports that provide natural explanations for what, at first, was thought to be supernatural. That antebellum stance that ghosts were a matter of optical illusion or products of "disordered imagination" was certainly challenged—but never defeated, and while the previous chapters' articles remind us to keep an open mind about ghosts, these reports suggest that one also shouldn't jump to supernatural conclusions.

I cheat on the dates with the very last article here, jumping ahead to 1919. It felt anticlimactic to end with a phantom that turned out to be a piano-playing possum. More significantly, though, that final ghost report reminds us that discovering natural explanations for specific ghostly encounters is something very different from offering proof that ghosts don't exist at all.

---

[1] *Cass County Republican* (Dowagiac, Michigan), Dec. 15, 1859.

Couldn't Fool Her.—The Lafayette, Ind., *Courier* tells an amusing story of some young ladies and gents of that place, who were taking a social walk near the cemetery, when a ghost appeared. They all ran but one sturdy woman of the strong-minded class, who stood her ground till the ghost got to her, when she seized it and thrashed out of his frightful disguise a mischievous fellow, who heard the project of walking about the graveyard discussed and hid himself there to give the venturesome party a fright. She led him back to the house and, in reply to the questions poured in upon her, said, "Can't fool me, I've seen too many men in sheets to get frightened at them."

Anderson Intelligencer (South Carolina), June 29, 1865

Thrilling Incident.

We have before us a private letter detailing events that recently occurred in a southwestern Ohio town, which gives peculiar force to the old adage that "truth is stranger than fiction."

Mr. Delos W. is a wealthy and influential man, residing near the village of P. On the Thursday preceding the prizefight between Gallagher and Davis, the old gentleman was thrown into a high state of excitement at learning that his only son, John, had gone to Cleveland with the avowed purpose of attending the fight, and his excitement intensified at still further discovering that John had helped himself to his (the father's) pocketbook containing $200. Mr. W. fumed and fretted over the conduct of his son and went to bed on Thursday night with a raging headache and marked symptoms of fever.

He was about the place in a more composed frame of mind on Friday, but the interview with John on Monday afternoon, immediately after the son's return, threw the old gentleman into a paroxysm of rage and grief, which was rendered doubly severe by John's insolence and his acknowledgement that he had lost $150 of the money in a bet on Gallagher.[2] Mr. W.'s frenzied feelings finally got the better of him, and he felled his son to the floor with a blow of his fist and, immediately thereafter, fell down himself in a senseless condition. Great excitement in the family ensued. The mother ran screaming for assistance, which

---

[2] William E. Harding's *The Champions of the American Prize Ring: A Complete History of the Heavy-Weight Champions of America* (1881) offers fight records of Charles Gallagher and Bill Davis. Harding doesn't specify a Cleveland bout, but he does note that "Davis whipped Charlie Gallagher in 44 rounds" in Point Pelee, Ontario—just across Lake Erie from Cleveland—on May 10, 1867. This newspaper article appeared in November of the same year.

was soon forthcoming in the persons of several of the neighbors. Mr. W. was found in an apparently lifeless condition with blood flowing from his mouth and nose. A subsequent examination by a physician led to the announcement by him that Mr. W. had died by the bursting of a blood vessel. So evidently had the vital spark fled that no efforts at resuscitation were made, and the "remains" were prepared for burial as promptly as possible.[3]

The funeral of the "deceased" took place the following Wednesday. Mr. W.'s body had only been coffined the previous day—up to which time it had lay draped in its shroud, in the parlor. Notwithstanding the wonderful life look of the skin and the color of the face, it occurred to no one to suggest a postponement of the burial till absolutely certain. The funeral was very largely attended, and everybody remarked the lifelike appearance of the deceased.

The "remains" were temporarily placed in one of the vaults of the cemetery, owing to the fact that a brick tomb, commenced for their reception, had not been completed.

At 10 o'clock on Thursday night, the village was thrown into a great excitement by a report that a ghost had been seen in the cemetery a short time before, and the old lady who had first seen it had been frightened into a fit from which it was doubtful if she would recover. Thinking that probably the ghost was personated by some scoundrel, who had played the same trick several times before, a number of persons armed themselves with shotguns, proceeded to the cemetery, and commenced a cautious inspection—their hearts keeping up an anxious thumping in the their bosoms in spite of their assumed bravado. They had not long to wait, for there flitting among the tombs, was a white object plainly to be seen. With trembling hands the guns were raised and fired, when—strange fact for a ghost—they saw the white creature fall between a couple of graves. Plucking up courage they cautiously approached the object and turned a dark lantern upon it. Their feelings can better be imagined than described when they found that the ghost was the lately "deceased" Mr. Delos W.

Whilst a portion of the party picked up the bleeding, senseless body of the old gentleman and started homeward with it, the remainder hastened to the vault. There they found Mr. W.'s coffin broken open and

---

[3] The quick funeral—and other aspects of this narrative—can be attributed to the fact that embalming a corpse before burial was only then becoming a standard practice. Indeed, embalming became widespread after its use with Civil War dead being returned home. Presumably, Mr. W.'s family had decided against following the emerging trend.

lying upon the floor, and the coffin of a deceased lady that had been lying upon it likewise thrown down from the shelf and standing on end partially broken open, displaying its ghastly inmate. The vault door, which was rather a weak affair, had been forced open by the resurrected Mr. W.

The party then went to Mr. W.'s house, where they found that the wounds were not serious and that he had recovered his senses. His story was briefly told: He had been carried to the cemetery in a trance. Early on Thursday morning consciousness returned to him, and the horrid truth flashed upon his mind that he was coffined alive. This led additional strength to his struggles to get free, and he finally succeeded in bursting the coffin.

Mr. W. is now fast recovering and seems good for a long lease of life.

> *The Wyandot Pioneer* (Upper Sandusky, Ohio), Nov. 21, 1867
> Reprinted from *Cleveland Plain-Dealer* (Ohio)

A HAUNTED HOUSE.
Rattling of Chains—Terrified Renters—
A Plucky Young Man Alone—
The Women in White—A Race at Night—
Glimpses of Garters—The Mystery Cleared Up

There is in the —— part of this city a small brick house which for two years past has borne the dreadful name "Haunted." We have no knowledge of its being at all historic, or of a murder or two, or any other crime having been committed in it to warrant ghostly manifestations. Yet there it stands, accredited with all the mystery which ever attaches to a house supposed to contain incorporeal inhabitants. Women and children avoid it in the daytime, and the men who live in that section have learned that, at night, the "nearest way 'round is the shortest way home."

As a publication of the locality of the house might be of injury to its owners, we refrain. During the past two years it has been frequently advertised in the "To Rent" column, and as frequently was rented, but the renters did not remain in possession long. The longest period it was held was two weeks, and the shortest ten hours. The occupants heard rattling of chains, the shuffling of feet, and saw doors which had just been locked fly open and shut to without the least noise. The conventional groans were missing in this haunted house, but clanking of chains, shuffling of feet, and the door manifestations were sufficient to so frighten the occupants as to make them leave without giving even a day's notice. Each and every occupant had the same story to tell. Finally, the owners of the house despaired of ever getting an occupant for it and allowed it to remain idle.

A young man who didn't believe in ghosts was heard to assert his disbelief and also his willingness to sleep in the house, and prove that there was no such indications of ghostly occupants as were spoken of. He was called upon to carry out his proposition.

"Being stout of muscle, strong of nerve,
He did not from his purpose swerve,"

And one night last week he might have been observed in a room of the house with a bottle of the ardent and two revolvers, lying in wait for ghostly intruders. Thus he remained until about ten o'clock, and seeing nor hearing nothing of spirits, he put himself outside of some and then went to sleep. Not long did he slumber. A noise aroused him. He arose and walked to the window, and saw two women clad in white (petticoats is the name the clothing goes by among the initiated) coming towards the house. They bore a chain and, as soon as they got upon the back porch, commenced pulling the chain back and forth. Hoping to catch them in the act, our hero crept downstairs, but while passing through the hall, made a noise which alarmed the women and off they went at a rate most surprising to our watcher. He pursued, but did not overtake them, and with the exception of knowing that they wore red garters—their rapid pace and the wind allowing him opportunities of observation—he has no clue whatever for identification purposes.

Being convinced that the rattling of chains and shuffling of feet heard by the former occupants was occasioned by these or other women, and that the alleged mysterious opening and shutting of locked doors was only the effect of the imaginations of the timid occupants, the watcher retired to rest, determined that on the morrow he would, if possible, solve the question he was constantly asking himself, "What is the object of these women in frightening off the occupants of this house?"

At an early hour he arose, left the house, and about ten o'clock circulated among the women who lived in the neighborhood—of a class popularly denominated the "low-down people." By judicious questioning he ascertained that there was in the lot of the haunted house an excellent well of water. From this well the neighbors had to obtain water or send a long distance for it and then get a poor article at that. When the house was vacated they had free use of the well, but when occupied they were not permitted to obtain water even for drinking purposes. To keep the house vacant was evidently to their interest, and they took up the ghost method, which was a "success" until a man who had commonsense enough not to believe in ghosts agreed to occupy the house and ascertain for himself whether there were such visitants. The neighbors thought he was to be an occupant and tried their game upon him with the result above stated.

Charleston Daily News (South Carolina), Sept. 16, 1869

An Indiana farmer thought he saw a ghost in a cemetery the other night. He procured his gun, thinking he would try the effect of cold lead on the apparition, fired, and brought down his own poor old white horse.

Public Ledger (Memphis, Tennessee), March 29, 1870

A Massachusetts Ghost Story.

A correspondent at Monson, skeptical as to the supernatural appearances, has been quietly investigating the circumstances attending the ghost excitement at that place a few months ago, and has solved the mystery to his full satisfaction. The story, as he tells it, is that a very young man became enamored last summer of a fascinating maiden residing about a mile from the village, and was accustomed to call upon her several times a week. An older brother, finding that the youthful Romeo was causing some gossip by his frequent attentions, resolved to stop them, and hit upon the plan of frightening him in the guise of a ghost.

Knowing that the lad was courageous, however, he "appeared" first to another member of the family. By strapping a broom upon his back with the bushy part projecting over his head, he successfully disguised his height and, by means of a big black dress, presented in the night the appearance of a woman about six feet and eight inches tall. Thus attired, he secreted himself in the new church and, when his victim came along, pounced upon him and chased him home, where he arrived breathless with fright. This incident produced much excitement in the community, but the intrepid Romeo, undismayed by ghosts, steadfastly continued his visits to the object of his affections.

The leaven of fear was working, however, and about a week later, the "ghost" accosted and chased a man on his way to the quarry at early daybreak, after which the 3,000 inhabitants of Monson were so wrought up that even men were afraid to venture out at night except in bands.

But love still conquered fear. The youngster continued his tri-weekly trips until one night, while returning home, the frightful ghost of whom he had heard so much confronted him at a lonely spot in the road. The first impulse was to run, but the ghost ran too; he walked, and the ghost assumed a measured tread and continued uncomfortably near; he slackened his pace, and the dreaded being stalked past him and remained before him or behind him until he reached home, frightened nearly to death. The ghost-personator, having accomplished his purpose, thereafter kept his own counsel and retired from the business, but the terrified people of the town saw a spectre in every bush, and the ghost was reported in half a dozen places after he had finally disappeared from view. The new church was watched for many a night; the woods were searched by bands of men, who took care to keep together; one man was so nervous as to shoot himself while in search of the ghost; and deadly fear for a time held the whole community.

Albany Register (Oregon), July 12, 1872
Reprinted from *Springfield Republican* (Massachusetts)

A Fine Ghost Story Spoiled.

For some time past, at a certain residence in Beaver Falls, Pa., the inmates have been frightened almost out of their wits by a continued rapping, which sounded as if in a closet in an apartment upstairs. Investigation at the time of the rapping failed to reveal anything and some people went so far as to say the house was haunted. The other day, as the lady of the house was cleaning the room, she heard the same curious sound, followed by what she called a "sneeze." She went to a window to open it, and while she was pushing the shutter, the sound became more distinct, and casting a glance upward she saw a large woodpecker sitting near the window and pecking away with all its might. It seems that a piece of timber the bird was sitting on led to the closet and when the bird would peck the sound could be clearly heard in the room. The family sleeps sounder o' nights now.

Middleburgh Post (Pennsylvania), July 14, 1887

Not far from Tombstone, Arizona, is a strange glen that has long enjoyed the reputation of being haunted. It is always cool there. Strange rushes of air sweep through it, and at a certain spot mysterious voices are often heard, speaking in audible words. Sometimes the listener can catch whole sentences. The place is regarded with superstitious horror

193

by many whom no wealth could tempt them to enter it after dark. A curious unbeliever in the supernatural has lately been investigating these phenomena. He finds that the coolness and sudden currents of air are due to the formation of the glen, which acts as a tunnel to intensify any strong breeze, and that the voices came from a ranch a long distance away. In fact, the place is a natural whispering gallery, and every word at the ranch can be distinctly heard at a certain spot in the glen.

Anderson Intelligencer (South Carolina), Aug. 25, 1892

SOLVED THE GHOST STORY.
A White-Clad Baker Says
He Was Going for Beer.
He Hurried to and from
Because Boys Annoyed Him.

NEWARK, N.J., May 18.—The alleged ghost that has been disturbing the residents of the lower section of this city has been found. Capt. Daly, of the Van Buren Street police station, saw a man dressed in white enter a saloon this morning early. He carried a pail, which he had filled with beer.

The captain followed the man and saw him enter a baker's shop at the corner of Jefferson Street and Elm. The man looked around before entering the place. The captain also entered the shop and, after questioning the white-clad person, learned that he was A. Lang, an apprentice in the shop.

The apprentice said that he was much annoyed by the boys in the neighborhood. Whenever he went to get beer, they chased him. The result was that he made flying trips to and from a nearby saloon, and the people seeing the white-robed figure fluttering along the streets at all hours of the night, concluded that it was a ghost, and spread the story that has been giving the police of that district considerable trouble.

Capt. Daly said that he was now convinced that Lang was the alleged ghost and that the spook mystery is solved.

Evening World (New York, New York), May 18, 1894

MAPLETON'S GHOST CAUGHT
EIGHT FLATBUSH YOUNG MEN
SOLVE THE MYSTERY.
The Ghost Proved to Be a Figure
Made of Straw Covered with a Sheet,
which Was Operated with a Wire
from a Tree by Two Mischief Makers—
They Escaped.

Eight determined young men, all unbelievers in the supernatural, started out from Flatbush on Monday night to convince themselves and the world at large that the apparition which has been appearing almost nightly at Mapleton was either a mischief-loving human being or a dummy operated by practical jokers. Other people who have started out to clear up the mystery of the Mapleton ghost have announced their intention in blatant tones, and somehow or other the ghost has always failed to appear when they were ready to bag it, but not so with the Flatbush young men. They said nothing about their scheme and, as a result, they succeeded in clearing up a mystery which has baffled the citizens of Mapleton, the police for miles around, and even a delegation of scientists from the Brooklyn Convention who went all the way down to Mapleton at a late hour in the night to investigate the ghost and came back without having had even as much as a glance at the spectre.

It is now nearly three weeks since the Mapleton ghost first appeared, and it has appeared so constantly that the residents of the place have been worked into a fever heat over it. There seems to have been an epidemic of ghosts all over the country of late, but none have stood a chance in the contest for popularity with the Long Islander. This particular ghost has not only scared the wits out of everybody for miles around Mapleton, but has also stampeded hunting parties which had the temerity to try to rout it out of the neighborhood; and one night, if stories are to be believed, it actually ran for some distance beside a Coney Island Railroad train, making horrible faces at the passengers and finally disappearing in the woods alongside of the track with a blood-curdling yell and a hollow, fiendish laugh.

If this ghost had made its first appearance in Mapleton without anything having happened just prior to its debut to form an excuse for its presence, the residents would not have been so panic-stricken when it came. But something had happened a few days before it first appeared which made the superstitious awake and tremble and the unbelievers shake their heads and wonder what it all meant. On Aug. 5 a young woman named Margaret Barning walked down the track of the Sea

Beach Railroad to a point some distance from the Mapleton station and, pulling out a pistol, fired a bullet into her heart. Death ensued almost instantly. Two or three nights later the ghost appeared near the spot where the young woman had killed herself, and then there was excitement in Mapleton such as the little village had never known before. Various descriptions were given of the apparition by people who said they had seen it, but all agreed that it looked very much like the spectre of a woman and was in all probability the troubled spirit of the unfortunate girl who had killed herself a few nights before.

The effect of the ghost's visit in Mapleton was remarkable. Nervous people refused to go out after dark, women spent sleepless nights, and when the men went out they armed themselves with either guns or clubs. The ghost's visit was certainly having a disastrous effect on Mapleton, and finally searching parties began to go out after it. One by one they were routed by the ghost, but still they kept organizing until finally the ghost got tired of materializing for the sake of scaring a lot of would-be heroes to death and failed to show up when the searchers came around.

This was the condition of affairs when Prof. Edward Drinker Cope of the University of Pennsylvania and Prof. Henry Faranbar of the Coast Survey went down to catch the ghost with the avowed intention of ripping it to bits and holding an autopsy over its body when they got it. They spent a cold, dismal night on the railroad track, but met the same fate that ghost hunters with avowed intentions always do. They saw nothing of a ghostly nature.

It is a customary thing when one village obtains any notoriety, even though it be through the medium of a ghost, for all of the other villages in the vicinity to get madly jealous, and needless to say, the village of Flatbush, which has never had a ghost of its own, scoffed at the idea of the Mapleton apparition being anything more than a "fake" of the worst description. When a Flatbush young man met a Mapleton young man, he would sarcastically inquire: "Say, how's that bundle of oats over your way?"

And then the Mapleton young man would grit his teeth and reply, "C'mover'n see." So often was the invitation extended that on Sunday there was a quiet meeting of Flatbush young men in the rooms of Windsor Hose Company, No. 3, of the Flatbush Fire Department, to determine what action should be taken to squelch the ambitious young men of Mapleton and wipe their ghost out of existence at one fell swoop. The young men at the meeting were Fred Cuthbert, Frank Mason, William Cross, W.T. Tibballs, Otto Siegman, William Siegman, Frank Probert, and John Probert.

For five hours they sat in conclave. It was finally decided that on the next night, which was Monday, the entire eight would start out and do up the Mapleton ghost if they were all transformed into air in the attempt. So the next night they gathered in the hose house in Windsor Terrace, all armed in one way or another, some nervous and some cheerful, but all determined to get that ghost or never come back.

The walk to Mapleton is not a long one and was covered in a short time. As the spot where the ghost had been in the habit of making his appearance was approached, some of the young men began to get nervous, a fact which Mr. Tibballs took advantage of to chant, in low and sepulchral tones, a dismal ditty about ghosts.

"Wow," suddenly yelled Otto Siegman. "What's that?"

The rest of the party huddled closely together and listened as out on the night air came a long-drawn sigh, followed by a series of moans.

"It sounds —" began Tibballs in a deep voice.

"Yes. What?" inquired the others in hoarse whispers.

"It sounds like —"

"Like what?"

"Like the voice of the hot tamale man," shrieked Tibballs, and then the others withdrew and held a consultation, which resulted in Mr. Cross approaching the disturber of nerves and saying:

"Now look here, Tibs, you've got to take a drop. We're here to get that ghost, and you're scaring the life out of the boys before they've seen it."

"All right," said Tibballs, "I'll not say another word—gee whiz, what's that?"

A series of piercing shrieks rang out on the air, followed by terrible moans. The ghost hunters turned pale and stood huddled together in a group, their knees quaking and their teeth chattering. Tibballs seemed to be worse off than anyone.

"It's g'good b'by, b'boys. We're all g'gonners. It's the ghost, and we might as well die here. Oh! Oh! Oh!" and the entertaining Mr. Tibballs let out shrieks far worse than those of the ghost.

"Get your guns and clubs ready, boys, for our lives," shouted Cross, and the frightened Flatbushians fumbled wildly for their weapons. Four had pistols and the rest clubs. The four with the pistols had just got them out of their pockets when Tibballs, who had been saving himself for a final effort, suddenly pointed his finger to the woods beside the track and, in a voice that could have been heard at Coney Island, shrieked: "My God, look ahead there."

The rest, following the direction of his finger, saw a sight which froze the blood in their veins.

197

In midair, not fifty feet away and gradually approaching them, was a huge white figure. The figure swayed gracefully to the right and the left as it approached. The young men, who had been rooted to the ground, finally began to recover themselves. The four with the pistols began firing recklessly in every direction while those with clubs hurled them fiercely at the approaching demon. But nothing seemed to stop it. On it came, slowing but surely, and the young men, completely rattled, fired a few last shots and then turned on their heels.

But not so Tibballs. That enterprising young man darted forward, and as the ghost reached him, he grabbed it, gave it a punch in the eye, threw it to the ground, and kicking it six feet in the air, landed it on the railroad track ten yards away. Then he made a grab at the air, clutched something, and with a broad grin on his face, exclaimed: "I thought so."

Then he fired his pistol in the air, and as he did so, two figures, closely muffled, rose out of the bushes a short distance off and began running rapidly away. No one chased them, unfortunately, and so the two scamps who are responsible for the Mapleton ghost scare will probably never be known. On seeing the ghost lying prostate on the track, the others came running back and, in about five minutes, were telling each other how hard it was to fool anyone from Flatbush with a bogus ghost.

For the ghost was nothing but a cross made of sticks, thickly padded with straw and covered with a sheet. Investigation showed that a wire had been strung from the top of a tree to the ground in such a manner that the ghost could be drawn up and down. In the daytime the jokers who have been manipulating the ghost probably secreted it in the top of a tree and took the wire away. The moans, groans, and shrieks were furnished, in all probability, by the jokers.

Triumphantly the Flatbush men took the ghost to their own village and set it up in the hose house, after which they proceeded to tell everybody in the vicinity just how they happened to catch it.

The young men of Mapleton have not been heard from yet, but it is understood that they are highly indignant over the invasion of their village by the Flatbushians and will put in a claim for the ghost which is still on exhibition in the Flatbush hose house. The Flatbush men say they will defend the ghost with their lives, so it may be that there will be interesting news from either Mapleton or Flatbush in the near future.

The Sun (New York, New York), Aug. 29, 1894

MYSTERY OF A HAUNTED HOUSE.

"A mystery has been solved in a house not far from San Gabriel, Cal.," said a resident of a neighboring little town, "a mystery that convinced several very sensible persons that ghosts do live and walk about o' nights. A certain rancher wished to go to the beach for the summer, so he rented his cottage for six months to some eastern people, and there is where the trouble began. The newcomers liked the place, but a few days after they had moved in, one of the members of the family went to the man who was working on the place and asked if there was anything peculiar about the house. 'No,' the man replied; 'why do you ask?' 'Well,' said the new tenant, 'we didn't sleep much last night. We went to bed early, and not long after my boy came and knocked at my door and said he heard someone trying to get in the house. I crept out into the hall then went all over the house, but I heard nothing, so went back to bed.

"'In a few minutes my boy called to me and said that he had heard the noise again. By this time the whole household was aroused. I went into the boy's room, but still heard nothing; then I put out the light and sat down to listen, and it wasn't 10 minutes before I heard the noise. It sounded like a person crawling along the floor of the next room; then something seemed to go bounding along like a ball, and we heard it strike the wall. Some of the children, who had followed me, were on the borders of hysterics by this time. I crept into the hall again, my revolver in one hand and some matches in the other, and toward the door of the next room. It was moonlight, and as I peeped through the keyhole I could see the room suffused with light, but apparently there was no one in it; yet there was the greatest scampering around you have ever heard.

"'For a second,' continued the tenant, 'I could not see distinctly, but when I looked around the room there was no one there; nothing to be seen but a ball, a big rubber ball, a sort of child's football, resting in the middle of the floor. I was dumbfounded; the windows were locked and there was no place in which to hide, so I finally backed out and went into my boy's room and told the family that it was the wind. But that didn't go, for as I was telling them, the ball went scurrying across the floor and the phantom was after it. Again I went out, and this time I held the door open and tried to look in. I waited some moments, but nothing appeared, and that was the last we heard of it that night.'

"'That beats me,' said the astonished workman. 'I have been around the house for two years and never heard that it was haunted. I believe,' he added, 'that I can get away with any ghost that ever walked, and if you will let me go up and try tonight I'll guarantee to find out the trouble.'

"So it was arranged: the man slept in the room which the boy had occupied, and the ball was replaced in the haunted room. At 11 o'clock the man was heard to go up and the ball started to roll about. The ranch hand crept to the door of the next room very carefully and at first made no attempt to open it; apparently he was listening; then he slowly opened the door, listened a moment, and closed it, and went down the hall to where the tenant was standing. 'Do you want to see the ghost?' he asked. 'Well, come on.'

"The tenant followed him, and after waiting for a few moments he saw, through the crack of the partially opened door, a little black animal suddenly appear in a broad band of moonlight and, riding up, strike at the ball with his forepaws, sending it whirling about the floor. 'A kitten!' ejaculated the new tenant in a whisper.

"'No, a skunk,' replied the man; 'a polecat—that's your ghost, and I would be careful how you run in on him.' It was true, and after some search, a small hole was discovered through which the animal had entered the room, where it amused itself playing ball by the light of the moon."

Daily Inter Mountain (Butte, Montana), Aug. 19, 1899

EXPOSED THE GHOST.
The New Haven Wraith
Only a Shining Monument.

NEW HAVEN, Conn, April 24.—The ghost of Mapledale Cemetery has been cornered, laid, exposed, resolved into its elements. The spook was a most ingenious combination of electricity, polished granite, and the laws of refraction. It was not CH_4, alias marsh gas,[4] as many wise young chemists of Yale supposed.

Terence W. Higgins, the caretaker of the cemetery, is the layer of the ghost. A better night for ghosts never fell than that which began at sunset last evening. The stars were hidden behind thick clouds. A veil of mist, torn now and then by raindrops, dulled the glow of the few arc lights along Winthrop Avenue and rendered all outlines indistinct. Mapledale Cemetery is bounded on the east by Winthrop Avenue.

When Terrence W. Higgins and a reporter entered the northeast corner of the cemetery, four policemen were guarding the little

---

[4] CH_4 is the chemical formula for methane.

enclosure. Not one of them cared to go inside. Scattered along the open iron fence at the north end of the cemetery—most remote from where the ghost had been seen to perform its dance—were a dozen Yale seniors, who scoffed, but did not draw near. There were also numerous young men of the vicinity.

Suddenly there shone in the southwestern part of the cemetery a tall form that seemed made of soft, phosphorescent light. It slowly swayed from side to side, as if dancing to the strains of solemn music. It advanced, now retreated, again advanced. It was real.

"There it is! There it is!" shouted twenty voices in darkness. Then fell silence, broken only by the scuffle of many feet up Winthrop Avenue.

"Come on, now," said Terrence W. Higgins, "and I'll show you what it is."

The policemen gripped their long night sticks with grim resolution and—stood stock still. Higgins stepped forward calmly with the deliberation proper when one goes to interview a ghost. The reporter, carefully holding down his constantly rising hat, followed him with reluctant feet.

"Don't go! It will kill you!" cried voices from the fence. The hat rose still higher. Oh, but that was a long journey over the grass! The tall, gleaming figure still swayed and threatened.

"You see now that it is the monument of Thomas C. Hollis, who used to be Sheriff of New Haven County," Higgins explained confidently as he sauntered. "The monument is tall and slender. It's made of Quincy granite with polished panels. There's an electric light in Winthrop Avenue northeast of the monument. When the light falls on the eastern panel of the monument it shines and looks like a ghost. When the light sputters, the ghost seems to dance. That's all there is about it."

And what Higgins said is exactly so.

Evening Times (Washington, DC), April 24, 1900

GHOST IN A CEMETERY.
Supposed Spook Proved to Be
Young Woman in White.

Seneca Falls, N.Y., May 10.—During the last two weeks a number of young men claim to have seen a ghost in Restvale Cemetery while on their way home from a fishing trip on Seneca River.

While returning home from Cayuga Lake on a bicycle last evening, a well-known citizen claimed to have seen a white object moving about among the monuments in the cemetery. He says that the "ghost" seemed to be in great distress, as he heard loud groans and saw streaks of fire issue from its mouth. He was greatly frightened and ran home as fast as he could operate his bicycle.

A large crowd visited the cemetery. The "ghost" proved to be a young woman from Geneva who is visiting the village. She was dressed in white and was accompanied by a married man who lives in the Fourth Ward. When caught by a couple of young men, the woman was sitting behind a monument lighting parlor matches and throwing them into the air while the man nearby was making loud groans. The excuse they gave for their strange performances was that they were trying to frighten a certain man in the Second Ward, whose attentions to the woman were unwelcome.

St. Louis Republic (Missouri), May 11, 1902

ARRESTED A GHOST.

A "ghost" was arrested by the police yesterday and it is now in a cell at the police station. For months it has haunted a vacant house in Otisco Street, regularly every night appearing at an upper window in white draperies and disappearing before dawn.

Friday a new tenant moved into the haunted house, and soon a call came to the police station. When Sgt. Jerry Dwyer arrived there he saw the "ghost" sitting in an upper window in broad daylight. In the street a swarm of boys threw mud and stones at the phantom and would not be driven away. The Sergeant telephoned to the station for instructions.

"Arrest the ghost," commanded the Captain.

The officers went upstairs and tremblingly approached the spirit at the window. "Yer arrested," said he as he tapped the spook on the shoulder. Then he discovered it was a plaster cast with white robes on, placed there to keep tramps out of the house when it was untenanted.

Inter-Mountain Farmer and Ranchman
(Salt Lake City, Utah), Oct. 7, 1902
Reprinted from *New York World* (New York)

GHOST WORE FEATHERS.
Grand Army Veteran Finds
House Is Haunted by a Goose.

The mystery of Germantown's "haunted" house has been solved, says the *Philadelphia Inquirer*.

For several days weird noises emanating from the house, an unoccupied one on Chew Street, filled the neighbors with alarm. Strange shadows were seen to flit across the closed blinds and the patter of footsteps upon the bare floors sent a shudder through the passerby.

None dared to enter or start an investigation until William Harkins, of 613 Mechanic Street, arrived on the scene. Harkins is a brave man, a veteran of the Civil War, and he excited the admiration of the crowd in front of the house last night by expressing a determination to locate the "ghost." He entered alone. A few minutes later there were sounds of a scuffle, and then a weird scream, and terror seized upon those without. Suddenly Harkins appeared on the threshold of the front door with a big goose in this arms.

"Here's your ghost," he said laughing. And the crowd melted away. An investigation revealed the fact that the goose was the property of William Logan, who conducts a poultry farm nearby. It had escaped a few days ago and had sought refuge in the house through an open cellar window.

Arizona Republican (Phoenix), May 14, 1904

FROG AS BIG AS A BULLDOG
Made Queer Noises and
Made People Think of Ghosts.

Mysterious noises have been heard at a house, corner of Toure and Royal Streets, New Orleans, for a long time past, until it has been termed the "haunted house."

The owners of the houses in that vicinity have received many complaints, and all the families near have moved out. There have been many attempts to "lay the ghost," but all were unsuccessful, and at last complaint was made to the police.

Wednesday night several police went to the house with clubs and lanterns, and after several hours' search, the cause of the noise was located under the house.

It turned out to be an immense frog, weighing nearly 12 pounds, which had terrorized the people in that vicinity by his deep croakings.

Bourbon News (Paris, Kentucky), May 25, 1906

RODE A WHEEL WHILE ASLEEP
The Mystery of an Iowa Ghost
Solved by an Accident.

Fort Dodge, Ia., Aug. 18.—The ghostlike apparition of a girl astride a bicycle flitting about the streets after midnight will not startle residents in the East End anymore. Clad in flowing white garments with hair streaming behind her and the gas lamp revealing her bare foot and ankles, the ghost rider has excited a good deal of interest as well as fright.

Several attempts made to follow the rider failed because the bicycle always disappeared. Last night a policeman, attracted to a crash and a scream, ran around a corner and solved the mystery. He found a young and pretty girl clad in a thin night dress who had suffered severely when the wheel she was riding struck a brick. The girl was dazed, but told the policeman where she lived. He escorted her home and startled her father, a merchant, who believed his daughter was safe in bed.

The girl said she had no recollection of her night rides. She had been flitting about the streets on her wheel and in her night dress asleep.

Daily Ardmoreite (Ardmore, Oklahoma), Aug. 19, 1907

"GHOST" WAS ONLY A MULE.
Mystery That Puzzled
Jacksonville, N.J.,
Is Solved by Citizens.

New York.—For several weeks persons living on the outskirts of Jacksonville, N.J., have taken a wide detour after nightfall to avoid passing an empty house on the abandoned farm formerly occupied by Joseph Halloway. The house had the reputation of being haunted. At night those who ventured near to the building heard strains of weird music emanating from the interior, and other strange sounds aided in creating the impression that ghosts tenanted the dismal looking structure.

Bolder spirits of the village finally decided that they would solve the mystery of the haunted house. Jacob Growther, Charles Spangler and Michael Doremus formed a committee of investigation. The trio approached the haunted house about nine o'clock. As they neared the building their ears were greeted by the uncanny music that had alarmed the timid wayfarers. Growther wanted to turn back, but his courage was bolstered up by the determined demeanor of his companions, who declared they would solve the mystery no matter what occurred.

One of the men carried a lantern. He led the way in through the open door. The strange music led them into what was formerly the kitchen. A strange form loomed up before them and a hollow rattle of the board floor marked the sudden termination of the music.

Under the glare of the light the mystery was solved. The "ghost" was an old mule belonging to Abraham Wallen, a farmer. As the men gazed on the startled mule the music started again, and the investigators then learned how it originated. The hairless tail of the mule beat rapidly over wires that the former occupants of the house had left on the kitchen window. Every time the mule switched his tail the wires gave forth a sound like someone strumming on a harp.

Now Jacksonville breathes easier.

Barbour County Index (Medicine Lodge, Kansas), July 22, 1908

BOYS FIND GHOST
AND FARMERS BREATHE EASY
HUGE ARCTIC OWL, CAUGHT ON FENCE,
TERRIFIED COUNTRYSIDE SEVERAL NIGHTS.

Chicago.—The mystery of the dismal cries heard at night by residents along the Fox River, north of Geneva, Ill., has been cleared up, and the good farmer folk now retire in the evening without fear of having their sleep disturbed by "ghosts."

The unearthly wailings began several nights ago, and from the fact that the sounds emanated from a point near the cemetery, the residents along the river valley were strengthened in their belief that the "ghosts were walking." Last Sunday two boys, while rambling through the woods near the graveyard, saw a large white object hanging on a fence. Going up to it they found it was a bird fastened by both wings to the barbs of the wire.

After considerable trouble the boys loosened the bird and brought it to a taxidermist in Geneva. The taxidermist pronounced the bird an arctic or snowy owl, the largest he had seen in 40 years of collecting. By the discovery, the "mystery of the ghost of Fox River hollow" was solved.

The owl evidently had become entangled in the barbed wire while chasing a rabbit or field rodent, and remained hanging there until it starved to death. It being a nocturnal bird the wounded and trapped owl uttered cries of pain and hunger at night. From the cries many persons coming home late at night and having to pass the cemetery were led to believe that the "spirits of the departed" were uttering warnings of an impending calamity.

Each evening after sunset the moanings began and generally continued at short intervals until midnight, when they ceased. It was not until after the cries had ceased each night that the residents felt they could go to sleep with any degree of safety.

Roundup Record (Montana), May 21, 1909

Horse Spook Proves to Be Electricity

WELBORN, Kan., Nov. 3.—About three months ago a horse was killed by a street car at the interurban crossing here. Since that time the place has been known as the "haunted crossing."

Nobody ever saw a ghost there, but it was generally supposed that the ghost of the horse was visible only to other horses, for almost every horse shied upon reaching the crossing, and it was getting to be almost impossible to drive past.

Two boys playing near the "haunted" place stepped on the car track and got a distinct electric shock. An investigation showed that there was a short circuit charging the rails, shocking the horses and causing them to shy and cut up fancy didoes. The traction company has chased away the spook.

Tacoma Times (Washington), Nov. 3, 1910

TRAIN FLAGGED BY GHOSTLY CONDUCTOR

'Tis strange, indeed, that in a cool calculating world like at this day and age of civilization and Christianity that there are some to be found who actually lend credence to fables and stories of hobgoblins.

Ely is not an exception to this rule. According to reports, many of her residents, within the past few nights, have wandered to the cemetery to be convinced of the presence there of a "ghost."

As the story goes, which originated in the mind of one of the railroad men on the suburban trains, ever since the former conductor on the road, each evening when passing the Ely cemetery, saw a ghost carrying a railroad green lantern and signaling the train, it appears in the same place at the cemetery. Not thoroughly convinced that he was laboring under an optical illusion or a wonderful stretch of the imagination, he told the story to other trainmen; they are also said to have seen the same phenomena and, in turn, told of the wonderful sight to others.

Hearing of the strange occurrence, a number of people have visited the cemetery the past few nights to witness the scene. Stories related by some of these have the ring of fables written in the days of Solomon: so complete was their illusion and so wonderful their imagination that, not only the glimmer of the lantern was seen, but images in the most hideous conceivable forms, bearing no relation to man or beast, were also observed perambulating the grounds. So convinced were some that there was animation, spiritual or otherwise, in these mental illusions that they feared to enter the grounds and satisfy themselves of their non-existence.

However, laying aside all fables, hobgoblins, optical illusions and mental hallucinations, there is unquestionably, reflected in the cemetery grounds by heat waves, a perfect reproduction of the railroader's green lantern, which at times owing to the density of the atmosphere and climate conditions, is more apparent than at others. This sight, it is claimed by some who have seen it, can be observed almost any evening now, after darkness has come on.

To witness the phenomena brings vividly to memory how many a man in these western deserts has lost his life in following these illusions. Mirages picturing in the distance, across the desert waste of sand, a sky-blue lake, its banks covered with foliage and animal life, have led men wandering from the usual path in quest of water. Day after day, until finally overcome by thirst and exhaustion, following always these reflections, have they gone on and on only to be lost and left to die a most horrible death. Those unaccustomed to these mirages cannot be too well informed of their death-alluring features. Even in Steptoe Valley, just below East Ely on a hot summer's day, one driving the old wagon road from McGill to Ely will observe a most perfect body of water, knowing full well that there is no such body of water within hundreds of miles.

Tonopah Daily Bonanza (Nevada), March 6, 1912
Reprinted from *Ely Expositor* (Nevada)

GAMBLERS IN GRAVE VAULT
Cemetery "Ghosts" Found
Playing Craps in Old Churchyard

Philadelphia, June 24.—In a dilapidated old vault in a churchyard containing the bones of some Colonial man or maiden, a group of roystering men was found last night, laughing, talking, smoking and shooting "craps." The vault in which they sat was the oldest in Old

Trinity burying ground, Queen Street, above 2nd, and it is falling into decay.

For more than a week residents of the neighborhood have heard uncanny sounds emanating from the churchyard after midnight, and the place was believed to be "haunted."

New York Tribune (New York), June 25, 1912

Ghost Mystery Solved by Arrest of Woman

SOUTH BEND, Ind., Aug. 22.—In the arrest of Anna Janzik on a charge of grand larceny the police believe they have solved the mystery of the "ghost" who has been frightening women and children.

The police say they caught the woman in the act of stealing potatoes from a freight car. She was attired only in a thin night gown.

The Janzik woman, it is claimed, has been visiting cars in the railroad yards nightly, disguising her movements through her ghostly garb. It is also stated an effort will be made to fix upon the woman the leadership of a gang which has been working South Bend for several months.

Seattle Star (Washington), Aug. 22, 1913

LAYING A GHOST.
A Simple Solution to the
Mystery of a "Haunted" House.

The mystery of a "haunted" house was explained in a recent number of *Science*.[5] It was a large, handsome structure in Boston's Back Bay district. The trouble centered in the third and fourth stories, where the slumbers of servants and children were disturbed by strange sensations.

It was a common occurrence for them to awake in the night with a feeling of oppression, "as if someone were tapping upon me." Sounds also were heard, as if someone were walking about or overhead. Once a child rushed screaming into the nurse's room, crying that a man was waking him up and asking why she let him frighten him so. In the morning the children were pale and sluggish, even cold water lacking its usual power to enliven them.

---

[5] Franz Schneider, Jr., "An Investigation of 'Haunted' House," *Science*, 37.958 (May 9, 1913), pp. 711-712.

Investigation at length revealed a comparatively simple, mechanistic solution in the escape of a large amount of furnace gas. Often the sulphur in it was so strong as to make the eyes water and to hurt the throat while the sensations of oppression were typical of carbon monoxide. The noises may have been actual sounds coming from an adjoining house, although any noises at all would probably be exaggerated in the mind of persons awakened in the night while suffering from poisonous gas.

Times-Herald (Burns, Oregon), Jan. 3, 1914

Hearing his piano playing in the night and not being able to see who was playing it, a Neosho man concluded his house was haunted. He watched for a few nights and finally caught a musically inclined possum running up and down the keyboard. The possum was captured and placed in a local zoo.

Butler Weekly Times (Missouri), July 20, 1916

CULTURED "GHOST" HAUNTS MD. SCHOOL

FREDERICK, Md., May 3.—"Tam-o'Shanter," who was haunted by ghosts; "Icabod Crane," that frenzied rider who clattered throughout the night; "The White Lady,"[6] and all of those well-known figures of "ghostology" are being paled into insignificance in Frederick County by a very ghostlike apparition which has paralyzed young folk with fright.

Continental School, a tiny country school north of Woodsboro, inconspicuous and never particularly famous for anything, has the distinction of being in the very heart of the ghost-ridden section of Frederick County. This "ghost" has intellectual tastes and visits, once as often as three times a day, this school. Clad in a suit of white, black stockinged, shod in shoes of white, and wearing a black silk hat, this "ghost" is as picturesque as any that ever performed on the printed pages of literature and to the school children, who shun the schoolhouse as if it were a pesthouse.

---

6 Tam O'Shanter is the title character in a 1790 poem by Robert Burns. Icabod Crane appears in Washington Irving's 1820 tale, "The Legend of Sleepy Hollow." The White Lady is a reference to Wilkie Collins' novel *The Woman in White* (1859) and/or to a widespread motif in ghost folklore, especially legends told in Britain, Ireland, and the U.S.

"Ghost" Plays Violin.

Authenticated reports have been received of a visitation by this "ghost" to the Continental Schoolhouse. 'Tis said that this figure appeared at the school one day at noon, entered, took possession, and proceeded to give a violin solo, relieved for variety's sake by wailing and weeping. The origin of the violin, the presence of which in the building was not suspected until its doleful tones were heard, is not known. 'Tis presumed the "ghost" accommodatingly brought it along.

Two theories are advanced concerning this ghost. Sheriff Charles H. Klipp has a sneaking suspicion that the role is being enacted by Clinton Baugher, insane, who nearly a month ago escaped from the Maryland Insane Asylum at Springfield. Baugher was sent to the State asylum only after he had threatened the life of Deputy Sheriff John Dutrow; after he had been locked in a cell in Montevue Hospital, the county's asylum for local insane; and after he had escaped from Montevue Hospital, and had been caught again by Officer Dutrow, who braved two menacing barrels of a perfectly good shotgun to capture the man. Two weeks after Baugher was put in the Springfield Insane Asylum, he vanished, and he has not been trapped since. It is presumed that he returned to his home in this county, which is the immediate neighborhood of Continental Schoolhouse, but none has ever seen him.

Honest-to-Goodness Ghost.

The other theory is advanced by the credulous. Those who believe in fairies, pots of gold at the rainbow's end, the laden ship sailing in at last, and such like, affirm that it is an honest-to-goodness "ghost."

So officials in the county have the unique sensation of starting on a man and ghost hunt. The capture of the first may mean the solution of the second. Of this the officers are sanguine, but the countryside is sure that, long after Clinton Baugher is caught, this ghost will continue to appear.

Washington Times (DC), May 5, 1919

STRANGE SHADOWS WERE SEEN.

From "GHOST WORE FEATHERS," page 203.

APPENDIX: The Brinkley College Ghost and the Debate over Reporting on Ghosts

In 1871, newspapers in Memphis, Tennessee, followed a local ghost story that grew stranger, more sensational, and more suspicious as it developed. The *Daily Memphis Avalanche* broke the story on March 5th—headlining it "The Most Remarkable Ghost Story on Record"—and then gave it in-depth coverage through the end of the month. The *Avalanche's* crosstown rival, the *Appeal,* led a campaign against devoting so much ink to the event, portraying it as a profit-driven publicity stunt that exploited and reinforced superstition. On the one hand, the Brinkley College haunting offers a curious mystery that can probably can never be solved. On the other, it illustrates how American journalists defined and debated their role in reporting on ghosts.

The Ghost Story

The *Avalanche* article that introduced readers to the Brinkley College ghost opens by asking if "disembodied spirits haunt the scenes which they frequented in the flesh? It is a mixed question: the theory that they do having as firm believers as it has firm disbelievers." It next sets the scene: a "palatial residence" with unsubstantiated rumors of having financially ruined its original owner and of being haunted.[1] If not actually inhabited by a ghost, the mansion had a certain eeriness due to its isolation and to the "weird aspect of the structure, to which may be added its surroundings, which strike the visitor as decidedly unattractive."

R.C. Brinkley owned the building in 1871 and had turned it into a school. Run by a half-dozen teachers and administrators, the so-called "college" served about forty to fifty young female students. One of those students was Clara Robertson, who was about thirteen-years-old. The reporter describes her as "of the nervous kind, while her health is rather

---

[1] The building was located at 683 South Fifth Street, where a large, industrial structure now stands. The original house was dismantled in 1972 with the intension of reconstructing it in Jonesboro, Arkansas.

what might be called delicate." Firm in her religious devotion, Clara is said to have "never been in any way connected with things spiritual or to have put trust in spiritualists." She acted as the key witness in the school's spectral visitation.

That specter had appeared to Clara "in the shape of a girl of about eight years of age, with sunken, lusterless eyes and strikingly emaciated form and features." This skeletal figure was "clad in a dingy and tattered dress of faded pink, which was partly covered with a greenish and slimy fold." Though transparent, the figure appeared sad. Clara's encounter with it occurred in a music practice room, and she ran off while simultaneously waving the phantom away. Her efforts to escape the ghost were successful—but only for two days. In the same music room, this time with two other students present, she "was startled by an unusual noise as if by some water being dashed over the floor." Turning their heads, all three spotted the apparition, and all three fled the room.

There was yet another sighting a few days later. This time, according to that same *Avalanche* article, Clara ran to get a teacher named Miss Jackie Boone, and together they returned to the music room. "As they opened the door," the reporter writes, "the figure stood plainly in view to Clara, but only imperfectly in the eyes of Miss Boone." Perhaps emboldened by the presence of the teacher, Clara asked the ghost what it wanted. It pointed toward the south and explained that "under a stump, some fifty yards from the houses, were secreted some valuables which she would have Miss Clara take possession of, and use to her advantage. Miss Boone heard a rumbling noise, but could not distinguish any words." The ghost then "vanished through the garret door." At this point, an adult had witnessed the spectral phenomenon, albeit not as distinctly as Clara—that is, according to that initial report.

Readers were then introduced to the next key player in the drama: Clara's father. Mr. J.R. Robertson, who had earlier dismissed his daughter's ghostly encounters as resulting from a trick, met with the college administrators to arrange an investigation. All the students were gathered together for questioning, and Clara was instructed to remain out in the yard. There, she saw the ghost a *fourth* time. The phantom addressed Clara by name, introduced itself as "Lizzie," and assured her that she wouldn't be hurt. "The vision spoke again and in a distinct tone related that Brinkley College property was [the ghost's] by right, title and deed, that its present pretended owners held it illegally." The ghost claimed that no living relations remained to rightfully claim the land, so she wanted Clara take possession. Ominously, "Lizzie" added that, unless Clara adhered to these wishes, "she never would do good to or for anyone."

Appendix

As fate would have it, Clara's father was a lawyer and one of his clients was a Spiritualist medium. At Mr. Robertson's request, the elderly woman led a séance with Clara in attendance. The skeptical father looked on as his daughter had a seizure that eventually subsided into a trance. A pencil was put into Clara's hand, and the marks she made on paper gradually "assumed shape and form, and finally became readable." Under the trance, Clara wrote statements that "corroborated all she had previously related. Questions were asked, and replies were instantly written on the paper." Specifics on where the deed was buried were given along with the explanation that, since Clara was best able to commune with the spirit realm, she was also best able to free the ghost from its earthly troubles. Asked about what to do if the present land holders refused to abide by the ghostly transfer of property, "Lizzie" again became demanding: "I WILL SEE THAT IT SHALL DO THEM NO GOOD IF YOU ONLY RECOVER THE PAPERS." The reporter offers readers an opportunity to see these messages from the Great Beyond in the offices of the *Avalanche.*

This first article ends by saying that, at press time, a team of diggers were "working like Trojans, with shovel, pick and spade," to unearth the deed of ownership. Unfortunately, they had only uncovered some brickwork, but further developments were awaited. Indeed, the public's curiosity became ignited when this article was released. By the next day, the Brinkley College ghost had become the talk of Memphis. Hundreds of gawkers swarmed the campus. Police efforts to stop the onslaught only inspired people to climb the college's fence, according to the March 6th issue of the *Public Ledger,* another Memphis newspaper.

This public response did not deter the *Avalanche,* which published a long follow-up article on the 7th. According to this report, after nothing more than that brickwork had been unearthed, another supernatural visitation, another séance, and more digging resulted in a major discovery. Clara had again seen the apparition in the pink dress, this time in the backyard of her home. "Lizzie" was unhappy that Clara had not yet found the deed, and after the girl managed to explain that the digging hadn't revealed it, the ghost "rejoined that Clara must go and seek it herself, or that others would get it." Returning to campus, poor Clara made the attempt. "She turned one spade full of dirt, stepped forward as if to pick something up and fell insensible." Another séance was quickly arranged, and "Lizzie" was summoned. Told that Clara was too high-strung for the task, the spirit consented to her father acting as proxy on the condition that the container holding the papers "should not be opened for sixty days. It also indicated the exact spot in the excavation" to find that container. The lawyer, the medium, and two diggers immediately went to campus. There, they unearthed a jar. "The jar bore evidence of long concealment, being covered with mold," the article explains, and "it was not opened, but through its sides could be seen several bags and packages, together with what appeared to be a large yellow envelope." The report ends by saying that Clara's father would honor the spectral request to keep the jar concealed for sixty days. In a sense, this jar is the *third* major character in the saga. Certainly, its discovery—presented as tangible proof of the ghost's authenticity—added a dramatic twist.

At the same time, the hastiness in the *Avalanche's* initial report started to show. Clara and her father's surname had been given as "Robinson" in that first article, and this second one openly corrected that to be Robertson. There's also an interview with Brinkley College principal, Mr. Meredith. He "did not question that Clara saw strange visions, but said they were certainly in her mind's eye, and insisted . . . that the unearthly vision had been seen by no one else on his premises." The other two students mentioned in the previous report had been fooled by Clara's actions into thinking there was a ghost, "but after collecting their senses they became doubtful and finally concluded that they saw nothing but a creation of their own fancy."

What about Miss Boone, the teacher who that first article cited as also having witnessed the ghost? On March 8th, the *Avalanche* printed yet another long article on the event. Along the way, it told readers that, given "the hurry of gathering first particulars it is very reasonable that mistakes should have occurred" and then it reprints a letter of complaint from Boone. The teacher says: "Miss Robertson at one time came into the music room, apparently very much excited, but having never given credit to the story of the ghost, I neither went back with her to her practice room or sent anyone else." Put beside Principal Meredith's statement that the other students had changed their minds about having seen the ghost, this disclaimer leaves Clara the only witness. Interestingly, that *Public Ledger* article printed on the 6th— one day after the *Avalanche* had broken the story—had said this: "So long as we were able to investigate the event yesterday, no other person [besides Clara] saw or heard the spiritual visitor, nor is the real appearance of the ghost credited by the teachers at the institution." Apparently, the *Avalanche* had misrepresented the facts in that March 5th article, but it did not hesitate to make retractions afterward.

On the 12th, the *Avalanche* featured a long, transcribed interview with Clara herself. For the most part, she recaps the sequence of events already reported. However, Clara does add some details about her not knowing anything about the building's reputation for being haunted; about the ghost's protruding teeth and deep, black eyes; and about Boone having never seen the ghost. She also says that the other students had been coerced to disbelieve in the ghost because "Mr. Meredith and the teachers made fun of them and laughed them out of it." The article ends by reporting that a child about six or eight years old, named Lizzie Davie, had died in Brinkley College in 1861. Those who attended her funeral "say she was laid out and buried in a dress of pink." Some "old and reliable citizens" also recalled a scandalous lawsuit concerning the grounds upon which Brinkley College was built. If the *Avalanche* was working at piecing together the true story, it was also favoring hearsay evidence for the ghost being real.

By the 14th, the *Public Ledger* commented that a 10-cent pamphlet about the ghost was selling well. Exactly one month later, the *Daily Chronicle* from over in Knoxville, Tennessee, reported that Clara's own father had written an account of the case, "including a great many things not heretofore published." It cost thirty cents.[2] But this was not the first method that Mr. Robertson had used to raise money from his daughter's extraordinary story. On March 19th, the *Avalanche* reprinted a letter addressed to Robertson, imploring him to open the jar "publically, in the presence of all who may desire to see the same." It was signed with twenty-three names. Robertson's reply, published on the 24th, includes this statement: "I propose to open the jar at the Greenlaw Opera House on Thursday evening, the 30th inst." To defray costs, Robertson proposed to sell tickets for a dollar per person. Perhaps to distract from the impression that he was exploiting his nervous daughter, Robertson explained that he would split the profits: "one half for the benefit of the Orphans' Home and the other half to Miss Clara."

Even this plan raised controversy, though. The *Public Ledger* expressed its disapproval of the developments surrounding the ghost, complaining in its issue for March 24th: "The jar business has been overdone, and is deservedly ridiculed by sensible people at present." Farther down the page, readers were told about Robertson's plan to split the profits with this commentary: "The spirits are determined that some money shall be made. But would it not be better and look less like a huge sell to divide the receipts between the orphans and Brinkley

---

[2] The price is given in an announcement in the *Public Ledger* on May 6, 1871. Titled "The Brinkley Female College Ghost Story," the 36-page publication by J.R. Robertson was published by R.C. Floyd. It is available online at Indiana University's Wright American Fiction site.

College? The latter gentleman was damaged and injured considerably, and his school was very much demoralized on account of the grand hoax and the intrusion of uninvited guests during the grave-digging scene."

The next day, the *Avalanche* reprinted a letter from Robertson that says, due to "some opposition," he would present *all* the proceeds to the Orphans' Home. He then adds that Clara and local Spiritualists "will give a séance on the stage." In other words, he would turn his daughter into a star attraction. The haunting was becoming a circus. Four days later—just two days before the public opening of the jar—the *Public Ledger* reprinted a letter from C.T. Quintard, head of the Orphans' Home, stating that "no part of the proceeds will be accepted" by that organization. This is followed by a satiric preview of the "voodoo performance" with its "sheet-iron thunder and chemical lightning." The writer mocks, "Let the thing go on, and give us a glimpse of the pickle jar, its contents, the little green specter, the mediums and clairvoyants, the *séances,* and lastly, give us sight of the audience, which will too truly represent a gullible public." Things were rapidly turning sour. If Robertson's idea for charging admission to a public opening of the jar had grown from his acquiescing to a request made in the papers, his mistake might have been renting the costly Opera House instead of, say, meeting in a free public park. His adding a séance with his daughter involved suggests his sense of showmanship might be at fault. Was the mistake his decision to capitalize on his daughter's ghostly experience, as his subsequent 30-cent pamphlet suggests—or had the whole thing been a money-making hoax from the start?

Or can we attribute the tragic conclusion to the narrative to the fact that Robertson was clearly *not* abiding by the 60-day waiting period stipulated by "Lizzie"? After all, the Brinkley College ghost had twice given warning that no good would come of disobeying her wishes.

Regardless of the reasons, events went from bad to worse. One day before the public opening of the jar, the *Avalanche* ran an article with this headline:

**Ruffians Entice Mr. Robertson from His House
and Force Him to Reveal the Hiding Place of the Jar.
Pistols Are Leveled at His Head.
He Is Choked, Beaten, Left Senseless on the Ground
and the Mysterious Jar is Carried Away.**

Indeed, what the paper had labeled "The Most Remarkable Ghost Story on Record" at the beginning of March had transformed into "One of the Boldest, Most Daring Acts of Violence on Record" by the month's end. It seems that a small number of Robertson's colleagues had met at his house and heard a noise in the backyard. He went to investigate.

About five minutes later, a servant named Joe came running in a panic. Joe led the group to find Robertson "lying insensible in a pool of blood, near a small stable in the rear of his lot." The group carried him inside, and a doctor was summoned. That doctor restored Robertson, who had several head wounds, one of which "appeared as if made with a knife or some sharp instrument, extending about four inches over the forehead." Also, there were "marks of a person's fingers upon his throat, as if he had been choked."

Robertson later reported that four men, armed with pistols, forced him to divulge the whereabouts of the famous jar. As it turned out, the jar was nearby in his backyard. The *Avalanche* explains, "Mr. R., fearing for his life, told them that the jar was underneath the seat in the outhouse attached to a rope, and told them how to get it." It was quick work to retrieve the jar from what some might consider a terribly odd place to have hidden such a remarkable treasure. Nevertheless, before fleeing with their plunder, the men choked and pistol-whipped Robertson.

The culprits were never apprehended. The jar was never retrieved.

The Debate

We've already seen that Memphis's *Public Ledger* began satirizing the Brinkley College ghost story once it had led to a proposed stage show. But another of the city's newspapers, the *Appeal,* had been voicing its disapproval of the affair as early as March 10th. Its issue printed that day says that a "kind of silly ignorance and superstition has found a home in Memphis. . . . Indeed, the scenes of the last week have been a disgrace to our city and all engaged in the swindle upon public credulity." Though not by name, the editor clearly blamed the *Avalanche* for printing "every lie connected with the ghost humbug" and for inciting the mob that swarmed the campus in search of the buried deed. The *Appeal* then showed the wider extent of the damage: "It is humiliating that the people of Memphis should be made the laughing-stock of the whole country. These published sensational accounts about ghosts would indicate that our people are illiterate, superstitious fools." In addition, Brinkley College and its students weren't alone in suffering, since children from other schools had had "instilled into their young and credulous minds a superstition which will never be eradicated." The editorial concluded by saying, "If there be any law for punishing the originators of this imposition, and its aiders and abettors, it ought to be rigidly enforced." The *Appeal* has charged its rival with unethical journalism and potentially illegal behavior.

The *Avalanche* fired back the next day. They accused the *Appeal* (by name!) of holding a grudge for not being the paper that broke the story: "There is a somewhat well-known fable about a fox which, after losing its tail, labored industriously to convince his fellows that tails were unfashionable." The *Appeal,* they went on, was "at liberty to apologize in any way that best suits them for failing to furnish the public with the news of the day." Their own coverage of the story would continue unreservedly. "The public interest in the 'Ghost' being unabated, our reporters have interviewed the young lady who so frequently interviewed the 'Ghost,'" and also obtained possession of other strange reports in connection with the mystery." The rebuttal then becomes a promotion for the upcoming Sunday issue, where the interview and additional information would appear, and it ends by cautioning the "weak intellects" at the *Appeal* to take care in reading that in-depth interview. In other words, the *Avalanche* justified its coverage by pointing to readers' interest in it and those readers' ability to judge it intelligently.

Also, on the 11th, the *Appeal* printed two letters of rebuttal, one from Mr. Robertson and another from his Spiritualist client who led the séances, prefacing them both by declaring that the paper would then "close our columns to everything that concerns the ghost humbug," But they were not true to their word because, on the 19th, the *Appeal* returned with even stronger language. "The Brinkley College ghost humbug has been a prolific source of evil. The startling, sensational reports that have appeared in a newspaper which seems to be a fit receptacle for the foul and vulgar tittle-tattle of courtesans and all the silly twaddle which the fools who believe in ghosts utter, have produced untold evils." Again, they mention children, those students unable to learn because they were too distracted by the fear that the ghost might manifest at *their* school. There is also mention of "Mr. S.W. Phillips, late keeper of Elmwood Cemetery," who apparently had a mental breakdown under the influence of the *Avalanche's* reports. "He is so ferocious in his madness that he has been securely fettered, and it is supposed his reason is forever dethroned."[3] The writer even appeals to

---

[3] As odd as this might strike readers in the 21st century, the *Public Ledger* had made the same diagnosis in their issue of the previous day: "Since the advent of the Brinkley College ghost, Mr. Phillips has been thinking and pondering over supernatural apparitions until his mind was overthrown and the light of reason fled from him, we fear forever."

the memory of Lizzie Davie, the girl who had died years earlier. "She was a bright, beautiful girl" carried to heaven, pleads the editor, "and now to have her bones dragged about Brinkley College a ghastly, frightful, hideous spectre—to make her party to some intrigue on earth about *money*—"FILTHY LUCRE" . . . is as offensive to her friends and relations as it is unpoetical and unbecoming in manners, morals and good taste." While their competition saw journalism as *following* the readers' interests, the *Appeal* presents the role of the press as *leading,* uplifting, and protecting the public's well-being and the community's sense of decency.

Along with implying this basic difference in defining the societal role of Journalism, the two papers were more basely engaged in barking and growling at one another, possibly because a public feud can lead to newspaper sales. For example, on the 26th, the *Avalanche* seemed to be alluding to poor Mr. Phillips when it lamented the maddening effect of the "ghost sensation" on the editorial staff of the *Appeal*. Since the story broke, those editors "have almost daily furnished undoubted evidences that the demon insanity has seized the ponderous intellects of its conductors." With far from sincere sympathy, this editorial asks, "Would it not be well to devote a portion—say, a tenth—of the proceeds of the 'ghostly jar' opening to the editors of the *Appeal,* whose intellects have been so sadly shattered by the agitation? . . . Instead of our suggestion being too generous, we doubt if the sum proposed will fully suffice." Those of us who look at the serious-faced, well-dressed people in photographs from the 1800s and think that people from that era must have behaved with far more dignity and decorum than people do now should read some of these historic newspapers to realize how very misleading those photos are.

These are only highlights of the debate held between the *Appeal* and the *Avalanche* that month. Once news of the jar being stolen from the Robertsons had ruined the presentation at the Opera House, both papers took their chance to make their closing arguments before the jury of readers. On the 30th, the day the jar was to be opened, the *Appeal* wrote: "The ghost story was a falsehood from the start; it had been kept alive by falsehood; it has taken the money of hard-working men, without giving them their money's worth in the ghost; it has encouraged superstition and ignorance, made false impressions upon the minds of the young, and finally has terminated in outlawry and robbery." Their views of the *Avalanche* appeared in the adjacent column. Counting on readers knowing that the jar had been hanging on a rope in the Robertson's outhouse, the editor joked that "his ghostship kept rather low company, judging from the fact that he was found in the jar in a certain cabinet in which Robertson deposits his *Avalanches* and meets his privy counselors." Apparently, taking the moral highroad does not prevent one from stooping to toilet humor.

The *Avalanche*, on the other hand, offered an editorial slightly longer than a full-page column. The writer asserts that the paper had carefully focused on objective reporting, since none of the staff were knowledgeable about ghosts enough to editorialize. "Expressions of opinions belong to editors," the writer says, "and reporters who make themselves partisans are unfit for their business. This principle was applied to the Brinkley College 'ghost' sensation. The reporters furnished what others did, saw and heard, together with such theories of different persons as seemed calculated to throw light on a mystery in which a large portion of the public became interested. No opinions were offered." Again, the *Avalanche* presents its journalistic role as respecting readers' ability to decide what to believe or disbelieve, adding that those readers will reject journalists who would tell them how to think. "The age has gone by when people educated to think for themselves are willing to accept anybody's *dicta* on subjects open to discussion." With the *Appeal* implied, the editorial suggests that to belittle anybody's beliefs—be it Spiritualism or otherwise—"with the charge of humbug, or pronounce those who believe it fools, imposters, charlatans, etc., simply because one cannot see any valid reason for their belief, convinces nobody."

The editorial then moves to the Robertsons before concluding. Refusing to attribute the ghost to either reality or delusion, the editor affirms Clara's sincerity: "No one believes her capable of duplicity." The integrity of Clara's father is defended next, noting that "his record for nearly twenty years is that of an honest, upright, Christian gentleman" and arguing that the idea that "he would deliberately blast the good name earned by a lifetime of probity, none believe who know him." The question of Mr. Robertson's mental health is also touched on, but as with his daughter, the editor leaves that unresolved. Similar ambiguity arises regarding the reality of "her little ghostship. . . . The jar is gone. It is doubtful whether a knowledge of its contents will ever reach the public," says the article. As such, a stalemate presides. "Believers in spiritualism will not abate an iota of their faith. Unbelievers who desired investigation will be disappointed. Those who decide without investigation will reiterate 'humbug,' as usual." This last comment, presumably aimed at their rival newspaper, is a fair point. To be sure, the *Avalanche* was guilty of some slipshod journalism, mistaking names of key witnesses and failing to verify secondhand information about other witnesses. Nonetheless, its reporters seem to have done far more investigation into the story than did the *Appeal,* which had positioned itself as too disapproving of the events to have examined them closely.

Finally, the *Avalanche* had been in error about the stalemated outcome of the Brinkley College ghost. There is evidence that the editors of *Appeal* became more open-minded in regard to articles that evoke a sense of supernatural wonder. A few of the ghost reports in the main chapters of this book were printed in later issues of the *Appeal.* In addition, on April 29, 1871—a single month after the famous jar had been stolen—the article below appeared in the *Appeal.* I present it as this book's final transcribed report:

> There are two trees standing opposite a house on Madison Street, that have a recent history more wonderful and startling than the developments of all the 'sperits,' ghosts and jar we have heard of. Those trees, apparently full-grown, were in vigorous bloom a year ago. During the summer a lady died in that house, and as her remains were carried forth from its portals, showers of leaves fell upon it from those mourning trees, and the grass had not covered her grave before every leaf and 'green thing' had faded away from their branches, and they stood forth in naked sorrow. Now, when every tree on the street is in bloom, those trees persevere in their winter nakedness, and refuse to be gladdened by sprouting twigs and sprightly leaves. They are withering away, and no one can guess the cause.

ABOUT THE EDITOR

Tim Prasil—it rhymes with "grim fossil"—is the editor of *Those Who Haunt Ghosts: A Century of Ghost Hunter Fiction* and *Giving Up the Ghosts: Short-Lived Occult Detective Series by Six Renowned Authors,* both anthologies of supernatural fiction. He also writes fiction himself—yes, ghost stories—and the audio and stage plays he has penned have been produced in Toronto, Boston, and Tulsa.

The *Spectral Edition* project began and continues as a weekly feature on Tim's website, The Merry Ghost Hunter. There, you can listen to audio files of him reading many of the ghost reports, recordings that were heard on *The Big Séance* and *History Goes Bump* podcasts. The Merry Ghost Hunter website also offers information on Tim's upcoming projects.

Made in the USA
Middletown, DE
11 December 2017